Lady, You're the Boss!

Apurva Purohit

Published by
Rupa Publications India Pvt. Ltd 2022
7/16, Ansari Road, Daryaganj
New Delhi 110002

Sales centres:
Allahabad Bengaluru Chennai
Hyderabad Jaipur Kathmandu
Kolkata Mumbai

First published by Westland Publications Private Limited 2019

Copyright © Apurva Purohit, 2019, 2022

The views and opinions expressed in this book are the author's own
and the facts are as reported by him which have been
verified to the extent possible, and the publishers are not
in any way liable for the same.

All rights reserved.
No part of this publication may be reproduced, transmitted,
or stored in a retrieval system, in any form or by any means,
electronic, mechanical, photocopying, recording or otherwise,
without the prior permission of the publisher.

ISBN: 978-93-5520-636-7

First impression 2019, 2022

10 9 8 7 6 5 4 3 2 1

The moral right of the author has been asserted.

Printed in India

This book is sold subject to the condition that it shall not,
by way of trade or otherwise, be lent, resold, hired out, or otherwise
circulated, without the publisher's prior consent, in any form of
binding or cover other than that in which it is published.

Lady, You're the Boss!

Apurva Purohit is an acclaimed Indian businesswoman and entrepreneur with over three decades of experience in the corporate world where she has built and scaled up a diverse set of businesses.

Apurva has been a leading voice in the Indian business landscape advocating gender diversity, what ails it, and what organizations and leaders can do to improve this critical imperative. Through her two national best-selling books, Apurva aims to empower women and encourage them to achieve their full potential.

Over the years, Apurva has won multiple business awards and has been named as one of the Most Powerful Women in Business as per the India Today Group and *Fortune India*. She was amongst LinkedIn's Top Voices and Your Story's Top 10 digital Influencers and her alma mater IIM Bangalore awarded her the Distinguished Alumni award in 2022.

Apurva holds a bachelor's degree in physics and completed her PGDM from IIM Bangalore. She was a state-level hockey player and played for Tamil Nadu state and Tamil Nadu University.

Also by the Author

Lady, You're Not a Man!: The Adventures of a Woman at Work

To
My mother – Asha Kanwar,
Sanjay and Siddharth

Contents

Prologue ... 1

Part One

A Minimum Life? ... 9

Imposter Syndrome ... 17

Strengths Not Weaknesses ... 24

Need to Feel Needed ... 31

Learning to Let Go ... 38

Last Woman Standing ... 44

The Lioness and the Dormouse ... 51

Subconscious Bias ... 58

All the Single Ladies ... 65

Token Woman ... 73

Finding Sisterhood ... 80

Real-Life Role Models ... 87

Menopause ... 94

Midlife Crisis 102
Somebody's Something 109

Part Two

Tough Love 117
Taming the Underling 124
Good Leaders Are Great Communicators 130
Prioritising: What Is Your First and Foremost Goal? 137
Curiosity Makes the Leader 145
Scylla and Charybdis: You Have No Choice But to Choose! 152
Perseverance 159
Planning the Implementation 166
Measurement and Monitoring 172
Creating Winning Teams 180
Kehna Karna Nibhana: Consistent Commitment 187
Culture Vulture 195
Personal Accountability: I Am Because of Me 203
Epilogue 211
Acknowledgements 215

Prologue

'Ma'am, *how* did you know this is the *exact same* problem I've been having with my husband?' young Neha excitedly quizzed me, getting her grammar all muddled up in her enthusiasm. She had just finished reading *Lady, You're Not a Man!* and got in touch with me virtually the moment she put down the book. 'It seems as if you were in the room with us while we were arguing!' she said. 'How did you know that I don't want to leave my child with my mother-in-law? You can't imagine how badly she has brought up my husband!' she whispered. Laughing, I told Neha that no, I hadn't peeked into her bedroom specifically. I certainly didn't have a third eye embedded into my forehead nor could I lay claim to soothsaying abilities, much as I would like to. The simple truth was that her story was the story of every young woman I had met in the thirty years of my career. And her call was neither the first phone call I had received attesting to that fact, nor would it be the last!

Lady, You're Not a Man! discussed issues that all working women have faced at some point or the other in our lives – from being guilt-ridden when our young children ask us not to go to work, to being convinced by our mothers/in-laws that staying at home after marriage is the right thing to do because after all, 'God has given us everything, so why on earth would we need a second income?' as if that is the only reason we want to work! The book took a peek into our bedrooms and boardrooms and pointed out how all of us had equally lazy husbands or difficult bosses and suggested ways of dealing with these troublesome, albeit lovable, beings in our lives as we went along our merry adventures at work.

I have witnessed so many women sacrificing their careers because they were not clear about their priorities and were accepting the status quo, or because they were not asking for help, or because they mistakenly believed that in the give and take of being a woman in a man's world, they could only partially achieve their dreams. I wrote *Lady, You're Not a Man!* to tell these young women that they could have it all too, because the distinction between women who have succeeded and those who have not, is actually not so much about aptitude and talent, but attitude and perseverance.

Like Neha, many of you wrote to tell me that it made you laugh when you figured out the 'you too?' moments and I believe several of you felt deeply consoled that your problems were not uniquely your own. You told me that the book had empowered you to become the heroine of your story and had provided several useful suggestions, which you had used to improve your lives.

However, as my conversation with all of you deepened, I realised that it was still incomplete. Without a doubt, many of you have done well in life and successfully found the balance between home and work. You are paddling your way pluckily through the turbulent waters of gender-agnostic environments. But somewhere in a little corner of your heart, you have also succumbed to the belief that there is a ceiling beyond which you cannot grow. After all, only 17 per cent of start-ups have a woman partner, just 5 per cent of senior-management roles in organisations are filled by women, and only 3 per cent of VC funding goes to women entrepreneurs. There are hardly any women in public spheres like politics or policymaking and even fewer women university chancellors and IIM directors.

Many of you, while having stable careers and being individually brilliant, have reconciled yourselves to being defined only as Sonu's mom or Vivek's wife. And these are the things you and I need to change.

I have met you in different personas: as businesswomen, professors, scientists, tarot-card readers, editors or corporate managers. And I have seen loneliness in your eyes. With whom do you share the particular tribulations that come attached to being a working woman? The stress over getting the next promotion or not getting it? The frustration in dealing with a male subordinate who thinks he should have been the boss instead of you or the investor who looks at you and not your male partner while asking for a cup of coffee?

You may not have met them but there are many valiant women exactly like you, fighting tough battles in the big bad world all by themselves. Under all our different skins and varying skin-tones, we are soul sisters dealing with precisely the same issues. Whether apple-shaped, pear-shaped or an hourglass type, at the core we are ultimately identical – a mix of confidence and self-doubt that makes us single-handedly take on the world one day, and a bundle of nerves the next. And I want to share the anecdotes of your sisters with you, so you recognise that this is not your battle alone and draw strength and succour from their stories.

It is a fact that even today despite their stellar achievements, women are still treated as second-class citizens of the world. Whether getting talked over at board meetings (or at home) or not getting funding for a start-up as brilliant as any man's or just not getting paid as much as male colleagues, there seems to be a cosmic endeavour to ensure that women remain firmly seated on the substitutes' bench and never get to play the match.

There is no doubt in my mind that many external prejudices and stereotypes are obstructing your path to glory. However, I believe that there are several mistakes you are making too, which are preventing you from achieving the peak of what you are capable of.

It bothers me to see that you still lack confidence and continue to have the tentativeness of a young novice, despite all those certificates of excellence on the wall behind you. It concerns me that you have become fed up of fighting for your rights incessantly and have thus decided to give up on the battle. I watch as you adjudicate poorly on your own behalf by downplaying yourself and minimising your abilities. As a result you are fulfilling a mere fraction of your true potential.

I know that there is an entire universe inside you, waiting to be discovered, but I see you sitting at the edge of your seat, always afraid that someone may throw you out of the room because you believe that you are an imposter who will get caught one day despite your accomplishments.

But here's the truth: unlike Cinderella, you are not going to turn back into a beggar-maid at the stroke of midnight. You have genuinely worked hard to reach here. You rode to the ball not in a carriage conjured out of thin air by a fairy godmother, but in the car you bought with your own hard-earned money.

You did not need a fairy godmother to get you this far, but you do need someone to tell you that you definitely deserve to be here! And that there are vast and unconquered opportunities still ahead of you. Because the one single unassailable truth is that your best version is yet to come.

For that to happen however, there is only one magic wand and it is firmly in your own hand – when you realise that only you can prevent yourself from being condensed or minimised.

The world with its inherent patriarchal order will wish to lock us inside a narrow box of mores and traditions. But we cannot and must not allow it to bonsai us. The glass ceiling, whether of our own or someone else's making, has to be shattered.

In my own journey, it took a long time to understand this and most of these wise thoughts came to me around the age of fifty, when finally I became truly confident about who I am and when menopausal changes, while playing havoc with my sleep pattern and metabolism, were also ensuring higher testosterone levels and thus higher degrees of aggression. Behaviourally I have inevitably been a late bloomer (what can I say?) and, I feel I could have done many things differently if only I had that extra dose of gumption earlier. But there is no reason at all for you to have to wait for that testosterone to kick in!

When you read this book, you will realise that it invites you to reflect on what you have achieved so far, the restrictions you have imposed on yourself and how you have many times swayed to a tune not of your own making, by adjusting and accommodating, by choosing to keep quiet and by allowing yourself to drift. As you reflect, I hope you will recognise that the time has come for you to decide for yourself what you want to do and that this time around, you get to choose what you want. Just remember that your prospects are limitless and infinite, and they will take you wherever you want to go.

Rumi, the patron saint of the Twitteratti, says: 'Are you a drop in the ocean or the ocean in the drop?' *Lady, You are the Boss!* is for women who believe that no boundaries should curb them, no shackles should bind them and no barriers should come in the way of what they can truly achieve.

I hope this book gives you the courage to dance to a tune of your own making and pushes you to the furthest limits of your potential in your adventures at work.

Part One

PART ONE

A Minimum Life?

He says you are too much. You talk, laugh, smile, feel too much. But baby, here is the real problem. He is too little to appreciate that it took an entire galaxy being woven into one soul to make you.

—Nikita Gill

Centuries ago our cave-dwelling ancestors began a pattern of behaviour that seems to be continuing to this day in workplaces across the world.

In those days, men had to go out to hunt while women stayed in their caves to care for the children and the elderly and thus each behaved in a way that aided them best in their respective roles. The men donned masks and body paint, puffed up their chests, yelled battle cries and made themselves larger than life to intimidate their prey. The women, sharing a small living space with so many others, shrank themselves as much as they could to cooperate with each other and to avoid communal strife.

Thousands of years of evolution later, many things have changed. For example, men and women alike leave their homes to earn a living. But some things have not. The brunt of the care for children and the elderly is still shouldered by women. But the most puzzling unchanged status quo is that men still don their metaphorical war paint and puff up their chests with aplomb while women continue to shrink themselves to take up as little space as possible, despite the fact that they are going a-hunting too!

A male sales head will confidently proclaim that he has achieved his target even if the reality is that he has barely scrambled past the 80 per cent goalpost! A company of five hundred employees becomes a thousand and a two-crore salary becomes four when the story is being told by a lad! A fellow just about competent to be a marketing head will declare himself entirely ready to be a CEO. And I am yet to come across the CV of any Indian male in which he hasn't asserted that he was the captain of his university cricket team and always was a topper to boot!

All is bluff and bluster (and par for the course) in the day of a macho corporate Zorro. After all, even Antonio Banderas wore a mask. However, this doesn't bother me much since I have learnt to moderate any grandiloquent statements the gentlemen around me make. So if HD* (husband dearest) says he will be back by nine, my mental clock auto-corrects it to 11 p.m. If one of my CEOs says, 'Don't worry boss, we will deliver the goods within forty-five days at 100 per cent quality,' I immediately make mental notes to tell our clients that seventy-three days is the earliest they can expect the shipment. And when my male friends tell me that they had the most amazing holiday in the most beautiful villa on the hippest island in the Aegean Sea, where they had perfect weather throughout the third week of October, you can be sure that except for the fact that they did go on vacation, nothing else is remotely accurate!

---

*You may remember him from *Lady, You're Not a Man!*

What worries me however, is that women too have not evolved significantly from their cave-dwelling selves! They have been shrinking and subduing themselves from time immemorial and continue to operate at sub-par visibility levels even in contemporary times.

We brush aside compliments, don't speak up, speak hesitantly when we do, never ask for raises, negotiate superbly on behalf of others but never for ourselves, and let others take credit for our work. Despite being given a senior role or promotion based on merit, we continue to behave as if we don't actually deserve to be there and deem that the roles of sales head, CEO, managing partner or principal are way above our station!

Sadly, it is not just our cave-dwelling ancestors who should be blamed for our public mousiness. It is also the way we have been brought up and are bringing up our daughters – by censoring and diminishing them to be lesser than they are. We train our daughters to take up as little space as possible – not laugh aloud or dress flamboyantly or do anything that draws attention. We do it for their sake, to protect them, but unintentionally and wretchedly end up teaching them that to be invisible is good for them. Then how can we expect them to behave differently when they grow up?

When my yoga teacher sternly reprimanded me for the nth time about my poor posture, I flashed her a guilty look and sighed in frustration. I had hoped these weekly classes would be an escape from the madness of work. But the teacher's constant, albeit well-meaning, prods about my hunched shoulders were making me feel like a slightly feeble-minded pupil!

She had tried correcting me patiently. But the moment

I took my attention off them, my stubborn shoulders hunched forward of their own volition.

How could I explain to her that I may be a confident CEO in my fifties, but to my overprotective shoulders, I was still the confused little girl trying to deflect the attention of the creepy local uncle, even though I didn't understand what he was looking at! I was still the timid adolescent girl navigating a crowded street. I was the young adult trying not to get groped on the bus. It is an instinct honed by girls across the nation to avoid attracting the wrong kind of notice. Almost from our childhood, we learnt to hide our bodies using books, clipboards and every object from quotidian life, which could pass for armour; we intentionally developed a poor posture and walked with our heads down hoping this would be enough to keep us from being pawed. We dressed down, spoke softly and walked as tentatively as we could, moving about cautiously in a world that didn't want us to occupy too much space in it.

When my yoga teacher glares at me for not getting my posture right, how do I tell her that fifty years of self-protective instincts do not evaporate overnight no matter how hard I try?

Both evolutionarily and behaviourally, the cards are frustratingly stacked against women. Men on the contrary have always been taught to maximise themselves. Whilst women shrink, slink, crouch and refrain from taking up too much space, men naturally move into it and claim it as their own.

A glaring example of this is the predominantly masculine noises we hear all around us – inside our homes; on our television screens; in public places, institutes and offices.

When I go to women-only colleges for workshops, all the students are vocal and boisterous. Certainly there are differences among those who speak up and those who don't, but that is largely attributable to differences in personality types. Bolder girls speak up and confidently express themselves, expecting to be heard – and that is a beautiful sight to behold. Quite a different experience awaits me when conducting workshops in co-ed colleges. There are no introverts and extroverts anymore. Only women and men! Invariably, the shy participants hanging back are women and the confident talkers asking questions are men!

Across classrooms and boardrooms, this pattern reveals itself without fail. In common spaces, women automatically register societal cues that designate them as second-class citizens, and lo and behold, they dissolve into secondary and silent characters.

In my own case I notice that although I have an important point to make in a board meeting, I hesitate. I avoid interrupting whoever is talking, which leaves me with limited occasions to talk, since the other board members, obviously male, are incessantly and continuously talking. I feel guilty if I take an extra minute to voice my opinion, because the board schedule has a time-bound agenda. My fellow board members, all male, are gloriously oblivious to any such dilemma as they interject at will, speak with utmost confidence about subject matters they are least qualified to have an opinion on, and drone on and on even as the poor company secretary starts fidgeting and looking agonisedly at the ticking clock.

And when I do find a pause in the proceedings (which only happens when said board members have been distracted by the arrival of tea, coffee and cookies) and muster up the courage to speak, I am likely to say, 'I have just a small point to make …' or 'May I only specify …' or 'Umm, maybe this is not the right way to evaluate competition.'

Just? Only? Maybe? Such pallid, insipid language! I know the points I am making are of significance, I know that nobody else in the room has arrived at these inferences. But evidently my tongue doesn't know this and continues using vocabulary that is destined to be snubbed.

It is no wonder that my fellow directors started taking me seriously only after several board meetings and repeated exposure to my inputs. It was not their fault; they were all very intelligent and thoughtful human beings. But if my own tone was hesitant, my body language timid and my words diffident, why would anyone have the patience to analyse the content when time was a constraint?

We think our work will speak for itself, good deeds will always be noticed, talent will not remain hidden for long, so we choose to keep quiet, either deliberately or because we have been conditioned to do so. I want to break your heart right here and tell you this is complete and utter moonshine, like the fairy tales we read in our childhood.

In order to be recognised, appreciated and successful, you have to be your own fairy godmother and your own advocate. And you had better hurry up because the boys who have read the same fairy tales were being programmed to go out, slay the dragon and blow their trumpets from the grandstands.

The only way to deal with this tentativeness is to stand up boldly, make your voice heard and your opinion matter. Like Kirti, a friend of mine. A famous author and well-known Twitter influencer, Kirti was called out by a mutual friend for promoting her books on Twitter. Our friend said this was rather forward of her. Kirti was unapologetic. 'Who will promote my books, if not me?' she asserted. And rightly so. If we don't talk about ourselves, I assure you no one else will.

If our voices are not heard and we are not forceful in our articulation, how will our opinions register in an uncaring and dismissive world? By being visible and vocal in private and public domains, we add our voices to the chorus that forms opinions and becomes the basis for any action. The wisdom of the crowd always prevails, and if we want pro-women actions, it is up to us to ensure we are a significant voice in that crowd.

We may live in a world that trains us into silence. But fortunately, we live in times when we know not to take such instructions silently. To begin with, let us fight strong, talk loud, laugh hard and assert ourselves without guilt. Let us take up as much space as we want, stand tall and walk upright with pride. Let us live unabashedly, loudly and wholeheartedly.

A life lived in fear is an abbreviated, feeble life. And that life is not for you, a woman who has the whole universe residing within her!

IN SHORT

- Women have been conditioned over centuries to minimise themselves.
- This reflects in their behaviour at work too, where despite being competent they are far more tentative, unsure and diffident than they need to be.
- We need to change this and the change can only come from within, when we reclaim our voices and proclaim our talent and skills to the world, loudly and unapologetically.
- If men can be their own publicists, what stops women from doing the same? After all we are competing in the same domain.
- Let's change how we bring up our daughters. Let us allow them to be as boisterous, flamboyant and visible as our sons. They deserve the same amount of space as their brothers.

Imposter Syndrome

I have a self to recover, a queen. Is she dead, is she sleeping?
Where has she been, with her lion-red body, her wings of glass?

—Sylvia Plath

I stared at our new head of HR with some consternation. She stared back, perplexed. The fact that she was highly competent was not under debate. Her terrific track record and dynamic thinking had led to her being appointed the head of the department at an age much younger than the norm. But as I sat there, trying to have a conversation with her that I'd repeatedly had before, I realised with a sinking feeling that she was not her predecessor.

Her predecessor, Sara, had been an aggressive and assertive department head who hadn't much cared for boundaries. She had unerringly understood the implicit authority of her role and therefore had been involved in the functions of all the other departments. She saw herself adding value to those departments and would make sure that she was not only part of the decision-making, but also an active influence there. Through intelligent use of her abilities and experience she had expanded the parameters of her role so well that HR was treated as a crucial voice at the boardroom table and not merely as a support department in the organisation.

When it was time for Sara to move to a higher position, I was sad to lose her. But I recognised that a person of her calibre needed a playing field proportional to her ever-expanding skillset. Enter the new recruit – our young but talented HOD from whom we expected great things.

Janice came into the organisation at a time when we were going through a huge sales challenge. But she made no move to pitch solutions or offer opinions about it. As we sat having this now-familiar conversation, I asked her why she wasn't a part of the sales meetings.

'I wasn't invited,' she replied glumly.

'I hope you realise that revenue is currently our biggest challenge? What's the concept of HR that we have built in this organisation? It's not just to recruit and train people. It's also to be involved in the business functions and see how you can be a source of support. Your role is exactly the same as that of your predecessor. You are supposed to be a partner to the CEO. Are you seeing yourself like that or not?' I asked, frustrated.

Janice looked like she desperately wanted to please but didn't know how. As she gazed at me deeply anguished, I felt like I had kicked a puppy. Truth be told, I identified with her more than she realised. And I was hard on her because I saw her on the verge of making the same mistake I had once made. With disastrous consequences.

I am talking about a mistake many women make repeatedly, a self-debilitating misconception they suffer from called, rather dramatically, 'The Imposter Syndrome'. The syndrome is defined as a psychological pattern in which individuals doubt their accomplishments and internalise their fears of being worthless. They feel that their position has been handed to them by a twist of fate or good fortune and that they have not earned it. This leads them to be tentative and uncertain, exactly when they are supposed to be pushing themselves to make the most of a new opportunity.

Flashback to three decades ago when I was a bright-eyed twenty-something who had only one goal in life – to get into an IIM. While appearing for the Common Admission Test, an exam that about two lakh entrants take and only two thousand crack, I was not nervous. I was a bright student. I had been preparing for it with single-minded focus and had aced all the practice tests.

When the results came in, no one was surprised to learn that I was the only person from my batch to have got through to IIM Bangalore, Ahmedabad and Kolkata at that first written stage. But the interview round was quite another matter. The conservative home environment I grew up in deemed all knowledge that was not in the school syllabus irrelevant. My inherent shyness didn't help matters. I performed poorly in the group discussion and interview rounds.

When the results were announced, I was shattered to find that I hadn't made it to any of the IIMs. My family went into mourning. I spent the next few months moping over broken dreams, staring forlornly every morning at our letterbox and willing the unlikely call letter to drop into it. And then one day, magically, it did.

This was their second list. I hadn't made it on their first. I couldn't care less. I packed my bags and rode off into the sunset. Given how precious this victory was to me, I worked hard to make the most of it. The first two months at IIM, I did well in every new subject that was introduced. Even the alien finance and quantitative mathematics courses were no match for my voracious determination.

Then as I slowly started getting to know my classmates better, I learnt that the majority of them were from IIT and had some impressive work experience under their belts. I started comparing myself with all the bright sparks around me and suddenly the fact that I hadn't made it on the first list took on new meaning. It must be because I was a mere graduate from a regular college with no work experience! That was who I was – a second-lister who had meandered by sheer luck into a constellation she was never supposed to be part of! I spent the next few weeks walking around with scarlet letters of shame plastered figuratively on my forehead!

And then the obvious happened. My grades started to dip and for the remainder of my first year, I did poorly in all my exams. The eight to nine months of failure were wrapped in not only misery but also mystery. How did I lose the plot so badly?

I was hurtling full speed in a downward spiral and I could not pull the brakes. From the shame of not being a first-lister to not being as qualified as my classmates, I let externalities convince me that I was not good enough. Imposter syndrome tells you you're a fraud for choosing to inhabit the role you've rightfully earned. Back then, I believed it.

Many years after this IIM debacle, a previous boss asked me to head Zee TV. The job would be a quantum leap from my then-current position. Hesitantly I accepted. The environment I entered was a highly charged one. Amid rampant internal workplace politics and intense external competition from the newly re-launched Star Plus channel, it was a time of crisis. Three months later, the CEO who got me into the organisation left it. Isolated in that unfriendly atmosphere, with my only source of support gone, I began to question my ability to get the job done. The ground was ripe for the imposter syndrome to raise its ugly head yet again! 'I am not trained for this job.' 'This position is higher than the promotion that would have come about in the normal course of my career.' 'This malevolent environment is just not conducive to productivity.'

But this time I was better prepared to handle these invidious beliefs, simply because I knew they were lurking like ghostly shadows around me.

I reminded myself that nobody was questioning my qualifications to be there except myself. Outwardly everyone was seeing the president of Zee TV even if inwardly I felt like a junior executive starting her first job. I knew I could help that organisation. I knew that my ex-manager had not recommended me for this position as a favour. The stakes were much too high for that. He had done so because he felt I was the most qualified person for this task.

Backing my own intelligence and reinforcing my sense of self-worth to myself, I realised, were the key to fighting the deadly insidious forces of imposter syndrome. This time around, I was committed to becoming my own ally instead of a saboteur. And I proceeded to own my role as president and did work I am still proud of.

The syndrome shows its worst form when we are given a platform to operate on and we choose to occupy only a small part of it. Quite like my newly minted HR head was now doing. 'I am too young. I am too junior. The CEO and I are not at the same level. I can't barge into meetings I am not invited to.'

We all suffer from this syndrome at some point in our lives. Yes, even that confident alpha male colleague who is ponderously explaining the impact of agrarian distress on the economic environment to you just now!

And my own experience tells me that there is a deceptively simple way to fight this enemy. Self-talk. It works like magic but we just do not do enough of it. In this highly connected world we spend so much time having partial conversations with best friends, half best friends, enemies turned friends, mere acquaintances and random aliens that we forget the most important person we need to talk to – the person belonging to the face that stares at us every day in the mirror.

It is vitally important that we reacquaint ourselves with her, talk to her and remind her of all the hard work, perseverance and talent she has, that have brought her to this juncture. The successes she garnered in the past because of her ability and the impact she generated because of her skill are not a twist of fate. They are her right and her due.

Then we need to go back to repeating a basic exercise we learnt in elementary school – Match the Columns. The moment we start matching the column of our skills with the column of the tasks at hand, we will realise that there is no better person to do those tasks.

Who will stand up and fight for us but ourselves? Especially when the ghosts are inside and not outside us? We can do anything we want. We are capable. We are in this place because we've earned the right to be here. And if we have to fight with our own selves to believe that, then fight we must. The imposter is not you. It never was.

IN SHORT

- Women suffer from 'the imposter syndrome', which insidiously tells them that they are not good enough to be where they are and that it is just happenstance that aided their progress, not their experience or skills.
- They are reluctant to fully occupy the platform they have been given because of this belittling belief and end up compromising their growth.
- Constant self-assurance is the trick to chase out the imposter from within.
- It is crucial to accept that the world knows what it is doing when it presents women with opportunities, and they must make full use of the breaks they get.

Strengths Not Weaknesses

*I take most things as a compliment.
I find it makes life much easier.*

—Dowager Countess, *Downton Abbey*

From the comfortable distance of thirty-five years I can look back and laugh at my adolescent self. Poor thing, she seems to have spent her teenage years mostly being either tongue-tied and shy, or moody and angry. A large part of those painful years however, was spent being hopelessly mortified at everything around me – the old Fiat car my father drove breaking down at awkward intervals, entailing all of us getting out and pushing it when we were all dressed in our finery; my sister laughing loudly in movie halls; my parents going to meet my teachers at school; or me developing a football-sized stye on the day of my cousin's wedding!

It is a medical fact that teenagers suffer from something known as cognitive distortion as a result of the mismatch in the development of different parts of their brains as they are growing up. This distortion results in exaggerated and unreasonable thoughts that cause them to misperceive reality and then subsequently feel bad. Every small thing that goes wrong, such as a stye in the eye, is either a catastrophe of ginormous proportions or it is a personal attack on their self. (Why did fate make me look so ugly with one eye half-blinded because of that huge stye just on the day of the sangeet when there are so many good looking boys around and everyone else is looking so gorgeous? I am doomed forever!)

However, as teens grow into adulthood, the laggard part of the brain responsible for calm reasoning catches up with the fast-paced anxious part and things start falling into some semblance of peace and quiet. While this biological evolutionary theory seems to have explained everything very neatly and tied it up with a cute bow, it appears as if the female brain missed reading this, because it continues suffering from heightened anxious brain syndrome despite moving deep into adulthood! What else can explain our peculiar penchant for always seeing the negative in ourselves rather than the positives? For concentrating on criticisms rather than praise? For seeing all flaws magnified manifold in ourselves? And thus remaining acutely anxious most of the time?

Certainly I see a wide disparity in self-confidence between the male and female managers who've worked under me. A female manager will come out of a presentation and immediately start muttering about all the things she did wrong. She will filter out all the positives and retain only the mistakes she made. While the male manager usually swaggers out of such meetings assured that he's just delivered the Gettysburg Address. Recently we had one such incident. One of our male senior heads was supposed to talk about a specific topic. Instead he gave a long-winded speech that jumped from his childhood to Aristotle while meandering through an example about an extreme sport no one had heard of. It had little to do with the topic at hand

and, frankly, made little sense. He came up to me with a self-satisfied smirk after the meeting and drawled, 'That went rather well, no?'

I goggled and gasped and wiggled my eyebrows, which is my default response with these pompous lads, since banging them on the head with a hefty hammer could be misconstrued as unprofessionalism!

It would be hilarious if this were an isolated incident. But when the pattern keeps recurring without break, then the joke is on us women. Two friends of mine – Rajni and Rajeev – recently left their jobs to become entrepreneurs. Rajni has set up a digital platform that offers integrated wellness solutions to corporate employees. She has been working for the past twenty years in this field. She had researched extensively before embarking on the project. The technology that she is implementing in her start-up is highly innovative. But a year has passed since she began working on it and there is no launch date in sight.

Every time she comes to me for a mentoring session, she shares how she has changed the platform yet again, how she has tweaked the services on offer or how she has improved the website. But she continues to leave each session unsure of the viability of her project and even less ready to go public with it than she was at the beginning of the session.

Rajeev on the other hand launched his start-up in four short months. He created a digital platform that aggregates bookings and appointments for hotels and clubs. He has had as tumultuous a time of it as Rajni – getting sidetracked by false starts, having to change technology partners and dealing with a lot of pressure from investors in trying to get conversions.

But at least he started. And because he started, he's seeing some success. This, in turn, is helping him move forward. Whereas Rajni is floating about in a pool of her own uncertainty. Every time I meet Rajeev, he is on an entrepreneur's high. 'Hey, Apurva, this service is going to actually change the way we live our lives, it's a blockbuster! Everyone I meet says they have never seen such a platform,' he exclaims.

I envy his confidence. Here's a guy who is helping businesses manage their bookings and he is convinced he is changing the world because of it. Rajni's platform has the ability to genuinely improve people's lives and, consequently, the actual potential to make the world a better place. But her confidence is non-existent because she can only see the problems in her platform. Her insecurities are so strong that she may never get around to doing anything either for the world or for herself!

Focusing on and magnifying weaknesses is not the monopoly of women alone. I look around at what happens in our organisations and I see a flawed system at work. When creating our training programmes, we typically analyse the skills of all the people in the organisation and figure out their strengths and weaknesses. More often than not, training programmes concentrate on how to overcome those weaknesses while taking the strengths for granted.

Great sports teams are built on the opposite philosophy. Good coaches know that the secret to a knockout performance lies in building on a player's strengths and minimising their weaknesses. If Sachin Tendulkar was constantly told to improve his bowling, where would our cricket team have been? Why strive to be an average all-rounder when you can be the world's greatest batsman? When we leverage our strengths to tackle challenges we become the best version of ourselves.

A very long time ago I knew a girl who worked with me in advertising where she started her career as part of the batch of management trainees we got every year. As seniors, we trained them for six months before sending them out into the big, bad world. There's a reason she stands out in my memory even after so many years.

Tanya was a slip of a girl, about four foot nothing. Really tiny and from a no-name college. All of us seniors subjected the trainees to time-honoured hazing rituals. We believed that we could not allow the trainees to be sent out in the world with a chip on their shoulders. It was our solemn duty to knock some sense and humility into them before letting them loose on egotistic clients and creative directors. Both girls and boys would cry in those programmes, thanks to the bullying that went on in the name of hazing.

But for Tanya, everything was water off a duck's back. Whatever criticism was levied at her was subjected to a curious moderation exercise. She would halt in her tracks and listen to the criticism very carefully. When I observed her during such instances I could almost see the wheels turning in her mind.

If she decided that what she'd received was a valid criticism, she would make a change in her behaviour. If she decided it was not constructive, she would dismiss it. For anyone who cared to notice, Tanya's opinion of the criticism received was apparent in her subsequent behaviour.

As I observed her during the training period, I learnt to identify the nuances of her moderation exercise. What she thought was relevant, she imbibed. What she thought was exaggerated or disrespectful, she discarded. But never

ever did she take any negative feedback personally or as a remark on her character. Her work was separate from her personhood and she was careful to maintain that distinction.

Tanya has done extraordinarily well in life. She's jumped fields, changed careers and pivoted with élan. In the last ten years I've not seen many people like her, people who have grown so much or taken on such diverse opportunities. Though we are not in touch any more, I will never forget the girl who was so clear in her thinking and more importantly, her evaluation of herself.

We all are a cocktail of strengths and weaknesses, strong and weak points. We need to learn to see both with an unjaundiced eye. There is absolutely no need to catastrophise weaknesses, whether in ourselves or in the platform we are creating. Life is always about the middle ground. Your platform will never be perfect, but it is also not likely to be tottering on shaky foundations only to collapse like a structure built by a corrupt municipal corporation! And you can always tinker with it later – but launch it at least? Building on strengths and working at minimising weaknesses is a constant endeavour. Even our own prejudices about ourselves should not be allowed to come in the way of marching ahead.

Tanya's level of self-awareness led to her confidence, which allowed her to embrace opportunities with gusto. She didn't let the anxious part of her brain colour her reality and allowed calm reasoning to dictate her behaviour.

I've witnessed what focusing on strengths instead of weaknesses can do to a woman's life. And I've intimately experienced how doing the opposite hurts. The stye is never as large as it seems, and more notably, it is temporary. Regardless of that, you have beautiful eyes. Make the most of them. A little kajal, perhaps?

IN SHORT

- Women tend to minimise their strengths and maximise their weaknesses, in complete contrast to men.
- Constantly worrying about your flaws and making them larger than they are is a sure way to get stuck in a rut.
- If you concentrate on your strengths and work at building on them, it will not only give you the confidence to move forward but also enthuse investors, bosses and colleagues to support you.

Need to Feel Needed

It's important to set goals which change.
Constant endeavour should be part of our lives.

—Swami Chinmayananda

It's my experience that women get extremely excited with the prospect of being needed. Men, meanwhile, stride through life in the fond belief that they are essential for the world to exist, so any external validation of this feeling is really not required. The sun shines on, tides come and go, and trumpets blow triumphantly only because the male human walks upon the earth – that's the way they look at life. Women are not born with this sense of entitlement, so they struggle to believe they are important and thus get super excited when someone makes them feel wanted. (I don't mean that in the Biblical sense as much as the warm and fuzzy feeling that comes from becoming a core and beloved part of any ecosystem.)

My first job as a freshly minted management trainee was at an advertising agency. Those were pre-millennial days when we were all insecure about our place in the world and pathetically grateful to the organisations that had deigned to hire us at a pittance. All of us began our training in the operations department, which was really just a fancy name to describe the gofers.

We were the coordinators between the tantrum-throwing, whimsical and crazy gods in the creative department and the beleaguered, stressed-out, work-hard-party-harder servicing types, who were at perpetual war with each other. The creative team was busy sitting on their Olympian heights thinking of the next Cannes-winning headline with which to sell the new detergent. And the servicing team was busy wooing the client at three-hour boozy lunch sessions. It fell on the ops team to do all the drudge work.

Our department's role was that of a plumber, or rather the plumber's assistant. But it was also the department that made things happen. Be it coordinating briefs with writers, writers with designers, layouts with client approval and then back again for changes; running to the typesetter and the printing press to catch the last courier for the release of the ad the next day – we kept the wheels of the organisation in motion.

All of us youngsters enjoyed that role tremendously and felt important and indispensable, especially diffident souls like me. So when that first year was up and we were finally getting transferred to our permanent jobs – strategic planning, client servicing, media planning and the like – I went through a bout of uncertainty and hesitation.

I was doing well, enjoying my work and, most importantly, feeling needed. Why then should I move? The boys in my batch obviously shared none of these doubts. They were raring to get out of their training knickers and the dead-end ops department and march towards the glorious career that indubitably lay ahead of them.

Eventually of course I made the rational and correct decision and joined the rest of my batch in their quest for success. However, it was a salutary lesson on the trap we can fall into if we anchor ourselves around our need to feel needed!

You have all been in situations like this – in organisations or departments where you are respected, liked, successful and (most importantly) vital to their functioning! The CEO thinks you are completely indispensable and your cabin is littered with BEST BOSS IN THE WORLD cups, stickers and wall hangings given to you by an adoring team. Your calendar is filled with meetings and conferences and one-on-ones. You walk into the office and everyone rushes to you, clamouring for your attention. Every moment is action packed and you are the pivot of that action! Atta girl, you say to yourself every morning as you breathlessly rush into work. If any of you have watched *Madam Secretary*, the CBS TV drama series, you'll know that in every episode, when the protagonist walks into office each morning, her team accosts her at the lift with panting tongues and puppy-dog expressions, to apprise her about the latest crisis that has occurred in some part of the world. And off she flies to resolve it, with much aplomb and verve. You are emulating exactly that in your own little niche and heaven seems to have no boundaries at that moment! Only a dunce would want to meddle with anything in that perfect picture!

But is the picture really perfect? Or is being appreciated and not taken for granted such a self-serving luxury for us women that we allow it to stymie our growth?

I don't want to be morbid, but the fact is that women have always lived with the feeling of being unwanted, right from the stage of being undesirable female foetuses to becoming the girl child whose birth is seen as a curse, to being constantly shushed because girls are not supposed to be heard, or rebuked for being too 'noticeable'. It would be infinitely preferable, dear girl, if you did not exist, but since you do, can you be invisible please?

No wonder women are particularly susceptible to this desire to feel needed. The mother who keeps babying her grown-up children, the wife who waits hand and foot on her husband, the secretary who will never share with the temp where she gets that perfect cup of coffee for her boss are all manifestations of this deeply felt need for need!

One of my mentees is the head of a business vertical in a large IT company. She is currently being groomed for a larger role in the organisation. As part of her personal development, I identified a list of milestones that she had to work on at different stages of the mentoring programme. The first six months went past like a dream, with Radha successfully meeting all her deadlines. Then overnight, she froze in her tracks. For the next six months, despite repeated reminders and gently nudging conversations, it seemed to me that she was making no progress at all! I finally had a tough talk with her to figure out what was going wrong. She launched into a detailed explanation of how for the last six months she had been managing her sister's family since said sister had twisted her ankle and needed her help. She was also managing her brother's immigration process to Australia and working with her former boss who had requested her support to finish a couple of projects. And all this while managing an intensive work schedule that required her to be on calls with clients operating in the US, at (obviously) US timings! No wonder she hadn't been able to do anything about her personal growth milestones!

Sheepishly, she admitted that she had a problem with saying no to people who asked her for help. While I admire her Good Samaritan outlook and noble heart, I remain convinced that she was secretly enjoying this ultra-dependence of everyone on her!

Until very recently, I was a manic multitasker, managing home and hearth and travel plans and staff schedules and school projects and laundry services, operating on a schedule any military general would have been proud of! Being praised on an almost daily basis by HD and son for my efficiency (I realised when I grew wiser that they were employing a very convenient motivating strategy with great success), the joy of feeling needed was enough to keep me going like a wildly spinning top. Then one day I realised my misplaced zeal was, err, misplaced. I was burning myself out while also not finding time to do what I truly wanted to do!

So how should we get out of this self-serving and misplaced joy we get in feeling that our tiny worlds would collapse if we were not around to hold them together?

I met Reena when she was a hotshot corporate lawyer in one of the largest legal firms in the country. She was handling an IPR matter for us, which was intricate and long-drawn. Over an extended period of sitting outside the senior counsel's room and amid high court hearings, we got to know each other quite well. She confided in me that while she was enjoying her job, she felt she had started stagnating in her role. As an expert on IP matters, she was much sought after and her views respected within her firm as well as within the legal fraternity. However, she longed to widen her knowledge base beyond her current niche. We won the case and I lost touch with Reena, till I bumped into her at a function where she was receiving an award. In the intervening years, she told me, she had given up her cushy and high-paying job and joined a much smaller firm where she had the opportunity to expand her scope of legal knowledge tremendously.

'I was shit scared to leave my erstwhile firm,' she said. 'I had spent fifteen years there and they gave me tremendous love and respect. My family thought I was demented when I told them I was leaving. I brazened it out at that time, but I was terrified inside.' She grimaced at remembering how tough a decision it had been. But look where she has reached now!

Thanks to our evolutionary and genetic makeup, human beings are wired for security and we find it extremely hard to move out of our comfort zones (and in the case of women, our comforting zones). The fear of the unknown is a powerful motivator to keep us stuck to the status quo. Added to that is the quixotic desire of women to remain ensconced in environments that keep playing 'you are wanted' in an unending feedback loop.

But in the very moments you are feeling the most comfortable and the most needed, you should be asking yourself some uncomfortable questions. Are you learning? Are you growing? Are you adding value to yourself? Or has being mission-critical become more important to you than your personal growth?

When you don't push the boundaries of your potential, you end up wallowing in the soothing but stagnating comfort of a mud bath. This may be relaxing, but it is also debilitating!

Each time you break out of the cocoon you have woven around yourself, you will emerge a stronger and more stunning butterfly, as I witnessed in the case of Reena and many others like her, who were plucky enough to walk out of their secure spaces. And if you are good at your work, you will become mission-critical wherever you are and whatever you do!

To grow, you have to break that cocoon again and again and yet again, however lovingly you may have built it. This cycle will never end. It should not.

IN SHORT

- We all like to belong and enjoy the feeling of being needed, but sometimes it can come in the way of our growth.
- After being at the receiving end of so many challenges and so much negativity from society, a woman is justified in seeking the security of an encouraging workplace and a supportive boss. But it is important to question whether that cocoon is stymieing your growth.
- Have the courage to jump off the cliff. You will be surprised at how strong your wings are and at the gusts of wind sent your way by a benevolent universe, to help you soar higher and higher! Be brave.

Learning to Let Go

Letting go means to come to the realisation that some people are a part of your history, but not a part of your destiny.

—Steve Maraboli

Vinita cornered me at my sister's fiftieth birthday party recently and launched into a litany about her eighteen-year career in one of the largest FMCG companies in the country. She had quit the job suddenly while on an international posting, and for four years thereafter had been trying to get back into the same organisation.

It was a social setting so I was listening to her half-heartedly while enjoying the general bonhomie around me and the fine whisky. But my ears perked up at her comment on trying to get back for four years.

'I was one of the fast-trackers in the organisation. After about fifteen years of consistent A-ratings, I was sent to work with one of our largest franchisee operations in Europe,' she recounted. 'I did well there too, increasing margins by 15 per cent every year. Everyone seemed mighty pleased with my performance. But then there was an issue with my boss.'

Here the story got a little muddy. She glossed over the details of what had actually transpired. 'Suffice to say that I complained. They offered to shift me to another location.

But I refused,' she told me grimly. 'So I quit and came back to India.'

'Okay, I get it, but then what is this bright idea about trying to get back into the same organisation?' I asked.

'After I came back, I realised I had made a mistake in not accepting their offer to shift me to another operation. I like the organisation very much. I want to go back. I know there are several opportunities for someone like me, with my experience and calibre. But they are not responding,' she replied in a woebegone tone.

'What do you mean you are not getting a response?' I asked.

'Every time I get in touch, they say there is a vacancy. They agree that I am the right fit for it. But then there is radio silence. I have tried across all their verticals, spoken to everyone I know there, but nothing moves,' she said dolefully.

'How long has this been going on?' I enquired, even though I knew the answer by heart now. I wanted to hear it from her again. Most importantly I wanted her to hear what she was saying. 'Four years,' she repeated.

I asked why she hadn't applied anywhere else. 'I want to work only in that organisation. It's the best in its field and I was happy there,' she confessed mournfully.

'My dear Vinita, YOU may want to work there. But THEY obviously don't want you to work for them! Don't you realise that? Otherwise wouldn't you have got something in four years?' I looked at her, exasperated.

'But why?' she wailed. 'I was a star performer!'

I wanted to shake her hard to make her realise the BOP (blindingly obvious point) she was missing! 'Vinita, obviously whatever transpired between you and your erstwhile boss has created some ripples within the organisation that they are not sharing with you.' I enunciated the words kindly but clearly to drive the message home.

'It's so unfair,' she cried. 'I was right and he was wrong.' I sympathised but also pointed out that she was now out of the organisation while he was still there. The hard truth is that organisations tend to believe their current employees rather than former employees. 'But it's so unfair,' she muttered on replay. 'Why don't they tell me the reason?'

I was awash with pity for her but there was not much I could do, so I left her peering into her gin and tonic and softly crooning to the melting ice cubes that life was unjust indeed.

A harsh reality of life is that many times we end up fighting not facts and direct criticisms but spectres of slander and untruths. Phantoms of rumours, backbiting, seniors taking a dislike to us because of their own insecurities and stymieing our growth. But how does one fight something one cannot confront? It's shadow-boxing at best and no one ever won a shadow-boxing contest – not even Muhammad Ali!

One of the reasons we women are not able to rise to the next rung is an unwillingness to step out of our comfort zones in the mistaken belief that being useful, invaluable and irreplaceable is the acme of our career. That attitude constrains growth, as we've already discussed in the previous chapter. The moment you become irreplaceable, you become part of the furniture and fixtures and are likely to get immortalised in the fixed asset register of your organisation rather than get promoted!

The other equally significant reason is that many times women just get stuck in the past. Men on the other hand have an uncanny ability to move on. They are easily able to let go of the good and the bad, the security and the comfort, with an eye firmly fixed on the next role, the higher salary offer or the bigger car.

If you've devoted a sizeable chunk of your life to an organisation, chances are you are invested personally as well. The mistake is when we assume those feelings are mutual. You can be liked, respected and admired, but it is highly unlikely that an organisation or its leadership will be personally invested in you the way you are in them.

Many of us make this mistake repeatedly. We don't get plum assignments, we are left out of the mid-year increment cycle, we don't get the role transfer that we want, all without a single negative word said to us by our bosses. And despite the clear albeit unsaid messaging, we don't get the hint because we weren't told in so many words!

Only on TV and in movies do people get closure from the party who has wronged them. In real life we have to get up, dust off the hurt and move on while learning to cultivate our own moral code.

My friend Priya was extremely attached to the marquee lifestyle brand she was working for. She had literally created the entire brand from scratch after joining a small organisation that had serendipitously innovated its way into being at the forefront of the indigenous handicrafts wave that had hit our fashion industry a decade ago.

She lived, dreamed and breathed the brand and had lovingly worked on its entire DNA, right from the slight curve in its logo to the designing of its hundred stores. But when there was an opportunity to expand it internationally, the role was given to her colleague. Priya took the setback like a trooper, didn't allow it to impact her work and carried on working in her usual cheerful go-getter fashion.

A couple of years later when the company got some serious PE funding, they wanted a COO as part of the succession-planning process. Priya had worked all along with the CEO as his loyal lieutenant, grudging not an iota of the hard work she had put in and the personal life she had sacrificed because of her passion for the brand. But the CEO and rest of the board decided to look outside the firm for candidates.

Priya was devastated. The labour she had put in for over a decade, the late nights, the early-morning flights, the sourcing of artisans by visiting some of the remotest areas of the country in extremely trying travel conditions, the brick-by-brick building of the hundred stores – everything had gone to nought! Life had snatched away from her what she truly deserved, what she had worked hard for with single-minded devotion.

But after a week-long bout of crying herself silly, she got up, hid her puffy eyes behind celebrity worthy sunglasses, applied blazing red lipstick, went into the office and quit! She encashed her thankfully sizeable stock options and set up an online venture in the same space. Today Priya is the poster child of online platforms and one of the better known and successful names in the e-commerce space.

Can we assume we will always be treated fairly? No. If we are lucky life will deal us only one or two blows. The truly lucky are those who refuse to allow the blows to hinder their progress.

There is a Zen story of two travelling monks who reached a river in the course of their journey. There they met a young woman. Since the river was in full spate, she asked if they could carry her across. One of the monks hesitated, but the other quickly put her on his shoulders, transported her across the water and put her down on the other bank.

She thanked him and departed. The monk who had hesitated remained preoccupied and agitated for quite a long while after that. Finally, unable to hold his silence, he spoke out. 'Brother, our spiritual training teaches us to avoid any contact with women. But you picked that one up on your shoulders and carried her!'

'Brother,' the second monk replied, 'I set her down on the other side while you are still carrying her with you, even now.'

It's an important lesson to remember in life's journey too. The unfair treatment, the needy bosses and the stultifying jobs are best left in the only place they deserve to be – the past. If we have to be swift in our voyages and successful in our ventures, we have no choice but to learn to let go.

IN SHORT

- Life sends many opportunities our way, but it also sends difficulties, challenges, inequities and injustice.
- When we have been treated unfairly, we want to stubbornly fight to correct the wrong done to us.
- Retreating is also a strategy. If we remain stuck in the past the wound will continue to fester and take over a larger part of our lives than it deserves to own.
- It is not necessary that the world will come to our support. We must learn to let go and move on.

Last Woman Standing

Nobody's taller than the last man standing.

—LaMichael James

Let me tell you a story about Manisha, a fiercely ambitious and devil-may-care friend of mine. Manisha studied HR at XLRI, the country's premier human resources institute, around the same time I was earning my MBA stripes at another venerable institution. She proceeded to get a job with a multinational bank straight out of campus and over the next eighteen years, steadily moved up the rung in the finance sector to become VP–HR. During this time, with characteristic aplomb, she had two lovely children, moved cities a couple of times and had a brief stint abroad. She recently returned to the motherland with yet another step up the corporate ladder. She had worked tremendously hard to reach where she is, and when she bought a plush apartment in midtown Mumbai, we all gathered there to toast her success.

Reminiscing about the decades that had flown past too quickly, we compared the bouquets and the battle scars that we had gathered along the way with the comfortable equanimity of distance and middle age. As we nattered away, she reminded me of an incident around five years ago when seething with frustration, she had come over for a venting session. Her immediate boss had quit and they were thinking of replacing him with an outsider. There were various logical reasons being submitted as to why she wasn't being considered for the role. What was evident, but left unsaid, were her two small children. Since the job demanded a fair amount of travel, there were doubts about whether she would be able to cope in this role.

She believed she was capable of taking on the assignment but felt frustrated at the brick walls she kept encountering. Hence the late-night advice seeking and multiple glasses of wine (watered down, since neither of us has a head for alcohol). We plotted and planned what her move should be. Armed with her track record, past accomplishments, a strategy of what she planned to do as GM, a rehearsed answer for addressing the elephant in the room in the form of her ability to manage home and travel, and the advantages she had over an external candidate, she sought an appointment with the head of HR and the CEO. And she walked away triumphantly with the role! We celebrated with un-watered wine and she went on to excel in her new position.

The next few years she remained so busy with the workload the promotion brought her that I rarely got to see her, and then she went abroad.

We talked about her trailblazing career after that one hiccup and admired the rows of trophies she had been awarded, both from her organisation and externally. She proudly told me that she was the only woman from her batch to have become head of HR. As she took me around her new apartment, I saw pictures of the family's international holidays and artefacts collected from trips around the world. Her mother-in-law declared that no woman in their family had attained the heights Manisha had in the workplace, and all of us basked pleasantly in the glow of a job well done. We had all been part of her journey and were so proud of her success. We knew that only 5 per cent of women in India reach the level she had climbed and that gave us a sense of immense satisfaction.

'Now I want to relax,' she smiled. 'I have more than I could ever have wanted.' I looked at her, flummoxed. 'God has been very kind to me and what's the point in slogging on and on? Isn't this enough?' she looked around, inviting me with a flourish to admire the sea view from her flat. Of course I wanted to be supportive; after all she deserved every bit of what she had got. But I was astonished by the change I saw in her.

Where was the fire-eating Manisha who had walked into the CEO's cabin and demanded her boss's job? When had she turned into this self-satisfied and complacent person who was happy to metaphorically hang up her boots? And where had flown her desire to climb more mountains and cross more streams?

Complacency in the workplace is a common fatigue experienced by both men and women. A positive spin all of us put on it is contentment. In some ways, many of us have become successful beyond our wildest dreams. We have markers of prosperity today that we had not even imagined yesterday. The latest BMW, foreign holidays whenever we want, thousands of people working for us, PE funding for our ideas, board directorships. It feels greedy to want more.

After working very hard for most of our careers, there also comes a time where we start feeling that our skills and talents have been utilised to the maximum degree and working for further improvement seems counterintuitive.

We believe we have given unstintingly of ourselves to the world, and now it's payback time, when the world owes us a living.

Both contentment and entitlement, sadly, have an underlying core of self-satisfaction, which I believe is the beginning that spells the end of learning. The mind tends to relax (read, becomes lazy) and that edge that has always been the driver for achievement becomes blunt.

Especially among women, complacency often creeps in when the definition of success becomes the fact that they are the only woman left standing at that level.

A study on women's participation in the Indian workforce, conducted by Anupriya Singh of Lal Bahadur Shastri Institute of Management, revealed that only 5 per cent of working women made it to senior leadership positions in the corporate sector. Women's representation at the board level is currently 2 per cent. Singh found that 48 per cent of women drop out between junior and middle level. At the junior level, women account for 28 per cent of the labour force. It dips to 15 per cent at the middle level, 10 per cent at the senior level and 5 per cent and less thereafter. Thus at senior positions, more often than not, women like Manisha are likely to be the only woman at the table.

No woman sets out to actively compete solely with her women colleagues. But having gone through the wringer over the years, I've witnessed that when you are the only woman left in the room, your source of self-worth suddenly springs from the fact that you are the only woman in the room.

A prevalent trope in media is pitting women against each other. Everywhere you look – movies, TV, books –

women are made to compete with each other, usually for a man's attention. You compete with your sister, never with your brother. You compete with your sister-in-law, never with your brother-in-law. This socialisation further fuels the shift in focus to other women.

Financial security is a privilege that can never be overstated. When we started out with our working lives, it was the driving force behind our efforts. But the importance we place on it later tends to distort our sense of success.

Financial prosperity should not be the marker of our success. It is a happy by-product of it. We can, and should, leverage it to benefit our life as much as possible. But it is toxic to consider it the trophy of our ambition. The world needs our brains, our experience and our creativity. With time and success, it is up to us to define what motivates us when we have achieved comfortable security. From my conversations with women friends – entrepreneurs, lawyers, doctors, bankers, engineers and so on – I've discovered that after financial security, impact creation is the greatest motivator for working people.

The ability to make a difference to people and ecosystems, whether it is our teams or shareholders, is what drives people who've attained success at par with their ambition. I think at every stage of advancement, women need to reassess their motivations for the work they are doing and reimagine the legacy they wish to leave behind.

Why is complacency among senior women a pet peeve of mine? I've observed an interesting conundrum with employees. Among the men who've reached HOD positions and the lone woman among them who's reached the same, I find the latter invariably better than the former. And that's because she's had to work twice as hard and be twice as competent to reach there. She's had to manage so many different roles, pressures and priorities in her life. This makes her a far more evolved and resilient human being.

I feel that by remaining where she is and not aiming higher, she is doing a disservice to both herself and her organisation. Her experience and competence will make her a great leader. But if she's decided that it's not for her, then it's a loss for herself and a loss for the world.

I invite you to reflect deeply about your current state of work and contemplate the questions I asked myself when I felt restless, yet too guilty to explore that dissatisfaction. There is no middle ground in life. Unless we are moving forward, we are sliding backwards. Martin Luther King Jr said it rightly: 'If you can't fly, then run, if you can't run, then walk, if you can't walk, then crawl, but whatever you do, you have to keep moving forward.'

If you are in that lucky 5 per cent of women who have reached almost the top, then you are absolutely justified to take it easy and enjoy the fruits of your labour. No way does my speaking out against complacency imply that your current achievements are not good enough. You must pat yourself on the back. You must feel a very strong sense of entitlement and be extremely proud of yourself. The remaining 95 per cent of your sisters did not make it this far. You are the crème de la crème. You absolutely must celebrate your success.

But after that you must assess your situation. 'This is where I've reached after decades of hard work. These are my talents and skills. Am I happy?' No one else can answer this question for you. Let nobody, including this book, tell you that where you've reached is not good enough. It is only for you to decide whether you've fulfilled your destiny or if you're still in the process of charting it.

If the answer to your self-questioning is that you are where you dreamed you'd be and are happy with it, then kudos to you. But if your self-reflection reveals that this is just one of the goalposts in your journey and not the destination itself, then it is time to get on with it. So proceed, my beauty, and read on.

IN SHORT

- Once we attain a certain position, a modicum of success or an aspired-to lifestyle, we become content with our achievements and settle down.
- But another word for contentment is complacency, which sets in especially when senior women look around the boardroom and see themselves as the lone representative of their sex.
- This sense of self-satisfaction and unwillingness to strive further is one of the several reasons why women reach the CXO level but don't grow beyond it.
- It is heartbreaking to see this, since in most instances a woman CXO is far more competent than the male CXOs around her. This is because she has fought so many more battles to get there.
- If you are genuinely happy with where you've reached and now want to relax, you're perfectly justified in your decision. If not, keep striving and growing. There's more to achieve.

The Lioness and the Dormouse

It's not my job to make you feel like a man.

—Astrid Leong, *Crazy Rich Asians*

Karishma Soni is a fiercely ambitious entrepreneur who turned her doctor father's single laboratory into a three thousand crore global empire. She also happens to be gorgeous and young, two qualities that frequently lead to her getting mistaken for the secretary, while the male junior executive in the room is assumed to be the boss!

Often, even when her identity is not under question, people simply refuse to take her seriously. It's hard for many people to believe that a young and pretty lady is capable of the accomplishments she has to her name. Despite these obstacles, Karishma has built a thriving business empire that continues to grow. And she is not bitter about these undermining experiences.

'While growing up, generations of men have seen women in only two roles – as a mother or a wife. They don't know how to relate to women at the workplace or as equals. They only know that women are either born to take care of men or need men to protect them,' she said in a recent interview.

In an earlier chapter in this book, we discussed how girls in India are trained from childhood to be quiet, to occupy as little space as possible, to not laugh out loud or answer back. For every action there is an equal and opposite reaction. So it is that our boys are rewarded for being boisterous. But this unequal parenting goes far beyond permitting boys to roll about in the mud and laugh with abandon or not policing their clothes, companions and life choices.

When little boys are constantly raised at the expense of little girls, they continue to expect the same behaviour throughout their lives. Men grow up to see themselves as the centre of the universe and all the women in their lives as assorted satellites fated to orbit around their glorious sun! This is a great disservice not only to women but also to men. We teach them to derive their sense of identity and fulfilment from their roles as protectors and providers and when that role comes into question, it results in a shattering sense of insecurity. Another consequence of this upbringing is the male ego, an all-consuming, all-pervasive beast that requires constant fodder and nourishment.

HD's aunt is a renowned eye surgeon. Sheila Aunty is a feisty woman and continues to do multiple and complicated eye surgeries even at the age of seventy-two. She is confident, bold and indefatigable when it comes to her iconic eye centre. At work she knows exactly what she is doing and dispenses eye care and advice with a surefootedness that is born out of finely honed talent and the experience of a forty-two-year career. The other day we visited her residence to meet the extended family who had gathered there for Diwali, and I was completely mystified by Sheila Aunty's wifely avatar at home! She was meek, docile and tentative in front of Raj Uncle, her husband, who is a retired college principal and seemed to be running his house in exactly the same manner that he ran his college! He ordered her around peremptorily, was dismissive when someone complimented her on an award she had won and quite churlish in his behaviour with her.

'Sheels is so poor at managing the house,' he told us peevishly, when there was a slight delay in the food being served. And Aunty had just come back from her clinic, whilst Uncle Pompous had been sitting on his backside reading the paper the entire morning! We all jumped to her rescue as she flapped around helplessly trying to set the table, while apologising profusely to him and all of us!

I was so angry that I was a hair's breadth away from kicking him! It still maddens me when I think about that incident, so much so that I am actually punching furiously at the keyboard as I write this down! I was angry not only with him but also with Sheila Aunty for putting up with his boorishness. She had been our heroine and role model when we were growing up, and to see her behave like a wimp was a huge let down that day.

Examples of 'the male as centre-piece' are littered throughout Indian literature, cinema and TV. From *Devdas* to everyday *saas-bahu* serials, women bend backwards, forwards and contort themselves in every angle possible to appease the troubled and brooding hero. His needs come first, his feelings are paramount and woe betide the world if the rotis served to him are not freshly made and piping hot!

But perhaps the instant example that comes to mind is the Jaya Bhaduri, Amitabh Bachhan starrer *Abhimaan*. The 1973 film by Hrishikesh Mukherjee sees popular singer Subir (Bachhan) entranced by the soulful, melodic voice of village girl Uma (Bhaduri). He falls in love with her and they get married. Subir convinces Uma to enter showbiz. But when her popularity outshines his own, cracks appear in the marriage.

Even though Uma harbours no desire for fame and is ready to give up singing professionally, it's too late. The couple is driven apart by Subir's jealousy. This being a Bollywood film of course, things work out eventually and they reconcile after some twists and turns – most significantly Subir confronting his own unfair rage and behaviour.

In real life things rarely work out this well, as the couple, on whose life *Abhimaan* was based, would tell you. Roshanara Khan became Annapurna Devi to marry Pandit Ravi Shankar, a disciple of her father Alauddin Khan. But the marriage became strained soon after as Ravi Shankar became jealous of the rave reviews his wife's public performances earned.

In a new biography titled *An Unheard Melody: Annapurna Devi, An Authorised Biography*, writer Swapan Kumar Bandopadhyay describes how bitter Shankar became when his wife's music performances outshone his own:

'She was on the rise. The connoisseurs hailed her as great. The surbahar also helped to establish her supremacy, because it is a more difficult instrument than the sitar, heavier and more satisfying musically. Ravi was justifiably jealous. And so he elicited a vow from his wife that she would no longer play in public,' writes Bandopadhyay.

Annapurna kept her vow. She never played publicly again, even though she and Shankar separated soon after. She kept a select roster of students and passed her craft to them. But while Shankar rose to become a music legend worldwide, Annapurna Devi's art was lost to the world forever.

These may be dramatic and extreme examples rather than the rule, but the fact still remains that working women even today believe that if their success is likely to lead to discord at home, it is better to take a backseat. Despite their accomplishments, they immediately resort to the childhood training of erasing themselves to accommodate their spouses' misguided sense of entitlement.

Recently at a panel discussion on women empowerment in the workplace, a speaker narrated an anecdote about his company. They wanted to promote a woman to a senior position – a position the bosses felt she richly deserved. He brought her in to discuss the move. But instead of happy cheer, her disposition showed tremendous unease and discomfort. She flatly refused the promotion. The manager was stunned and insisted on knowing why she would not accept the role. It took much cajoling before she finally revealed what was going on in her head. She said she could not accept the promotion since her salary would then become higher than her husband's!

I was slack-jawed for a while upon hearing this. But now I realise actions like this are more commonplace than we realise. We don't hear about it because we don't talk about it.

Over the years some conversations about women and inequality in the workplace – sexual harassment, equal pay, double standards, etc. – have gained volume. There are some topics we actively discuss and practices we move to ban. But stories like this rarely get revealed because the women making these adjustments feel guilty and hypocritical even as they martyr themselves for peace at home.

The quick switch that Sheila Aunty routinely practised of playing the doormat at home after being the boss at work, the handing over of all financial decisions to men, the ease with which women become supportive listeners and cheerleaders of their men's exploits, the hiding of the award won at work lest it upset the big guy at home are all symptomatic of this malaise.

However, increasingly I see that the next generation of women is not willing to play second fiddle at home. They are staunchly refusing to be quieter, plainer and more colourless versions of themselves in social or domestic environments.

When after twenty-five years of being married I apologetically requested a separate bathroom for myself, my young and recently married niece was flabbergasted. 'But Apu Aunty, that was my first condition for getting married,' she squealed. 'We also have a marriage manifesto,' she solemnly informed me. 'What does it contain?' I asked her, puzzled. 'Either of us can stay separately if our work requires it. We will take one independent holiday each with our friends. Both of us will take equal time off when we have a baby,' she rattled off at express speed. 'And most certainly, no uncle jokes!' she grinned naughtily. 'What's that?' I wondered. 'He will not ever crack pathetic uncle jokes like "Heh, heh, see how well she has trained me," if someone sees him doing household chores!' she said, pointing an admonishing finger at her beaming husband.

My heart blossomed with pride while listening to her. I was supremely impressed and thrilled with her confidence and her husband's genial demeanour. Our sons are growing up with a healthy sense of self; they are comfortable in their skins. And our daughters are growing up with unapologetic ambition and derring-do. They are making sure that both sexes walk tall and stand shoulder to shoulder with each other. Our girls are refusing to tiptoe around the male ego and equally our boys are sweeping their partners in their arms, and twirling merrily all over the ashes of the bonfires of vanity!

We must have done something right in their upbringing. Who knows? Maybe it's finally time that the child truly became the father of the man and we get reverse mentored by our daughters who can teach us a thing or two. Maybe that dawn has indeed come when we learn to be true to ourselves, not by hiding but by showcasing our coloured plumes in all their vibrant glory in each and every moment we live.

IN SHORT

- While working women have been fighting a long and arduous battle in the world outside, they have also had to contend with the male ego at home.
- To keep home affairs calm and male feathers unruffled, many times they choose to mute their achievements and accept secondary-citizen status at home.
- But millennials are far more confident than earlier generations. The millennial girl wants to be acknowledged publicly and privately for her triumphs and accomplishments.
- Maybe we should be reverse mentored by this generation and own our successes on every occasion.

Subconscious Bias

Stereotypes fall in the face of humanity. We human beings are best understood one at a time.

—Anna Quindlen

On a visit to a well-known tech firm to conduct a workshop with their women employees, I was most impressed with the large pool of competent and talented women in their middle management. But I was sorely disappointed that there was not even a single woman employee in the senior leadership team.

When I quizzed Anand, the CEO, he was mournful about this. He assured me most solemnly that he was a pro-woman recruiter, desperately wanted gender diversity in his office but couldn't find any women in his team who were ready or keen to take on the stressful responsibilities that a senior role entailed. He informed me that he personally had been headhunting extensively for a couple of critical positions but had been unable to find any women to fit those roles, either inside or outside his organisation.

I was very pleased with his enthusiasm and earnestness in correcting this unfair imbalance, left him looking glumly at more CVs and went away, delighted with having met a male leader who was such an ardent advocate of diversity.

But a completely different tale met me while talking to the women in the organisation during the workshop. I started the session by asking them what was holding them back from accepting promotions for the next level. Did they believe they didn't have the necessary qualifications or did they believe they would be unable to cope with the pressures of senior managerial roles? I wanted to understand why they were voluntarily choosing to stagnate instead of moving ahead.

Their collective protestations stunned me. They told me they were dying to be given more responsibilities and indeed were thirsty for opportunities to prove themselves, but were not being offered those roles. When I asked the HR team present at the workshop why they hadn't pushed for filling those vacant senior positions with women from their existing talent pool, pat came the reply that all the senior roles involved late nights, heavy travel, unreasonable client expectations and a huge amount of pressure. They believed that their women employees would not be able to cope with these insane demands and would refuse to take these assignments or would end up burning out or compromising on their work or family if they did agree! As good employers, they didn't want to impose such a burden on the women.

But before making these assumptions, had anyone actually checked with these ladies whom they were so valiantly protecting, and asked what their opinion on the matter was? There was deafening silence in the room when I asked this question.

Each time someone has asked me if I've encountered any bias in the workplace because of being a woman, I have always said no. I have always believed that in my career I have got the same opportunities as any man in my position. But this experience brought those assumptions to a screeching halt. I started looking back and wondering about all the opportunities that had possibly passed me by because nobody even cared to check whether I was ready for them, in the false assumption that I wasn't. How would I even know that I was the subject of bias if I didn't even know it was happening to me?

Patriarchy has long been the popular villain for gender inequality at the workplace and elsewhere. Men have been in hierarchical positions of power from the beginning of existence. Thus ingrained in them and in the systems around them is a view that women are inferior, less capable and in constant need of protection and support. In its most benign state, this inculcates a systemic response geared towards making women weaker than they are, than they need to be or deserve to be.

Anand's bias, despite his pro-women stance, was not hypocritical. He had been indoctrinated with a stereotype that was not true about the women in his team and he didn't even realise that this bias existed in his mind. He was certainly well-intentioned when he worried that he would put extraordinary pressure on his women managers by promoting them, but he also was being unfair to his women managers by being paternalistic.

I assess Anand's bias not from a moral high ground, but with the inside knowledge only the guilty can possess. I once hired a CEO, Hitesh, for one of the companies I manage after doing due diligence on his background. He had the right credentials and his references were stellar. Added to that he gave all of us a feeling of great comfort and confidence with his deep gruff voice, measured tone and solid demeanour (he was well over six feet tall and built like a barrel). All of us felt assured that he could navigate the company through any storm. He spent two years at the organisation and then one day quit abruptly, citing unexplained personal reasons.

His sudden departure got me, the HR team and the people who worked directly with him searching within ourselves for the reasons for his move. After a lengthy analysis we realised that he had been unable to handle the pressure of the three months prior to his resignation. The organisation had been facing headwinds and revenue pressures at that time. I was puzzled that he threw in the towel when the going got tough because innate strength was a quality I'd always associated with him.

Only once I started connecting the dots and reviewing his performance, not only in our company but also in previous organisations, did the mystery begin to resolve itself. Closer inspection revealed that whenever a significant crisis had arisen in the organisations under his charge, he had not been the one to resolve it. He had preferred to ignore the problem rather than taking charge and facing it head-on.

Hitesh's physical attributes matched accurately the stereotype of the strong and silent alpha male who comes striding out of the sunset to solve the community's woes with the music score of a spaghetti western movie playing in the background. His statuesque demeanour and deep bass voice communicated leonine strength and dependability to me, while inside he was just a little mouse! I grudgingly admitted to myself that I, like Anand, had acted on bias rather than on empirical evidence.

At any given time, the human brain is bombarded with eleven million pieces of information. We can only handle forty. To navigate the world without being inundated and overwhelmed, the brain creates patterns that help sort this information. Forming stereotypes is one such pattern. And by assuming that people behave according to a certain stereotype, we begin acting out of bias. We are also genetically coded to be positively biased towards people similar to us.

Once we take into consideration that the majority of managers and recruiters are men, the absence of women in the upper echelons of corporate India begins to make a lot of sense. People will naturally choose candidates they identify with the most.

Even the most well-meaning of us, both men and women, are biased. Instead of railing against a genetic trait that skews the scales against women, let's ask what we can do to help people around us (including ourselves) step out of the narrow corridors of perception bias.

The incentive to dismantle subconscious bias lies not just in diverse gender-equal hiring. When leaders take the time to assess their preconceived notions, they enhance their level of objective comprehension and critical reasoning skills. In short, they become better at their jobs.

As far as gender bias goes, there is unfortunately no quick fix for reaching into the subterranean regions of male minds and shaking out the cobwebs. The only way to deal with these perceptions is to co-opt more and more men into the diversity conversation. Every time I speak on this issue at any organisation, I ask that men also be part of the proceedings. There are several initiatives across the globe where men are increasingly being encouraged to be part of this process of recognising and thus changing subconscious behaviours and mindsets, and we must all actively support such initiatives.

Equally we need to be patient not in accepting but in explaining to men what we believe qualifies as biases. The famous 'silent treatment' women adopt to manage conflict will not work here! It is imperative to call out the big as well as the small biases we see playing out around us every day. Don't call me 'sweetheart', don't assume it's the male at the table who will pay the bill, don't automatically decide that my drink will be a mocktail and look shocked when I ask for a strong shot, and yes HD cooks and I don't! The more time women spend discussing with men what they want, what they value and what they don't, the more we will be able to remove the misconceptions in their minds. Equally we will understand their point of view. Which is yet another reason we need more women at the workplace, in the boardrooms and at the negotiating tables.

Finally, we have to consciously stop ourselves from playing to a stereotype. The Pet, the Mother, the Seductress are some of the slots we naturally and effortlessly manoeuvre ourselves into, like obedient clockwork dolls in a dystopian fairy tale. And every time a woman leaves her job to stay at home, it reinforces the perception that the workplace is not her natural domain and God always intended womenfolk to be housewifely.

Biases are created out of patterns we reinforce repeatedly. Mindfully and laboriously, we need to erase these behaviours in ourselves and in doing so, erase them from the minds of all the folk around us.

IN SHORT

- The human brain perpetuates stereotypes because that is the only way it can make sense of complex information and the data overload it is bombarded with.
- Thus despite best efforts, the stereotypes operating around women continue to be part of the subconscious biases that exist at the workplace.
- Women get slotted in traditional moulds unconsciously and because the biases are subterranean, they become very difficult to challenge.
- The only way to erase these biases is to call them out constantly.

All the Single Ladies

I got my own back.

—Maya Angelou

The prejudices and biases we discussed in the previous chapter have become such an inescapable part of the world surrounding women that we don't even notice them any longer. People assume that women can't drive well or open a can or change the light bulb and mostly we give these biases a pass and let them think whatever they want. Partly because we are fed up of proving a point all the time and partly because it is quite convenient to get someone more manly to open the can or drive us where we want to go. Much like my son pretending that there was a Santa Claus way beyond the regulation age of awakening to myths till we started wondering whether he was a bit dim. Only to realise that by age two he had quite adeptly grasped the reality, but chose to keep up the pretence in order to get his presents!

Beyond a point I don't get agitated if at a party you ask my husband where he works and what he does and then condescendingly ask me about my favourite city for shopping! I smile beatifically, pat the sofa next to me and say, 'Come sit by my side and I will tell you all about Marrakesh's hidden markets and Le Marais in Paris.'

But the preconceptions that surround bachelor girls make even a hardened pragmatist such as me gasp. Having got married in my early twenties, I completely bypassed the peculiar barbs that single women in India are bombarded with, but some of the stories they tell me would try the patience of any monk.

For example, I recently met a fabulous young lady at a talk I gave at an SME forum. She's a successful entrepreneur in her own right who's done a brilliant job in turning around and scaling up the business she inherited from her late father. Her life story intrigued me so much that we chatted for hours.

Ayesha is single. I was fascinated not by her singledom but the story of how it has affected her work life. She told me of a recent audit review at her firm. As is the norm, every audit review ends with a risk-management discussion with the senior management. Post the review, the auditor asked her what she viewed as the biggest risk to her business. 'Me,' she told him nonchalantly.

I almost choked on my coffee as she recounted this to me. Did she really think she was the biggest risk to her business? 'Well, of course I don't think that,' she clarified. 'But this issue has cropped up on various occasions in my life. So I decided in the spirit of full disclosure to be forthcoming with the auditor about the challenges facing the organisation and tell him what so many people have repeatedly told me,' she smiled naughtily.

Take for example an encounter she had in her early days as boss of the company. Ayesha's father had recently passed away. She had unexpectedly become the face of the business at a very young age but was eager to shake things up and accelerate growth. She was twenty-seven at the time. She'd gone to meet a big industrialist to pitch some ideas. The industrialist asked her, 'Why should I give my business to you?' She was ready with what made her company the best suited for the job and rattled off all the reasons with great verve and enthusiasm. While agreeing with all her claims, the industrialist shot back, 'Yes, all this is fine, but I have one fundamental issue with your business.'

'What?' she asked, slightly fazed.

'I see you as the biggest risk to your business. Tomorrow if you get married and move away, what will happen to your company and by association my supply?' he queried.

She smiled as she recounted this story. 'It's been ten years. I am thirty-seven now and the people I meet still consider me the biggest risk to the business. The foremost question on the minds of prospective investors and collaborators is the risk of being left in the lurch when I'm suddenly swept off my feet by a prince charming and leave everything I've worked so hard for years to build – both mine and my father's legacy – to ride off into the sunset with him.'

The question seemed completely absurd to her. Why would she leave everything and go away? But apparently that's how men see single women's work – as placeholders while they wait for their prospective husbands and even more prospective offspring. Getting married sometime in the future was a vague possibility in Ayesha's case, but what was crystal clear to anyone who knew her was the dedication and hard work she had put into reviving her dad's business and turning it around so dramatically. But regrettably the subtext after every such meeting was that her ability to work would be forever and irrevocably altered once she got married. While it was gratifying that Ayesha was handling these prejudices with a sense of humour, the fact that this question would not have even been contemplated had Ayesha been an Ayush was galling in the extreme.

As the only single woman in a firm with an otherwise decent representation of female employees, Indrani explains to me how her marital status disadvantages her. Her boss always asks her to stay back and finish the work of other women. 'Let her go home. She has small children waiting for her. You finish the work. After all, you have no such responsibilities,' is his reasoning.

Often, bosses refuse to entertain pay raise requests from single women: 'Why do you need a pay raise? You don't have a family to provide for.' It frustrates these women very much. 'What do you mean? So what if I am single? Won't I have financial requirements of my own? Don't I have parents to look after or a future to secure?' they rant to me. Married people, or even unmarried men, are never asked to justify their raises. An unmarried woman has to justify even her paycheck.

Mehnaz is the thirty-five-year-old COO of a small financial services firm. She has been constantly hearing barbs over her unmarried state since her mid-twenties, under the guise of well-meaning advice.

'It's not that I am against marriage,' she wailed to me. 'But I can't get hitched to just anybody for the sake of getting married. He has to be the right guy.'

Unfortunately, she has rarely ended up meeting the 'right' man who is not intimidated by her independence!

She finally got so fed up of the pressure that she agreed to meet a few men. 'From the beginning I knew it was doomed,' she told me about her interaction with one of them. She was in Goregaon and the guy was in Worli, but he expected her to meet him there. 'He wasn't even willing to meet me halfway. I had to go all across Mumbai to where he was, because after all HE was the superior partner in the future relationship.'

Nonetheless she swallowed her misgivings and braved the Mumbai traffic to conduct her personalised swayamvar. The first question posed by the shortlisted groom was, 'So do you intend to work after marriage?' 'I am the COO of an organisation. Obviously, I intend to work after marriage,' she retorted incredulously. 'Maybe you can consider becoming a teacher if you insist on working,' he magnanimously suggested. 'Why teacher?' she asked.

'Not that I have anything against teachers but I was so flummoxed with that suggestion that I just had to know,' she recalls.

'If you are a teacher, then you can be at home after half day to take care of our children,' said the husband and dad-in-waiting coyly! Suffice to say Mehnaz is clinging to her singledom fiercely after her brief dip into the dating pool.

Gloria Steinem aptly said, 'We are becoming the men we wanted to marry.' Today's educated working woman does not need to marry for security, but she certainly wants an equal partner in every sense of the term. Most of my single women friends are not single by choice; they would like to have a spouse to share life's ups and downs with. But they rarely encounter a male who is comfortable with the concept of marital equality. And in the absence of suitable choices, they would much rather remain single than settle for someone who would diminish them.

Though she rarely sets out to make a statement, some view the single woman as a radical. She doesn't exist for her husband or children. She exists for herself. Her salary is not to pay for school tuitions or family vacations but to spend on herself. She is such a threat to a well-ordered patriarchal world that she needs to be controlled and censored at every turn and punished for her choices. Let her stay back late, give her extra work, don't pay her much money – these are the punishments for the husband and children-less nature of her life.

Others may not see her as a threat, but she is a lesser being to them. She exists to make life easier for married folks who have too much pressure at home and outside it. If unmarried women can take that pressure off, well that's because they should. What else are they going to do with all the extra time and money they have?

'If I am single, I must be promiscuous,' my friend Shirleen says of how the world views her. 'At the very least I should have no hang-ups about sleeping with anyone in the office kind enough to take note of my attractiveness.'

Shirleen recounts an incident – rather, a horror story – from when she had just started working. She was young, inexperienced and easy pickings in the eyes of a predatory boss. He showered her with inappropriate remarks and sexually laden innuendos at work. Initially she shrugged those off with an uneasy laugh because she didn't have the courage to stand up to him.

One weekend he started texting her, sending compliments about her looks and asking her out for a drink. She didn't know how to refuse politely, so she didn't reply at all. On Monday morning her boss icily commented in front of the whole team that Shirleen obviously wasn't a dependable person since she didn't even bother to see her messages over the weekend.

After fortifying herself with self-talk, Shirleen went into his cabin to 'explain' herself. She told her boss that her strict conservative father commandeered her phone during weekends to curb any 'disreputable' activity. The boss was embarrassed to know her father may have read his flirty texts and left her alone for the rest of the time she worked there.

For Shirleen this was a bitter victory. She had protected herself by infantilising herself. The fact that she was an independent adult was of no consequence to her boss. Her consent, or lack thereof, had not been a barrier to his advances. But he respected the fact that she was her father's property, a fiction she had sold to him by undermining herself.

Every time I hear examples of the myriad, nuanced and delicate ways in which my supremely strong single friends navigate a muddled and unfair world, I am filled with awe and respect. In the face of a society determined to define their unworthiness, they are fiercely and unashamedly living life on their own terms. And having boatloads of fun while doing so.

One of my single friends has chucked up her career and has become a healer full time. She told me, 'I have saved up enough to be financially secure and I don't have anyone to leave my money to. So why shouldn't I do exactly as I please?' The last I heard is that she is off to Glastonbury, which apparently is the heart chakra of the world (!), to conduct a healing workshop! Now isn't that cool! A freelance writer friend took off to Himachal on a whim to live in a village and volunteer at the local school. Looking at the breathtakingly beautiful updates of her bohemian lifestyle on Facebook, I realised that once upon a time matrimony may have been the final prize to aspire to. But no longer is it true.

Now more than ever, the world has become boundary-less and label-less and in becoming so, it has become truly empowering. Today there are many different and differing ways to live, each offering its own rewards and heartbreaks. And if my bachelorette friends' adventures are anything to go by, the joys of singledom are spectacular in their own right.

IN SHORT

- Single women have been the frontrunners in demonstrating to the world that women and men are equal and deserve to be treated on par.
- By flying in the face of traditional expectations and conservative mindsets, they have indicated their freedom and demonstrated their courage.
- As we see the numbers of single women increasing in a more open and diverse world, we need to stand in support with them so that they have the space and the empowerment to live life on their own terms.

Token Woman

Definitions belong to the definer, not the defined.

—Toni Morrison

I had imagined I would feel a great many things when I finally got to sit on a board – the relish of having made it; the satisfaction of being surrounded by top achievers across different fields; the reflected glory of the polish from all that chrome, glass and leather around me. I was savouring the thought of saying, 'With great power comes great responsibility,' with a bravely suffering look to people all around me. What I had not imagined even in my wildest of fancies was that I would be deified – albeit in the 'Goddess who must be revered but largely ignored' fashion!

It took some time to dawn on me what it meant to be the lone woman in a boardroom populated largely by alpha males who at first glance looked like grizzled versions of extras from *Men in Black*. There were flowers, compliments and plenty of references such as, 'For heaven's sake, there's a lady present!' Self-appointed knights dressed in, err, black, regularly rushed to open and close doors for me. I was gallantly told by all the gentlemen in the room how I had enlivened the previously dull proceedings with my fair presence. One respectable member of the board coyly divulged to me that I had brought much-needed glamour into the boardroom. Universally all my ideas were commented upon and exclaimed over with much ado, and equally universally politely dismissed. And that was if I ever got a chance to complete my sentences or be heard in the first place!

Getting talked over is a familiar foe for all women, but the glamour comment got my goat. 'They think I'm here to be glamorous, do they?' I seethed to myself. To countermand this completely ridiculous perception I immediately twirled my wand around and became the absolute opposite of the glamour queen – the earth mother!

Now the self-appointed matron in the boardroom, I cajoled, scolded and disciplined my way through most meetings. I would sternly offer admonishment or kindly mete out criticism to men two decades senior to me. I dictated agendas as though I were setting homework and offered the solace of my cosy shoulders to the management team after tough meetings. I remember an instance when I actually came within a whisker of patting the CEO on his shoulder and saying 'there, there' after a particularly brutal quarter results meeting. He was looking at me longingly for exactly that reason, but I desisted (I think)!

There couldn't have been a better mother than me and we soon settled into a happy family routine at the board meetings thereafter.

Many senior women I know ask my advice on what it takes to get onto a board. They believe that getting onto a board is mandatory to reach the next rung in their careers since it showcases their achievements to people outside their organisation and prepares them for larger responsibilities. While this is certainly true, I do urge them to reflect on a few things.

Firstly, I tell them it is important to judge what their contribution will be on the board. Will they bring a specific functional perspective or a particular industry expertise that is missing? What outside angle can they bring that will synchronise with what the board requires? It is critical not to get onto a board just to be a mute spectator.

Secondly, being on a board is no longer a simple matter. With the Companies Act, 2013 becoming more and more draconian with time, there are a lot more expectations from board members in terms of monitoring the governance practices of an organisation and being mindful that the business is being run with integrity and diligence. By sitting on a board and attending four to six meetings a year, one will never learn what's happening inside the company. Despite the many questions one may ask or how engaged one is, no one will ever get to know the intricacies of the organisation from the distance of a board chair. And thus it has now become more of a liability than an asset to be on a board.

The third and most important thing I tell my women friends is to truly understand the issues that come with being the solitary woman director in the room.

Alas, being the token woman on the board comes with a mountain load of baggage that needs to be dealt with delicately and firmly. Most organisations treat women directors as a tedious requirement that the law expects them to comply with. The male board members treat women as if they are a different species altogether and very much an inferior sort at that.

Finally, women themselves subconsciously behave in yet another fashion, by either assimilating or resisting these treatments. Both these behaviours unfortunately lead to the same tapered end of becoming typecast, as it happened to me in my starring role as mother of the board.

In 1983, Harvard business professor Rosabeth Moss Kanter identified four distinct role traps that women habitually get pigeon-holed into while trying to navigate male bastions of power. These stereotypes arise mainly from men's perception of a woman in charge in the workplace. But more importantly, they also endure because of women's willingness to conform to these roles.

The most common stereotype of the woman at work is the Seductress. A woman who takes pride in her grooming and likes to dress well is immediately labelled a distraction in the workplace. Her efforts at climbing the corporate ladder are looked on with suspicion. People readily believe that she schmoozed her way to the top rather than acknowledge she may be talented and hardworking enough to have earned the role. The Seductress's femininity is what places distrust upon her. Both men and women are wary of her and that's why when my fellow board member told me that I had enhanced the glamour quotient in the room, I pivoted immediately towards the polar opposite maternal mode.

The Mother is a typical and the most traditional role a woman in the workplace embodies. She is completely non-threatening sexually and will be described as a frump, matron or schoolmarm in terms of appearance. She is caring, compassionate and warm. Her leadership is valued in the emotional labour she provides and not in the industry expertise she brings to the table.

The third stereotype Kanter talks about is the sweet, cute and girly mascot of womanhood, which is adopted by the contingent for amusement – the Pet. She is teased and mocked relentlessly. She will put up with the teasing lest people think she is not a good sport. The childish silliness assigned to the Pet undermines her credibility. This cutie pie bimbette is much loved for her antics. But she will never be taken seriously. She won't be considered for promotions and important leadership positions. She is even going to be excluded from serious conversations and decisions about the organisation.

The fourth stereotype is the assertive and no-nonsense woman at work, the Iron Maiden. Unlike the Seductress it is her competence and not her sexuality that makes her a threat. She is described as tough, mean, hard, scary and mannish. The Iron Maiden is a bully who lives for her work, has no personal life and no feminine allures to soften her harsh edges.

If she were a man, the Iron Maiden would be described as a go-getter, a deal-closer and a leader. But because she is a woman, she is bossy. Think Margaret Thatcher or our own Indira Gandhi. Modern time has seen labels like feminazi and man-hater added to the traditional canon of descriptors reserved for such a stereotype. The Iron Maiden can, and likely will, make it to the top. But she will be considered horrid for doing so.

Why do women bother substantiating the silly stereotypes they get endowed with? For Kanter, who has done groundbreaking research work on tokenism throughout her career, the answer is simple. It is easy and sometimes a matter of survival to concede to a dominant culture because it can be the path of least resistance to success.

Bitch or Bimbette. Mother or Seductress. Either we willingly walk into a box presented to us. Or we resist walking into one box by walking into another ourselves. We forget that the choice to not squeeze ourselves into a set precedent is ours and ours alone. Are we aware that each time we choose to embody a particular stereotype, we are complicit in accepting the treatment we get?

So what can we do? Across the world, women are fighting back. For example, the late Aston University professor Judith Baxter re-analysed Kanter's four role traps in the modern context and was pleasantly surprised by what she found. Not only did she see newer, more positive versions of these archetypes that women have coined for themselves to resist traditional power structures in the workplace, like Queen Bee, Superwoman and Xena (the warrior princess), but she also saw women leaders in the workplace skilfully navigating between the four roles to fulfil their professional objectives.

Baxter highlighted the example of Germany's chancellor, Angela Merkel, who flits between iron-fisted chancellor or 'mother' at home and 'charming female bantering with male heads of state' at Eurozone tête-à-têtes. This reclamation of agency from labels that have been thrust upon us to more proactive styles that we mindfully choose to adopt is indeed cause for celebration and a worthy example for all of us to follow.

In any case, owning multifaceted leadership styles is the natural next step ahead not only for women but also for men, as we learn to work in a volatile and ambiguous environment requiring flexible managerial skills.

The typical binary world is increasingly losing its context, especially as we deal with a generation of millennials and Gen Z, unencumbered as they are both by historical hangovers and conventional mindsets.

So as you move in to claim your role as a leader in an amorphous new age, can you be Earth Mother in Season One and morph seamlessly into Seductress in Season Two and then jump to Iron Maiden in the Finale? Can you?

IN SHORT

- Traditional stereotypes surrounding women have typically fallen into four distinct roles traps – the Seductress, the Pet, the Iron Maiden and the Mother.
- Unfortunately, women have chosen the path of least resistance and played to these roles in order to fit social norms and the dominant patriarchal culture.
- We need to break out of these set patterns of behaviour in order to shatter these stereotypes forever.
- By creating newer and more multi-faceted leadership styles we will evolve a more relevant managerial style to deal with the changing contexts of a new-age workforce and work environment.

Finding Sisterhood

Sisters in battle, I am shield and blade to you. As I breathe, your enemies will know no sanctuary. While I live, your cause is mine.

—Leigh Bardugo, *Wonder Woman: Warbringer*

I was delighted when my long-time friend Gauri finally agreed to have lunch with me. We used to be thick as thieves and our monthly lunch meetings had been both witness and markers of our progress, from the twenty-five rupees per plate meals at Mahesh Lunch Home (one small fried fish each and one plate of rice with free curry) to the five-star meals at some of the hallowed restaurants of the Taj. But then she became a partner at one of the top management consultancy firms in the country and scheduling a get-together with her became well-nigh impossible.

It's no secret that the work environment at management consultancy firms is ruthlessly competitive and making one's way to the top is a long and difficult journey – one that Gauri had been assiduously working her way through. She had finally succeeded and was now one of the only two female partners among a hundred male partners.

But while the scent of victory was sweetly perfumed, it was also accompanied by sharp and unpleasant gusts of performance pressure and stress. Every day Gauri left home at 7.30 in the morning, returning well after 9 p.m. I knew the last time she had taken a vacation was five years ago so I was lucky that she had been able to sneak away for lunch.

When Gauri walked in for our date, I was stunned to see how haggard she looked. I had expected her to be tired and overworked, but certainly not so desolate. Overruling her plea that she was on a diet, I ordered her favourite dishes and once she had polished off her beloved tiramisu, I gave her my signature basilisk look and launched into my interrogation.

'So what's up? Spill the beans without leaving out a single beanlet. And don't waste your breath telling me all is well. It clearly is not.'

One of the biggest advantages of a decades' long relationship is that no one wastes time posturing, so the beans did gush out forthright!

I knew about the internal politics and external demands of Gauri's job and she informed me that she was dealing quite adroitly with those. Managing difficult clients, ensuring expected billings, surpassing targets and the horrendous travel schedule, all the expectations from a partner were grist to her mill. She said that she was thriving in such a hardcore environment. So, no. It wasn't the work pressure that was getting to her. It was the fact that she had no one to talk to!

The only other woman partner at her firm was posted in another city. Most days, and most meetings, she was the only woman in the room. She was good friends with all her colleagues, but she had no way of letting off steam and was rarely able to let her hair down at work the way she saw the men around her doing, notwithstanding their thinning pates.

'I am lonely,' she confessed morosely.

I wanted to hug her tightly, hoping that the warmth of a friend's non-judgemental embrace would give her some succour. Like Munnabhai, I am a big believer in the *'jaadu ki jhappi'* concept, but try as we did to prolong the lunch and the brief magic of soul-sisterly warmth we had created around ourselves, it was soon over. We both returned to our offices, each to fight her own war.

Sociologists Tetyana Pudrovska and Amelia Karraker studied thirteen hundred middle-aged men and fifteen hundred middle-aged women for a paper titled 'Gender, Job Authority and Depression'. They found that job authority increases symptoms of depression in women but decreases them in men. These results are not surprising. The social isolation faced by women in authority leads them to suffer from a poorer state of mental health than women at lower rungs. According to the researchers, women in senior positions had to also deal with a barrage of interpersonal tensions, negative stereotypes, prejudice and resistance from subordinates, colleagues and superiors who were largely male, which made matters worse.

The intense scrutiny senior women face by virtue of being the only woman at that level puts huge pressure on them. And as we discussed in the last chapter, it also forces them to continue playing by the rule book of stereotypes that has been crafted for them by men. Prof. Kanter says, 'For token women, the price of being one of the boys is a willingness to turn occasionally against the girls. Put up or shut up is a way of going along to get along because noise is trouble.'

These are not mere consequences of a high-pressure job. These are the consequences of being a *woman* holding a high-pressure job. Being the only woman in the room, dealing with the prejudices stemming from being the only woman in the room and then having no one to share that experience with compounds the isolation that senior women feel.

Research on loneliness reveals that it is as lethal as smoking fifteen cigarettes a day! Isolation will not only wreck our mental health, but it will also create havoc with our physical health as well.

So we have no choice, ladies. We have to become proactive, look for our version of Wonder Woman's Themyscira and create communities from scratch if we have to. We urgently need to do this not only to battle the loneliness we feel but also to break free of the stereotypical roles and outmoded notions we are expected to abide by.

When I was running Radio City, I was the only woman in the boardroom, as usual, among a bunch of grave and sombre financial investors. (No, their demeanour wasn't anything to do with our performance; we were rocking the radio industry. It was just their default disposition!) One day, just as a meeting was about to begin, one of them started to whisper to me hoarsely, 'RSVP! RSVP!' I couldn't understand either his peculiar code or his sudden compulsion for secrecy, so bluntly and rather loudly I inquired, 'What's RSVP, Anil?' 'Royal Strap Visible Please,' he responded, red-faced, pointing to an errant bra strap visible on my shoulder.

Though momentarily discomfited, I later had a good laugh with him over the fact that while he seemed to know the intimate acronyms convent girls use, I had no clue about them! Once back in my own office however, I wondered how differently such a situation would have been handled if another woman had been in the room with me. For one, no female colleague would have been driven into an apoplectic fit over a peeking strap like men seem to be, and for another, an eyebrow would have been raised, a signal understood and a surreptitious adjustment made without anyone being the wiser!

In creating communities, we will find the power to be ourselves. But traditionally, social spaces have been designed for men – golf courses, bars and exclusive clubs a la *Mad Men* – and they remain largely and stubbornly true to these historical legacies. Women who have wanted to leverage the power of sisterhood have been held back by the sheer lack of spaces to convene and converge. But today we can create our own space on social media, a powerful and accessible platform. The best example in recent times of the intersection of social media and sisterhood has been the #MeToo movement. It is a reminder of our strength, of the fact that when women actively reach out to form a coven, not only do we find support but we also drive change.

For a woman sitting at home and feeling angry about the injustice committed against her, it need not be a lonely moment any longer. She can talk about it on social media and she will find support and encouragement. Magically, this also bolsters the courage of other women to come forward and share their stories of harassment at the hands of the same man! Together the survivors experience redemption through their sisterhood.

Whether it is sharing #MeToo stories or creating groups sharing the same interests like WOW-Women On Wanderlust or the hundred sarees campaign, social media has spread its tentacles so far and wide and deep that you can find a sister in support whatever your unique specifications may be.

Sometimes when I am fed up of being surrounded by men, more men and so many men around me, I imagine myself in an all-girls' commune somewhere far away on an island full of light and fresh air. I fantasise about how nimble I would feel – having shed all the layers of pretence and artifice along with the coatings of forbearance and resignation with which I arm myself on a daily basis to navigate the world of men.

I imagine this retreat to be like Themyscira, the island home of superhero Wonder Woman and the Amazons. Warriors of fearsome strength and valour, these women live together, fight together and swear to die together. They have no need to subvert or undermine themselves. They are free to embrace their power. They are all sisters who fly together on shared wings of openness and authenticity.

But we forget. We have no need of the mythological Themyscira or to escape into whimsical flights of fantasy. We have all the power we need right here. We have each other. We just need to make the effort to find our way to each other, to be there for each other and to support each other through thick and thin.

Whether you've been friends since nursery or have only met a few months ago at the yoga class or follow each other on Twitter, mark out your soul sisters and create your own circle of magic with them. Find the time to invest in these relationships not only for their sake but also for yours! I know you are brave and strong. You wouldn't have got where you are without these attributes. But equally you don't need to fight the good fight alone. Especially since so many of your soul sisters are forlornly flying around just as lonely as you are, looking in life's jigsaw for that corner in which to fit themselves and find anchor.

Alternatively, you can start smoking fifteen cigarettes a day and hope for temporary succour!

IN SHORT

- Working women face an uphill task every single day in trying to achieve desired business outcomes while fighting against a prejudiced social order and navigating inherently male-dominated ecosystems.
- The intense scrutiny senior women face by virtue of being the only woman at that level also puts huge pressure on them.
- The only way to manage this stress is to find like-minded women and create a support system around yourself.
- By investing in these relationships, you will find power and succour and help to create the change you seek.

Real-Life Role Models

What's the point of winning awards citing you as a powerful woman if you don't empower other women?

—Arundhati Bhattacharya

When I was six, my mother asked me what I wanted to be when I grew up. 'Mother Teresa,' I replied, gazing at her solemnly. Lest you believe I was a child prodigy with a heart of gold or even worse, a precocious and dreadfully prissy little girl, let me assure you I was not. But my sentiment was innocent, sincere and heartfelt.

I did not grow up to become a selfless charitable woman who spends all her waking hours taking care of the underprivileged. I am an honourable capitalist and driving the P&L (profit and loss) of my organisation is important to me. I enjoy wealth creation for myself and for all my stakeholders. But in keeping with my childhood ambitions, I have always looked for opportunities to create impact in whatever way I can. So while my fantasies have been slightly grand – I become a strict principal roaming around with a scowl and a cane in my hands – in reality I have tried to be a teacher and mentor wherever possible. As a happy consequence of being in leadership positions since the age of twenty-three, I have had several opportunities to mentor and guide women either in my own organisations or elsewhere. And over the course of numerous conversations with them, I have come to the conclusion that there is a crying need for more women role models to help these young women navigate the unchartered territories of public spaces.

Women are flooding into the workplace in India in unprecedented numbers today. Many of them are the first generation of women in their families to work. They have fought courageously with parents and in-laws for the right to work. Every single day they withstand tremendous personal pressure just so they have the freedom to earn a living.

However, when they enter the workplace and look around, 95 per cent of the leaders they see are male. This triggers two thoughts in the subconscious mind of these young women. The first is the conclusion that 'leader equals male', so naturally a woman cannot aspire to be a leader. And secondly, they implicitly see a biased environment and probably demur from having conversations about the challenges they face at work with male supervisors. That's not because male leaders are any less receptive than female ones. It's because they innately identify with the latter and feel intimidated by the former. Consequently, they will either underperform or after a point, leave that organisation.

What the scarcity of role models can do to a generation was driven home to me while listening to an episode of Malcolm Gladwell's *Revisionist History* podcast. In the episode titled 'Miss Buchanan's Period of Adjustment', Gladwell deconstructs the consequences of the US Supreme Court's landmark 1954 ruling ending segregation in schools.

While the Brown v. Board of Education ruling marked the end of separate schools for white and black children and was hailed as a great victory against racism, it ironically rang a death knell for black teachers. As schools began to be integrated, teachers in massive numbers had to be let go since many weren't required. And while society was finally willing to allow black and white children to be educated together, it was yet to reach the stage where parents were okay with black teachers educating white students. As a consequence, most of the teachers who were let go were black.

What no one paid attention to was how this would affect the black students. Robbed of teachers who were like them, and more importantly, understood them, the performance of black students plummeted. Top-performing black students from previously segregated schools became mediocre or below average. Their graduation rates, chances of following through with higher education and moving up in life was so severely negatively affected that even now, seventy years later, they have been unable to catch up!

Having role models is the biggest and most important driver of diversity. When people ask me what I have done in my own organisations to ensure diversity, my immediate response is that the only thing I have done is ensure there are enough senior women around!

A woman will stay on in an organisation when she sees senior women around her because this sends out several subconscious messages to her. She feels empowered thinking that if they could do it, so can she. She feels that it is a safe place for women. She is excited to dream about reaching the level she sees other women attain in that workplace. She tacitly believes that the organisation has no inherent gender biases because it has people like her in senior roles.

If you are a senior woman in your organisation, you should use your hard-won position to not only right the wrongs done to you but also ensure these wrongs don't happen to young women entering the workforce today. That can only happen when you play a visible role in the workplace. To build each other up, we have to invest long-term sustained efforts in coaching and mentoring women leaders of tomorrow. Cloistering ourselves in an ivory tower with that 'Power Woman' award is an exercise in self-aggrandisement and nothing else.

Let me share what a study produced jointly by the Geena Davis Institute on Gender in Media and the J. Walter Thompson Company has to say. It revealed that female role models in film and TV are hugely influential in driving women to improve their lives. In the study, 90 per cent of women from across the globe said they felt that female role models in film and TV have been hugely impactful in their lives.

What Indian films and TV have to offer little girls was revealed to me through a dreadful example. While visiting a friend, the five-year-old daughter of her house help offered to entertain us with her dance moves. We readily agreed. What followed horrified me worse than the scariest movies I'd ever seen.

The little girl gyrated her breasts and hips while crooning the seductive refrain of the latest chart-topping item number. She had no idea of the meaning behind what she was singing or the moves she was making while dancing, but was confident that this was what she was supposed to be doing.

A study by IBM looked at movies made over fifty years in Bollywood to identify biases. It confirmed the largely decorative status of women in films. It also found that male characters had profession-driven roles with their occupations ranging from scientist and army general to singer and professor. Meanwhile the women characters were appearance- or relationship-driven. For the handful of women characters who had any profession, it was restricted to teaching and secretarial roles.

Our boys grow up seeing themselves as doctors, CEOs and presidents. Our girls grow up thinking they are worth only the contextual roles defined by their relationships – mother, daughter, wife, etc. By the time they enter the workforce, much of the damage has already been done. When they see men occupy the majority of leadership positions, it only emphasises the truth of their early socialisation. That power means male. That they are destined to play forever the supporting cast – a Mona darling, the sidekick of an all-powerful gangster or a wheelchair-bound sister to showcase the nurturing 'family' side of the hero!

It is thus even more important that the women I am talking to in this book stand up and be counted as role models. The presence of strong role models in an organisation will give rise to a host of new archetypes our young ladies can aspire to play – the legal eagle, the iron lady, the prudent financial controller or the collaborative manager. The lack thereof will leave them reconciling to the stereotypical and submissive roles of supportive secretary or glamorous receptionist.

Young women look to us for guidance, experience-backed wisdom and for that silver bullet that helped us reach wherever we have. As senior women it is our job to help decode those steps for them. Especially when we know they are being pressurised by society to play passive and secondary roles.

Madeleine Albright rightly said, 'There is a special place in hell for women who don't help other women.' So reach out and pull them up behind you. But while doing so, definitely remember to tell them that, once upon a time, you too were just like them.

Rajeshwari, a young woman working in a new-age housing company, came to me lacking in confidence and raw in experience. But she was burning with ambition to grow. She had sought me out after a lecture I had given at CII as part of their women-empowerment programme.

You could make out that she was from a very middle-class family and had to really push against the pressures of her conventional upbringing, both to educate herself in the first place and then to ensure she continued working. Through the duration of our monthly mentoring sessions, I witnessed her rapid progress and growth into a great accountant and professional.

Despite a poor start in life and constant pressure at home from her unemployed husband and domineering mother-in-law to give up her job and start a family, she showed indomitable willpower and remained focussed on her job. One day while discussing some of the problems holding her back at home, I casually mentioned how I had been elbow-deep in dirty utensils when she had called me at home the previous evening.

She looked flabbergasted. 'Madam, what are you saying?' she squeaked. 'You wash dishes?' 'Yes, when I don't have help at home!' I said. That domestic troubles befell me too and I had to clean dirty dishes made her feel far closer to me than all the talks we'd shared through the months about upskilling, widening her understanding of finance and business, and her own personal problems!

She left our session that day with the unshakeable belief that I was a kindred spirit. Her ambition was bolstered by the fact that she could see in me a little bit of herself.

One of the less vocalised worries plaguing younger women is that the lives of successful women who came before them have been easier than their own. They see the martinis and the foreign holidays and are convinced that these women had certain exclusive opportunities available to them, which helped them succeed.

Not only is this thought scary but also very overwhelming. So much so that many young women feel unequal to climbing those Olympian heights where all their goddesses reside. The biggest disservice we will do to younger women is to perpetuate this belief further.

Let's shatter this corrosive thought and pound it out of their hearts and minds. That is the best way we can empower them and that should be our foremost legacy to them – I am just like you. See my roughened hands from all that scrubbing. And if I could do it, so can you! After all, being a role model is not about being an inspiration. It's about being an aspiration.

IN SHORT

- One of the best ways you can support the cause of gender diversity is by becoming a role model yourself.
- Young women require visible role models to give them the confidence to aspire for more. You cannot let them down.
- But be a relatable role model. Show them you are the same as them. If you present yourself as someone who is so special that no one can follow your path, you would have failed in this responsibility.

Menopause

Change is disturbing when it is done to us,
exhilarating when it is done by us.

—Rosabeth Moss Kanter

The insomnia came out of nowhere. I was forty-five when I suddenly stopped sleeping at night. While HD snored next to me, I spent my nights tossing and turning, the light bulb in my head stubbornly refusing to switch off. My nights were neatly sub-sectioned into phases of trying to sleep and falling asleep only to wake up feeling too hot or too cold, interspersed with hallucinatory moments of thinking that I had, against all odds, fallen asleep!

The stress from the lack of sleep made Swiss cheese of my brain. Previously acknowledged for my laser-sharp focus and eagle-like ability to swoop into the core of the issue, I found myself meandering about in a foggy and muddled mental state, making desperate attempts to camouflage the confusion in my mind from the troops.

For a number of years, I bounced like a yo-yo between sleeplessness-induced stress and stress-induced sleeplessness. I tried every cure, juggling allopathy and quack remedies, including sleeping pills, white noise apps, aromatherapy, oil-rubs, pillow sprays and magic potions straight out of the

Harry Potter books. Most male doctors either dismissed my concerns or misdiagnosed them.

Only a female doctor hit the nail on the head. She told me right away, 'This is the start of your perimenopause. Please be aware that you will go through these symptoms for quite some time, like five to seven years!'

I was stunned into silence. I had associated menopause with women in their late fifties and early sixties. While I didn't fancy myself a spring chicken, this stark reminder of ageing was a sudden and rude shock.

The body didn't care about my feelings on the matter. In the months and years that followed, I revolved in a whirlpool of mood swings, irritability, impulsiveness, abject pessimism and energetic enthusiasm. I was impatient, quick to anger and prone to making rash decisions. My once powerful memory bailed on me. Previously I'd fancied myself a heroic captain at work, managing my crew on the high seas. Now I felt the *Titanic* threatening to capsize on me.

It was now that an adolescent memory came to me unbidden. I recalled how my usually bright and cheerful mother would suddenly break into tears at all hours of the day. I didn't know what was happening and I don't think she did either. In the typical fashion of self-obsessed teenagers, I shrugged it off with a 'crazy grown-ups' eye-roll.

Now that I was facing this maddening metamorphosis myself I finally empathised with what she had gone through. When our mothers and grandmothers were going through menopause, they had two choices. Either to take it in their stride or to suffer in silence. They may have become gloomier, quieter or depressed. But they never asked for help. After all they had been conditioned since childhood not to call attention to their 'womanly' troubles.

Why am I calling attention to it now then? What place does a woman's reproductive health have in a book about career and leadership?

Many of you I am talking to are at the cusp of perimenopause and also overloaded with work in your professional capacities. This is really the first generation of women who will be working in substantial numbers in the public workspace while facing menopause. The majority of earlier generations of women going through menopause were housewives. Secondly, perimenopause is coming earlier than it did ever before. According to a study by the Institute for Social and Economic Change (ISEC), about 4 per cent of women between the ages of twenty-nine and thirty-four experience signs of menopause. The figure goes up to 8 per cent for women between the ages of thirty-five and thirty-nine!

Women going through menopause or perimenopause face added stressors today, which have greatly exacerbated the symptoms and degree of suffering they endure. In fact, menopause is being recognised as an emerging health crisis in India.

We will soon have a silent epidemic affecting a reasonably large chunk of our workforce, and we cannot afford not to talk about it. For all of you who have spent decades in building a thriving career and sterling reputation, the vagaries inflicted by menopause are likely to undo that hard work unless you know it is happening to you.

Ladies, if you want to achieve success in the workplace, there are certain life phases that will demand your dedication. Your willingness to work after marriage. Your willingness to balance work and parenting. And finally twenty years later, your ability to deal with menopause. Because we don't talk about it, read about it or even know about it, when the symptoms come out of the blue we don't know we should take it seriously. And worst of all, we give in to the raging hormonal impulses instead of fighting them.

There is nothing to panic about and of course you don't have to start preparing twenty years in advance. But you need to know that there is one more obstacle coming your way in case you think that you are done with all the challenges a working woman faces. Forewarned is forearmed.

I stared astonished at my friend Neelima as she detailed her new life plan to me when we bumped into each other at Khan Market. She, who had been a high-flying executive living in a plush Mumbai apartment with her husband and two children till yesterday, had become a free-ranging bird today. She announced she had separated from her husband and, at forty-eight, had moved to Delhi to live by herself.

I was shocked because I had always presumed theirs to be a happy marriage. She agreed, saying that they had been happy together. Her move was not precipitated by any problems or issues in their marriage. She had chosen to live alone suddenly, after almost three decades of marriage, because she wanted to 'discover' herself.

She shared that she had got married almost immediately after college. They had the usual spats and disagreements inherent to any marriage, but overall they had been good for each other. They'd raised two beautiful children together. But getting swept up in family life so young had left her no room to explore herself as an individual.

So she had quit Mumbai (and her marriage with it), shifted to Delhi and was living in a barsati (a small one-room rooftop apartment). I was perplexed. Barsatis look good in movies when they are used as a trope to show a young woman living the free life of her dreams, all bedecked with fairy lights (the barsati, not the heroine). But in real life, frankly, they are quite uncomfortable and grimy (which is why you need the fairy lights). I couldn't imagine living in a barsati at the age of even twenty, forget fifty! And my face, never my political ally in the best of times, must have shown my horror.

But she was unfazed. She was enjoying the freedom of living in an eight-by-ten feet room. Ironic, given her Mumbai flat was around five thousand square feet! Her children had grown up. She was exhilarated at having shrugged off all attachments and ridden off into the sunset by herself. I remained perplexed until it hit me that it was menopause talking.

Unfortunately, she was not the first friend of mine to make a rash life decision.

Around the same time, Sudha, a similarly aged friend, told me she had read whatever she could lay her hands on about menopause once her doctor had confirmed the symptoms. According to her, the physical and emotional metamorphosis of menopausal women was at par with the extreme changes undergone by adolescents during puberty – thanks to hormonal swings and imbalances in the body. Unfortunately, while we have all been so understanding of teenage angst, none of us acknowledges the issue of menopause, which being a specific 'womanly' problem has been conveniently swept under the carpet.

So Sudha had spectacularly decided to make dramatic changes in her life as commanded by the hormonal swings of menopause! She had been staying in the USA with her family for fifteen years. Her husband was completely Americanised and her daughter genuinely thought America was home. But menopausal Sudha moved her family back to India overnight.

Her sixteen-year-old daughter was devastated and was literally counting the days until college when she would go to an American university and never come back. Her husband had no job in India. He worked with an American firm remotely and thus had to adjust his entire schedule to work at night. Their family life had completely gone out of gear. But Sudha remained resolute.

'For twenty years I've done what they wanted to do. Now they have to do what I want to do,' she insisted. 'But you're harming your family, aren't you, by demanding this?' I queried. 'So what? To deal with this difficult time in my life, my chakras need to be on Indian soil for perfect alignment,' she intoned.

While I am all for women empowerment and for us taking ruthless control of our lives, I also wonder how many of these words were hers and how much belonged to her reading on menopause. She had devoured so much on the condition that she was playing out what the books told her to do.

The sheer variety of menopausal examples quite startled me. There was my mother who had borne it in silence and expected the same of me. There was my suddenly hippie friend 'finding' herself in a barsati in Delhi. There was my expat friend who had uprooted her family overnight after fifteen years abroad. And then there was me. Sleep-deprived, exhausted, hormonal me.

Menopause can create cataclysmic changes within all of us. But because of ignorance and the lack of conversation around it, there is nowhere for us to go and even understand what is happening to us. All of us who were going through this stage in our lives were desperately hoping to anchor ourselves and find meaning amid the chaos through different actions. Even the friends who had resorted to changing their lives overnight hoped to come to terms with what was happening to them through external changes. I don't know whether either of these women was doing the right thing. But I do know that major life changes are best not made in the midst of so much turbulence.

A single symptom of menopause can give rise to a host of new unrelated ones. If like me you suffer from sleeplessness, then know that insomnia leads to depression, cognitive impairment, irritability and even mild symptoms of PTSD. You are trapped in a vicious cycle of mood swings and unproductivity that feeds on your agony and creates more despair.

When you go through menopause, you will invariably also be dealing with other life changes. Whether you are facing bittersweet regrets or pondering over your mortality or simply experiencing the trauma of the empty nest, the physiological and philosophical cocktail you are subject to can be unpleasant at best and wrecking at worst.

No one would willingly choose the trial by fire that is menopause. But it is a process of transformation that all women have to go through, whether we like it or not.

Thus it is important to know that this will happen, and to read about it, prepare for it and talk about it. The one piece of advice I keep on reinforcing is to practise awareness and mind management. We have to recognise what is happening and link it to how we are feeling. Knowledge is empowering and critical in helping us make informed, reasoned choices instead of impulsive ones. Realisation precedes corrective action. And once you know, you can ensure you do whatever is possible to alleviate the trauma. Meditate. Exercise. Use the power of the sisterhood. Commiserate openly with your girlfriends. Share your problems with your family.

As an inveterate silver-lining advocate, I also believe that menopause is not gloom and doom alone. The one constant about change is that it always has an upside! And the big positive here is that with your testosterone increasing to male-like proportions, your confidence also shoots up to masculine heights! So instead of allowing menopause to play havoc with your emotions, you can and must channelise the self-assuredness it gives you to finally tell the world, your aunt, the nosy neighbour downstairs and your husband (the last one is optional): 'I really don't give a damn!' And mean it!

IN SHORT

- Among the many challenges and hardships women face in their adventures at home and work, there is one more looming on the horizon – menopause.
- Unfortunately, despite the intensity of changes it wreaks on women, it is a topic that has been kept well below the radar so far.
- It is important to understand its implications by reading and talking about it, so when it comes it is not an unexpected or alarming guest.
- Knowledge will help us deal with it better. Forewarned is forearmed.

Midlife Crisis

*I live in that solitude which is painful in youth,
but delicious in the years of maturity.*

—Albert Einstein

I was thirty-five the first time I was called 'Aunty'. I found that immensely funny. Maybe the boys who had shouted that word to me across the road while puffing up their chests to distract from their milk moustaches thought I deserved the label. Or maybe rating women into categories of desirability based on age was a sport that helped them feel more like men. Aunty is a much-maligned and pejorative term in our country, designed to summarily demote women from attractiveness to matronly-ness. However, it was like water off a duck's back at that time. I narrated the story to the girl-gang, we insouciantly shrugged it off our shapely shoulders and went about being our usual flamboyant selves.

In the preceding fifteen years I had built a fabulous life that I enjoyed immensely. I had resolutely scaled the evolutionary ladder from naïve teenager to confident senior leader one step at a time and didn't intend to look back. The mirror smiled at me lovingly every morning and the few lines on my face were cheerful crinkles rather than mature wrinkles, which I thought added great character and depth to my face! No street urchins were going to make me question how hot and happening I was.

Flash-forward a decade. Ranbir Kapoor walked into our studio one fine morning. The millennial heartthrob had come for interviews to promote his latest film and was immediately thronged by crowds of young women (and some men) desperate to inhale his essence. They accosted him to click selfies, that millennial version of autographs, and he pandered to all of them with good humour. He was introduced to me and while we were chatting, I found myself engulfed in a disconcerting feeling of maternal protectiveness! He reminded me of my son, even though he is a generation older. I worried that his last film hadn't done well and hoped that this one would be better. My tender heart rued how thin he seemed. I wondered whether he ate properly. I mentally castigated the film industry for expecting actors to starve for appearance's sake.

And that's when I suddenly realised I had become OLD! When earlier, proximity to a good-looking male would send several butterflies and a host of other woodland creatures fluttering in my stomach, today the only feeling that consumed me was motherly love!

A twenty-one-year-old Apurva or even the thirty-five-year-old Apurva who had laughed off being called an Aunty would never identify with this crazy lady I had become, the one who just wanted to feed the movie star in her office a hearty Punjabi meal. The collision that is the reckoning with one's midlife occurred at full force for me in that moment. I realised that unbeknown to all of us, the girl-gang had transmogrified almost overnight into a version of my mom's lady friends!

Horrified, I noticed we were spending our entire lunch sessions either commiserating over subtle but certainly not imperceptible signs of ageing or discussing various illnesses real and imagined, much like the women at mom's kitty-party sessions, which end up being a virtual trip through a medical clinic!

The immutable fact about middle age is that no one is immune to it. Maybe it will be a slow dawning of truth for you. Or maybe, as in my case, it will be a sudden explosion that hits you unexpectedly.

While midlife issues are gender agnostic, arguably women have it worse. While men supposedly age like fine wine, we are considered crinkly crones by forty. Nearly four generations of heroines were deemed to have reached their dotage around their early thirties and retired accordingly, while our current crop of sixty-something heroes continue to romance the latest twenty-one-year-old entering the movie industry.

Being confronted with one's mortality is never pleasant. Dealing with the psychological attack on our self-worth while also fielding the existential crises that are sure to descend around this time is daunting. Added to that is the onset of perimenopause, which we just discussed. Cue the cascade of regrets, nostalgia, what-ifs and if-onlys.

Men suffer from midlife crises just as much as women do. But they deal with it far better, give or take a few tattoos, leather jackets, motorbikes and flirtations with twenty-six-year-old PYTs (pretty young things). And that's because men manage to retain their sense of selfhood, through the turmoil of work, marriage and child-rearing, while women completely immerse themselves in these tasks.

We juggle being good wives, mothers and professionals. We rush home from the office to oversee homework and organise playdates and rush back again to finish the project report on time. We make sure the kitchen cupboards are stocked with food when we go away on work trips, including labelled meals and refrigerated parathas.

We baulk at the pressure and dream of solo getaways where all we will do is drink cocktails on the beach, dressed in wispy (albeit non-revealing) resort wear! We fantasise about eating meals that we didn't need to shop, cook or plan for. But as we discussed earlier in the book, secretly we love being needed this much. We enjoy the feeling that everything will fall apart if not for our herculean management skills – both at home and in the office. And though we miss the person we used to be before being drowned by responsibilities, we don't grudge the sacrifices because of the joy this brings us.

And then suddenly that life as we knew it is gone. The change takes effect gradually but the realisation hits us like the bucket of ice water that those ALS challenge participants doused themselves with to participate in the viral internet challenge. The marriage has settled into a comfortable harmony that no longer needs conscious upkeep. The children have grown up and moved out. The career has achieved a level of success we could once only dream of.

We now have in our grasp that holy grail that seemed too fantastical to be true – time for ourselves. Yet when the key expectations and duties that defined our lives for so long are no longer present, our first reaction isn't happiness or relief. It's a sinking feeling of emptiness. When this empty-nest syndrome strikes, men continue to have their hobbies and interests and friends to turn to. We don't even remember what ours had been in the first place. Consequently, the desolation becomes inescapable.

But it doesn't have to be this way. A temporary mourning period is acceptable. Lamenting the emptiness and wallowing in suffering as a way of life is not. Life is asking us to reboot, but sometimes we are too stuck to move. When my son moved away from home, I too experienced the gut-punching pain that comes with the wrenching of a family nucleus. Of course I was reassured that some things will never change when the next month said son landed back home carrying bags of dirty clothes to be laundered, all the while announcing how independent he now was.

But I digress.

My own reboot was baby steps at first. A theatre date with the hubby, a hangout session with a dearly loved but not oft seen friend. Gradually as I felt life seep back into previously ignored corners, I was energised enough to kick things up a notch. I reconnected with old school friends. Fortunately, there are no outside witnesses to our meetups where fifty-year-old women squeal and giggle like tweens and call each other 'girlie'.

Then came the crown jewel experience of my life reboot – a solo trip. Three days of wining and dining by myself at a resort. It was not so much the physical luxury as it was the emotional space to rediscover who I was when I was not being a wife, mother or boss. I finally realised why *Eat Pray Love* has become such a cult hit with middle-aged women. Spending time with yourself is addictive. Once you start, it's a habit you will keep going back to.

It's okay at this stage to be a teensy weensy bit more selfish and to put your needs first. It is critical to do a lot more self-care. It can be disciplined self-care like being conscious of what you are eating and exercising daily to help with hormone regulation. It can be indulgent self-care like weekly spa days or taking weekend trips on your own for some 'me time'. It could even be learning to fight for the remote or learning to say NO loudly and clearly! 'Please note I am going to watch *GoT* and not the hundredth version of a cricket league.' 'I do not want to eat what you decide to order.' 'I will keep the curtains drawn and the AC at sub-polar temperatures should I elect to.' 'And I will certainly not get up and start organising lunch the second I have sat down to read the papers just because you are hungry!' Aah, the freedom of saying NYET!

It's also okay to finally and totally stop giving a damn! Your best friend may point out that you have added yet another tire around the midriff; the sleazy neighbour will continue to talk to your décolleté rather than to you; husband dearest will be astounded that the fridge is not stocked with his favourite beer, despite the fact that you have been travelling on work the entire week; any of these things would have had you tearing your hair out or overcompensating defensively in your manic thirties. But now you just couldn't be bothered. 'And here's how my middle finger looks, dear neighbour,' you may say in a very ladylike manner (Rhett Butler would be proud of you)!

Most importantly, it is okay to accept that you don't need to be the adept multitasker you have been all your adult life. Now is the time for you to free up your plate, delegate responsibilities and live every single moment precisely the way you choose to do so.

One of my pals, Nidhi, had an epiphany in her mid-forties when it dawned on her that she had spent a lifetime accumulating expensive Kanjeevarams but had never had enough time to attend occasions that could justify wearing one. Faced with a cupboard full of beautiful but unworn

Kanjeevarams, she decided to do something about it. She started wearing her Kanjeevarams to office. Every day at 9 a.m. she would walk into the office and bedazzle everyone, decked out like Rekha at the Filmfare Award functions! We adored her for her savoir-faire and carpe-diem-ness and were much inspired by her.

We have all spent the first forty-five years of our lives accruing security and stability while fulfilling all the roles demanded from us. In this first phase of our lives we burdened ourselves with expectations, imposed as much by others as our own selves. Let's spend the next forty-five years having fun and doing only those things that we choose to. Now, which Kanjeevaram will you wear tomorrow?

IN SHORT

- Midlife crises for women are far more painful than for men, because they come with other life changes like an empty nest and menopause.
- But this can also be a great time to reboot and rediscover yourself.
- Finally your responsibilities of bringing up your children (and husband) are over and you can concentrate on yourself.
- Use this time to rediscover and re-ignite your passions and make choices that appeal only to you.
- At this stage in your life, you have the self-confidence, the maturity (and the money and the time) to know and do what you want. So get, set and zoom away into the horizon of your choice!

Somebody's Something

She's always been somebody's something.
She's been everything but alone.
A daughter, a lover, a wife, and a mother –
She's lived every life but her own.
She'd say, 'That's just called being a woman.'
She's always been somebody's something.
She wonders what it might be like to be somebody else.
She wonders what it'd feel like to be free.
When she tries to imagine being nobody's nothing,
That's someone she'd never want to be.

—Kaci Bolls

When I proudly sent the very first copy of my book *Lady, You're Not a Man!* to my mother, she looked at it, then immediately called me up and aggrievedly asked why her name was not there! Since the book was prominently dedicated to her, I was a bit taken aback. 'But look at the first page, Momsie – you are right there,' I said in a mildly exasperated tone. I could hear the turning of pages over the phone and then a few moments later she muttered crossly, 'But it just says "To Mummy" … Where is my name?'

And so it is for all women. Our entire life gets telescoped into one brief appellation, and just like that, in a jiffy, we are reduced to merely being somebody's something.

Tinku's mummy and Raju's sister and Mrs Khanna and the daughter-in-law of that nasty Mrs Bhatia who lives in 504. It almost seems that we have no identity of our own except as an appendage to a man!

Even our family name is not ours to own forever and must fall by the wayside as we adopt our husband's name after marriage. Or we can choose to sound very splendid and roam the earth with a double-barrelled Smythe-Winston or Kapur-Sud title. I assure you that brings its own set of challenges however, and is not something I would recommend since it also comes accompanied by unwarranted and repetitive explanations to be given to the passport officer, the electricity company and the Aadhar card system, which asks us rather nosily to explain why we have a surname that is different from our husband/father/son's name. Thus all it ends up being is a very grand but meaningless (and painful) gesture to defy the patriarchal order!

The loss of a name is mere semantics at the end of the day; after all a rose by any other name smells just as sweet, as the great bard wrote so many years ago. The much bigger loss for women is the forfeiture of individuality that takes place after they get married. The transition from Miss Swaminathan to Mrs Shankar is more than a name change; it is like sloughing off old skin and with it, discarding childhood friends, city, hobbies, TV habits and sometimes, painfully, even family! A woman is the paraya dhan after all and must transform, at the cost of her personality, into a new avatar that has very little in common with who she was pre the one 'chutki sindoor'!

But you are no longer the coy bride of two decades ago and today I am talking to the poised, smart and self-assured woman who has recently and bravely dealt with: 1) the morphing of a sweet little baby who loved her mom into a sulky teenager who bangs doors and scowls like someone from *Assassin's Creed*, 2) being called aunty by the cute neighbour, 3) working with insolent millennials who were born exactly at the moment you were getting your first salary check and who keep reminding you about it – 'What is a fax, ma'am? … You didn't have Google? How did you find out things? … Wow! You were born in 1978? That's around Partition, isn't it ma'am? How cool! Did you know Gandhi-ji?'

And having dealt with these life-changing events with immense verve and flair (and reached thus far in the book) I want to invite you now to the post-interval stage in which you prepare yourself to soar to even further heights, above and beyond the limits of your imagination, and see for yourself what you are truly capable of!

So let's begin the pre-take-off prep.

Step one and the single-most important thing to do at this juncture is to rediscover and reclaim your lost self. Who were you before the layers of daughter, mother, wife, boss accumulated on you as time went by? What did you smile about when you were young? Do you remember what brought a frown on your face? Did you like dance or poetry or just the adda that happened in the evening near the building gate?

This is the moment you look into the mirror and reacquaint yourself with that stranger you see there. And when you stare closely at that image, you will realise that not only have you forgotten who she was, but she is also coated with so many artificial layers that you will have to actually excavate the real person that lies beneath, section by section. So go ahead, take a hard brush and exfoliate the residue of the struggles, the hardships, the criticisms and the compliments. Figure out what you believe in and stand for without the pressure of ambient prejudices. And get in touch with your unvarnished spirit and your core essence.

It is supremely difficult to do that, I assure you, to hear again that forgotten voice from a distant past, to see yourself as an individual, to drown out the cacophony of expectations. But only when you do that will you start revealing the unashamed, unapologetic, phenomenal and beautiful person underneath.

My sister-in-law Raksha was once a glamourous globe-trotting air hostess. She gave up her job and her creative outlets when she married my engineer brother-in-law. He was building an engineering firm from scratch and she joined him in his efforts to build his business. For thirty years she served as his right-hand person, managing the firm along with him despite having no interest in this technical field.

Raksha never grudged the work nor shouted from the rooftops about her sacrifice. She enjoyed being her husband's partner and was proud of having created a successful business with him. But the day their two children began working in the family firm, she walked away from it.

She announced to us that she had done her duty. Now it was time for her to focus on her own interests. She was going to explore her creativity in full force. She had always been interested in fashion and grooming. Apparel and textiles were of particular interest to her and in the hardcore engineering works that had surrounded her for so long, their colours and textures had faded into sepia tones. But now she was determined that she would go back and bring them to fruition. Within months she had sourced a set of artisan women from Hubli in Karnataka, worked with them to create intricately embroidered sarees and was soon ready with her first exhibition!

The family turned up in full support to attend her show and we were all completely impressed by what she had managed to achieve in such a short time and the fun she was having while fulfilling her heart's desire. After the event, I stayed back to help her fold the few sarees that had been left unsold, but she wouldn't let me touch them. She lovingly caressed each one, crooning to them like they were her offspring, gently swishing them this way and that until she was surrounded by expertly folded piles. She confessed to me that she felt each of the sarees had a personality of its own, centred on the old artisans who had lovingly and diligently embroidered them, and that she sometimes even talked to them! I rolled my eyes, laughing at her exaggerated romanticism, but felt hugely proud of her and the dramatic volte-face she had accomplished. From running an engineering company to becoming a successful creative designer!

Her journey should be the journey of each of us, where in the second phase of our lives, only we have a lien over its course and its path. This phase of our lives is about us. About our growth, our evolution and advancement – and it should be in the direction we wish it to be and at the pace we want to drive it at.

We have reached thus far by dint of immense hard work and perseverance. We have become successful entrepreneurs, senior lawyers, managers running not-for-profit organisations, school principals and marquee investment bankers. We may choose to do a 360-degree turn and take our life in another direction, or we may choose to continue on the same path with renewed vim and vigour; the vital thing to remember is that this is just the halfway mark. We have accomplished but a fraction of what we are truly capable of doing.

But for that we need to accept the challenge of becoming once more the best version of our new self and invoke the leader within!

To become the leader of your destiny, of your organisation or of yourself however, requires certain traits that you need to cultivate and develop. To know what those are, you must read on, my dear ...

Picture abhi baaki hai, mere dost!

IN SHORT

- For the first half of our lives, most of us have been an addendum to our fathers, brothers, spouses and sons. It is now time to reclaim our lost identity.
- This mid-point in our lives comes with opportunities to make choices that are not dependent on the people around us.
- It is an opportunity to uncover our lost individuality, rejuvenate that essential self and start the journey towards building its best version, answerable to no one but ourselves.

Part Two

*Out of every one hundred men, ten shouldn't even be there,
eighty are just targets, nine are the real fighters,
and we are lucky to have them, for they make the battle.
Ah, but the one, one is a warrior, and he will bring the others
back.*

—Heraclitus

Part Two

Tough Love

Everything depends on upbringing.

—Leo Tolstoy, *War and Peace*

As a lady boss – whether you are running your own clinic or investment firm, or you are managing your family and their crazy schedules with the savoir-faire of a general while dealing with thousands of employees in your organisation – you need to have a specialised toolkit at your command to become a spectacular leader and manager. You certainly don't want to settle for anything less than being spectacular. After all you are not just any leader. You are the boss lady!

So in this part of the book, I want to share with you some nuggets of wisdom I have gathered along the way up my own career ladder. These are stories of building high-value organisations one patient brick at a time, of putting together talented players and teaching them to behave like a team. They are tales of setting grand strategies at the start of a year while never forgetting that the execution is just as important. They tell you that having a macro-perspective is a great leadership trait (and kudos to you for being such a visionary), but the job gets done only when you get the plumbing right, and the pipes and drains all clean and working. In this part we discuss that to succeed you need to have passion for the task and compassion for people in equal measure, and manoeuvring and balancing both these critical facets are the biggest challenges you will face every single day of your managerial life. So let's begin, as they say, at the very beginning.

I don't know whether you have noticed, but leadership is having its moment currently and everyone and their aunt wants to tell you what they think they know about it. It's very much like having a point of view on cricket; whether we know anything about the sport or not, every one of us 1.2 billion Indians has an opinion on the India vs Pakistan series, Sachin's finest innings or who was the better captain – Sourav, Dhoni or Kohli. The topic of leadership is a bit like that, and every senior manager who has been a CEO, ex-CEO, or an almost-CEO, and is obviously of the masculine gender and thus prone to pontificate, can give you the lengthier version of a TED talk on his personal opinion on leadership before you have so much as smiled at him prettily.

I am a lady boss however, and you all know that a no-nonsense, practical and sensible approach to leadership is our default style. We don't preach or sermonise. We don't stand up on platforms (in any case I have vertigo and two-inch platform heels are the best I can manage) and hold forth grandiosely. Instead we give pithy tips and subtle suggestions to stimulate everyone around us to think, and our leadership lessons are drawn not from the majestic high ground of theoretical thought, but from the minutiae of everyday living.

Precisely because these lessons are from the perspective of ground zero, where the real job of living and managing gets conducted, I believe they are all the more effective and also easy to apply. Indeed, one of the most important leadership lessons I learnt quite early on and constantly propagate is from the arduous yet oddly satisfying business of being a parent.

I offer this thought to you – that if you can get the core of parenting right, which is essentially to convert that little angel who is pulling at your dress and throwing a tantrum just as you are leaving for an already-overdue appointment, into a decent human who will be kind, polite and make a meaningful contribution to society, you have already learnt all that is required to be a good leader. Parenting, with its tear-your-hair-out moments interspersed with bouts of uncertainty at the lousy job you are doing and sprinkled with itsy-bitsy crumbs of smugness at those rare intervals when that little person is behaving well, is where you learn the vital art of leading. If you have understood that, I would almost dare suggest that you don't need to read this book any further! But never mind me, do carry on.

The essence of leadership in its basic, primal form, stripped of all jargon and affectation, is the ability to impact people's lives and help transform them into better and more productive professionals and human beings. Whether you are an entrepreneur running a small firm with three employees or a lawyer with just one clerk in attendance or the head of a mammoth MNC with a million employees spread across the world, the core of leadership is about positively influencing people and helping transform them into their best versions.

Now re-read the last sentence. How is that different from parenting, except that parenting entails a life-long commitment in comparison?

I remember in the initial days of setting up Radio City, while we were evolving the basic foundation of the organisation we were trying to build, we conducted a workshop with a leading HR firm to develop the values that would define our culture.

As is their wont, the HR firm organised multiple exercises designed to help us get in touch with our inner selves and ascertain what our organisational vision would be. The exercises included colourful balloons and myriad hats, whiteboards and team spirit, and yards of green twine with large nails attached at regular intervals, whose purpose I still haven't fathomed since we didn't get around to using it. We all earnestly got into the spirit of creating the VMV (vision-mission-value) statement, which would be the defining lodestar for the company for many years to come.

The workshop progressed along expected lines, several HR truisms being volleyed about with great enthusiasm. I particularly remember 'innovation led', 'people focused', 'process driven', 'customer first' being used repeatedly and vociferously. It always impresses me that all good HR trainers have the uncanny ability to channel the spirit of childish enthusiasm and boundless eagerness even in the most hardened executive or cynical loner in a team.

As the workshop progressed, I stopped the trainer midway and firmly told him that one of the values that I most certainly wanted to make part of the Radio City culture was tough love. He gawked at me in utter disbelief. If my memory serves me right, he goggled too. Then he led me to the side of the room and in a horrified undertone informed me that tough love was not 'corporate' enough to be used as a value. With its parenting subtext, it just did not have the seriousness or solemnity an organisational value required. According to him, all VMV statements had to be explicitly stuffed with gravitas and had to have a minimum of fifteen words with multiple prefixes and suffixes to communicate their importance. This was no child's play after all, he expostulated. I wanted to point to the clown's hat he was wearing while giving me this lecture, but since he was on the verge of an apoplectic fit, I desisted. The poor chap's internal wires had already started a-twisting and a-turning in shame at the blasphemous thought of seeing 'Tough Love' painted graphically on our corporate corridors and on our coffee mugs!

But I persisted, and as you read more of this book it will gradually dawn upon you that perseverance is one of the virtues I am particularly fixated on. So naturally, tough love did become one of the values that Radio City practises even to this day.

Now you may ask why I was so keen to make tough love a core value at Radio City.

One of the most challenging struggles we face in our journey to become good leaders is to find the ideal mix between discipline and empathy or between managing processes and managing people. Every stage in the leadership pipeline is fraught with the danger of upsetting the delicate balance that is required between being people-oriented and result-focused. Or between caring and outcome. The equilibrium can be destabilised at an organisational level when budget cuts have to be enforced, which could potentially mean retrenching employees who have worked in the organisation for years. It can happen at an individual level when a sales executive misses his targets because of issues in his personal life. How does the manager balance the P&L and the person sitting across the table? Is it okay to miss sales numbers? Or frankly, should it not matter a damn that the employee's wife is sick and the only thing that should be seen while admonishing him are the quarter's unachieved numbers?

I had suggested 'Tough Love' to our trainer simply because applying this particular parenting principle to many such difficult situations has made them far easier for me to deal with. Isn't it a fact that if your child is throwing a tantrum or refusing to eat his food, or behaving in an atrociously impolite manner with your neighbours' aunt, you will discipline him, scold him or send him to stand in a corner? He knows what he has done is wrong and that you are punishing him for a particular misdeed. He also knows that despite being punished, he is loved and cared for. Indeed, because he is loved, he is being disciplined. And that's how parents practise tough love!

Similarly, managers need to be tough when performance is being discussed, while making every effort to ensure that the employee is being treated empathetically. They have to know the vital difference between judging a task and not the person, and censure the act and not the actor. If passion for excellence and compassion for people can coexist and work in tandem in a managerial operating style, there is no better demonstration of great leadership. People are not fools, and your team member will recognise that you are giving her feedback only to help her improve. She knows you value her and care about her, and that is the conscious effort you have to make in the tough love style of management.

Being a parent or a leader is not a test of popularity. It is a solemn duty we all have, a commitment we make that whoever passes through our circle of influence – our children, our executives or our managers – will become better at what they are doing through a series of interventions, some pleasant and some not so. If we have to be good leaders, tough choices have to be made and disagreeable calls need to be taken. Leadership is not a congeniality contest after all. But if we can do so with our humaneness intact, with our mind driven by results and our heart filled with empathy for people, parenting would have taught us a valuable lesson in management indeed!

IN SHORT

- One of the best places to learn leadership skills is the parenting academy, which teaches tough love.
- The principles of tough love include knowing when to discipline your child so that they grow up to be a better human being while reinforcing your love for them at all times so they are never in doubt that you care. This ensures that they understand your desire to improve them is because you value them. These are the same principles you need to apply at work.
- Balancing performance orientation with empathy for people is the toughest synchronisation for a leader. Understanding the ethos of tough love will make the job simpler.

Taming the Underling

The measure of a man is what he does with power.

—Greek Proverb

A lady asked me the other day to help her figure out how parents can teach their children to manage a crisis. Her contention was that while practice is a great way to become perfect, crises by their very nature are one-off events and therefore no one can prepare anybody to manage them.

Most sensible parents, I told her, are aware that they can't protect their children always nor will they be around each time to deal with the crises their kids face. Thus one of the most important life skills they try to teach their offspring is resilience. We repeatedly drill into our child's head that they need to get up after a fall and ride that bicycle again, or reappear for the test they failed, or stay put in that first lowly job and gain experience, despite having graduated with honours. We pray and wish for our children not to stumble, but equally we teach them how to get up and run once again should they fall. But to teach them resilience, we first have to instil courage in them. We need to tutor them to have the resolve to take that exam again, the nerve to jump into the deep end of the pool, the determination to get up on that cycle despite the scraped knee.

As parents we know courage will be the only companion that will see our children through any period of stress and that is an important legacy we would like to leave with them.

Then why do so many managers, directly or invidiously, work at eroding the courage and confidence of their juniors? This is one problem that I have not been able to fathom even after thirty years of working. It is obvious to me that leaders will want to accomplish great things in life and the only way they can succeed is if their teams do well, which will happen only if the teams have the resilience to deal with the turbulence that they will face in their work, for which they need to have courage. Ergo, the first principle in being a successful leader is teaching the troops confidence! Then why do managers behave inappositely? Perplexing!

One of my batchmates, Vishal, narrated this interesting anecdote to me recently about his boss who is a very well-respected marketing guru. 'Come what may, Basu never ever has anything good to say about me,' he grimaced. 'Every time I go to him with a strategy, an idea or a plan, he dismisses it disdainfully, saying you can do better, son! And although several times we have ended up implementing exactly my suggestion, it is never acknowledged as such,' the litany continued. 'When I was younger, at every single appraisal session of mine, Basu would say, "You still have to mature as a marketeer. I can see you have potential, but you are not there as yet. Keep trying. Push yourself beyond the limited outlook you have currently."'

As we continued chatting, Vishal told me reflectively, 'Initially I was in awe of him and thought that he was pushing me to excel for my own sake. Then I realised several appraisal years later that I had become like the growth prospects of the Indian GDP; invariably the potential is there, but it never seems to be achieved! And once when I asked him what he thought I should do to improve, Basu had no specific or concrete suggestions to make! That's the day I realised that the problem was not with me but with him. Whatever I did, I would always remain the bridesmaid and never the bride with Basu, because he didn't want any of his juniors to grow.'

I could hear the despondency in Vishal's voice. I remembered how starry-eyed he had been as a young brand manager when he had first started working with Basu. Not only did he have the opportunity to work in one of the most marquee marketing organisations in the country but it was also with Basu, the company's much-lauded marketing head.

Many times we are dazzled by talented, charismatic and respected senior leaders and we feel the need to seek their approval precisely because of the aura surrounding them. We are so overawed with their personas that we don't even realise how they are slicing at our self-confidence one snarky comment at a time.

In our book club we recently discussed *The Little Prince* by Antoine de Saint-Exupéry.

There was widespread discussion around the interaction between the Little Prince and a fox he meets on his travels across the planets, and how the fox teaches the Little Prince about love, one of the most valuable lessons in the book.

'Come and play with me,' proposed the little prince. 'I am so unhappy.'

'I cannot play with you,' the fox said. 'I am not tamed.'

'Ah! Please excuse me,' said the little prince. But, after some thought, he added: 'What does that mean – "tame"?'

'It is an act too often neglected,' said the fox. *'It means to establish ties.'*

'To establish ties?'

'Just that,' said the fox. *'To me, you are still nothing more than a little boy who is just like a hundred thousand other little boys. And I have no need of you. And you, on your part, have no need of me. To you, I am nothing more than a fox like a hundred thousand other foxes. But if you tame me, then we shall need each other. To me, you will be unique in all the world. To you, I shall be unique in all the world …'*

'I am beginning to understand,' said the little prince. *'There is a flower … I think that she has tamed me …'*

And of course the message is about how by giving our time and our effort and our emotions to somebody, we build a special relationship with that person, and it is this love that makes each of us unique. But I have pondered on the use of the word 'taming' as a parallel for love and wondered whether there is an underlying cynicism in the context. Maybe the author is trying to tell us that often the reality is that we want to control the people we love. And that love is nothing but a desire for ownership. I think that is also the lesson in this tale, which is why it is considered not just a children's book but equally an important fable for adults.

I so wish that the current strong and mighty captains of industry would move their narcissistic gaze away from their own reflection and realise this. So many senior leaders I know behave in a manner calculated to reduce their juniors to timid, unsure professionals who will then remain perpetually dependant on their great leader to save their souls, shelter them and care for them. Leaders such as Basu believe that they know best and their disciples should follow them unwaveringly and steadfastly. And the price for their devotees' loyalty is the protection of the guru. Managers like him live in an imaginary land where they see themselves in technicolour glory striding across stormy deserts and choppy seas while their followers march singing *Chale Chalo* behind them for all eternity. It reminds me of the 'taming' the fox explains to the Little Prince.

But you are the new age leader who doesn't need to tame anyone or rely on only their loyalty to buoy you. You have confidence, intelligence and the self-assurance to deal with strong team players. More importantly, as a woman you understand the power of partnerships and of collaboration. You have successfully partnered with your husband and collaborated with parents and in-laws in raising your children. Since prehistoric days when your foremothers lived in caves, they understood the strength of the collective over the singular and the same ancient wisdom courses through your veins.

A leader is only as good as the team she has around her. And as leaders we need to have teammates who have intelligence and nerve standing beside us. The moment we teach courage to our team, we may also embolden them to question our judgement, to have opinions contrary to ourselves and to not think of us as demi-gods, which in any case we aren't. And that is perfectly fine. The advantages of diverse opinions and brave teammates far outweigh the disadvantages. I would trade an army of timorous followers for three brave warriors watching my back (though they may argue with me incessantly in private) any day!

IN SHORT

- Wise leaders understand the importance of having brave teammates around them, who have minds of their own.
- They encourage dissent in thinking so that the solutions that emerge have had the benefit of diversity.
- Thus courage is one of the primary skills they seek in their teams or strive to inculcate in them.
- As a boss lady, channel your inherent strength of nurturing and learn to be an enabling rather than a debilitating boss.

Good Leaders Are Great Communicators

The single biggest problem in communication is the illusion that it has taken place.

—George Bernard Shaw

If I asked for your definition of communication, what would you say?

People of whom I've asked this question on multiple occasions have come up with a plethora of rather interesting responses. 'It is to outline a point to someone.' Bang on. 'The way people speak with each other.' Right-o. 'It is talking.' Beautifully simplistic. 'It is effectively telling people what to do.' How very CEO of you.

I personally find the Oxford English Dictionary definition of communication most elegant because it is both short and to the point. Additionally, it is also highly relevant to the modern business leader. Let's examine this definition that describes communication as 'the successful conveying or sharing of ideas and feelings.' The reason I find this definition particularly pertinent is that it highlights that communication is not only about transmission but also about reception! In order for it to be classified as communication, it needs to be *successfully* conveyed and understood. Now tell that to Mr CEO who is very pleased with himself after a town hall where he droned on endlessly using the seventy-six multicoloured slides his executive assistant had prepared, of which only a fraction registered with his audience! Or the entrepreneur who presents a business plan to a potential investor in which every third word is an acronym specific to his industry. The dazed look your investor is giving you is not from admiration at your vision, my dear, but because he is still trying to make sense of this: 'So the moment we have 35 per cent of our ACK in place, we would have delivered an innovative PBX solution to the customer acquisition challenge faced by BFSI and our gross margins on the Zena vertical will become 3X.' Wow!

You may remember that I mentioned in an earlier chapter that I have learnt some vital lessons on leadership in the quotidian-ness of life and parenting. And so it happened that I figured out the trick of great communication smack in the middle of a kids' animated movie!

How this came about was as follows. I have an age-old tradition with my son. We call it 'Back to School' day. The premise is very simple. Throughout his schooling, on one of the final days of his summer vacation, we would carve out a day – me from work and he from his furious cricket playing – and go shopping for all the supplies he would require for the coming school year. We would also indulge in a movie and a meal outside. No matter how big the shoes grew and how advanced the textbooks got, two things remained constant. The movie always had to be an animated one and the meal always at McDonald's.

That particular year, the movie was *Madagascar 2* and my epiphany struck during the denouement when Alex, the lion, and his father are being rescued by their friends who land up in a hastily put together aeroplane. While the brave and motley crew of animals fly the aeroplane, Alex and father hang some thirty feet below in a large iron bucket. Connecting them is a series of monkeys in chain-formation, holding on to each other, not unlike the *Ring a Ring o' Roses* nursery game so popular in our childhood.

Now Alex, being the alpha lion (literally and metaphorically) and finding himself in a particularly sticky situation, attempts to shoot off quick instructions to his friend Marty, the zebra, who is near the flying plane. The only problem is, Marty can't hear him. So Alex needs to rely on the monkeys forming the link to pass the message on. Alex screams to the monkey nearest to him, 'She's got a gun. Let's get out while we can! Pass it on!'

A comical sequence of monkey gruntings ensues, and the message reaches Marty via a very aristocratic British-sounding primate. However, what's happened is a round of Chinese Whispers. 'She's got a gun. Let's get out while we can! Pass it on!' becomes 'Let's have some fun and take out the dam. Basset hound!'

While my son giggled in delight at this sequence, I realised how easy it was for 'let's get out while we can' to become 'take out the dam' in any organisation. After all communication is nothing but a flow of information passed from top to bottom and back again via a chain of primates (ahem), a loop that is repeated for every project, every department and every implementation plan.

Fortunately for Alex and gang, this miscommunication ends serendipitously. The dam gets busted successfully, enemy turns on enemy and mission accomplished, they return home to the adulation of the entire savannah. Now just imagine a communication gap like this between a leader and his team, where one thing is being said but the complete opposite being executed. Would that lead to a happy ending? Absolutely not. Equally imagine when the troops are trying to pass a message up to their leader and the leader is blissfully floating on an aeroplane twenty thousand leagues above sea level and can't or chooses not to hear their desperate pleas.

Miscommunication is an unfortunate by-product of all organisations, big and small. Given the levels of hierarchy that exist between the CEO and the on-ground teams, not to mention the various ways in which an organisation is cut up – regionally, functionally, by cluster – there is ample scope for even the clearest of messages to be distorted. The problem has been compounded today, ironically, by the same technological advancements that are meant to improve connectivity: our wireless networks and multiple screens. As a consequence even people working on the same project no longer sit together, cooped in the same cubicle or lab or around a massive work station, as it happened earlier. They are working out of their homes or from wherever they are holidaying or from another continent in a different time zone, on their laptops plugged in at airport lounges or from cafes. There is limited face-to-face interaction and we all have to rely on hastily typed emails, WhatsApp code language and emojis to convey what we want to say (needless to say, I find that I use the frowny face emoji all the time). And therefore, communicating what needs to be done and the onerous responsibility of making sure that it has been understood by everyone across the width of a far-flung team have become key success factors for the leaders of today.

It has become mission-critical for leaders to be effective transmitters of information and outstanding communicators through simplicity, consistency and clarity of message. While making sure that there is a comprehensive system of reinforcement so that communication across the length and breadth of the organisation is crystal clear and understood by all.

Given the slightest opportunity, people will construe your message in the manner that they deem fit and confidently convey it to others in this new shape and form. This keeps happening until it has gone through so many mental prisms that by the last exchange, you can be sure the message being passed on is almost entirely opposite to the one set in motion! And the organisation has begun pulling in different and conflicting directions rather than towards the single-minded vision you thought you articulated so beautifully in your townhall.

Thus clear and consistent thoughts, simply articulated and repeated ad nauseam, is the only formula of good communication. The best way to do this is to channel that innate nagging mother (or wife or girlfriend). 'Did you get what I just said? Want me to explain it again? Do you require any further clarifications? Are you sure? NOW, TELL ME WHAT YOU UNDERSTOOD!'

And then repeat it all over again!

In our organisation we actually have quizzes after each town hall to make sure that everyone has understood the plan. And they get prizes for getting the answers right too!

That, of course, is not all. Effective messaging is only one half of the communication game. The other aspect, just as critical, is listening. It is something all of us attend to far too little, and the problem is only exacerbated at a more senior level, where instead of listening to what their teams and organisations are saying, leaders become inordinately fond of their own voices. But listening is the bedrock of collaboration and successful team management. Listening to your team, not only with your ears but also with your mind, body and soul, helps you improve your decisions and form the right opinions to drive action.

In one of my earlier organisations, we had a CEO who was a formidable individual. One of the traits that made him so impressive was his uncanny ability to know exactly what was going on in any of our offices, often better than the respective office managers themselves. Such was his knack that we often suspected that he had secret cameras and microphones in various locations. It was only after thirty years that the secret of his success dawned upon me. Today, I can walk into any of our smaller, more far-flung stations and guarantee that I will know the environment of the branch better than the branch manager herself. Does it mean I've put some hi-fi spy surveillance systems there? Certainly not. I might stalk my teams on Facebook on occasion, but even I wouldn't stretch to hidden cameras and microphones! My only secret is that for all my years as a leader, I've been listening with my ears, eyes and mind wide open. Management by walking around and observing what goes on, talking to as many people as possible – in the lift, in the canteen, in corridors – has helped me know exactly what makes our organisation tick (or not). I therefore only require the tiniest exposure to a particular branch before I can correctly gauge the myriad issues that could be plaguing them, what needs to be done next, which initiative to push and which to drop, and how to ensure the branch delivers the desired results.

Nuanced decisions based on factual and timely information gathered from ground zero and unadulterated by false perceptions can avert disasters. Remember the *Titanic*? That is the sheer power of listening. And along with the ability to effectively get one's message across to the team, it forms the crux of being a great communicator, in itself a prerequisite to being a great leader!

IN SHORT

- One of the biggest missteps leaders make is in assuming that they have communicated their expectations just by articulating them at the annual conference.
- Between the talk from the rampart and the walk on the ground, multiple steps need to be taken, including simplifying the communication, keeping the messaging consistent and repeating it as many times as possible.
- Management by listening and walking around is a powerful tool for access to speedy and timely information, often critical in averting disasters.

Prioritising: What Is Your First and Foremost Goal?

Things which matter most must never be at the mercy of things which matter least.

—Johann Wolfgang von Goethe

In the last chapter we discussed how clarity of thought is the first step in successful communication. Only when your mind is clear can you articulate your strategy logically, but ah! There lies the bulk of the problems of our planet, and definitely of the little companies you and I run!

Realistically speaking, the majority of humankind has a very jalebi-fied approach to thinking (jalebi: a circular Indian sweet made up of complex whorls). The root of most problems in organisations, I find, lies in the inability of a leader to be focused and logical in his or her approach and to move from point A to point B in a straight line, rather than by jumping around like a grasshopper. Unfortunately, organisations are stuffed with grasshoppers in more ways than one. This lack of logic results in businesses bouncing about from action to action in a 'one step forward, two steps sideward and one step completely outside the arena' manner, which is highly wasteful and inefficient. Furthermore, the various segments of the organisation are also unable to move together in a concerted and organised manner because there is no clarity about the end goal.

The ability to un-jalebi one's thinking and be absolutely clear on the foremost priority of your business, project, career or next meeting is yet another important component of the journey towards being a great leader.

When I pose the question, 'So, what's your F1?' to any of my employees, I think their minds race immediately towards Formula 1 and whizzing cars, but for me F1 is the very first priority at the top of any list of strategic choices: the non-negotiable goal, your foremost agenda, your North Star. And just like the sailors of yore followed the North Star to get to shore safely, it is the direction set by this F1 priority that one must unflinchingly follow if success as a leader has to be guaranteed.

All of us find ourselves confounded by the immense range of possibilities in front of us at several junctures in our lives – what should we look for in the career we are choosing? Where should we invest our hard-earned money? What should be the focus for this year's organisational strategy – top line, margin or market share – and so on and so forth. We want to have everything, but our limited resources require us to pick and choose between, for example, the size of the apartment, its proximity to work, and good childcare facilities around the property we plan to buy. What should be your F1 when at first glance all three are equally important and desirable?

Unfortunately, another word for focus is sacrifice and human nature is such that we are not able to give something up by making a mindful choice. Consequently, and sometimes injuriously, we end up falling between a stool and a chair in these situations, a place most uncomfortable to our backsides I assure you!

At this stage it is imperative that we select a clear F1 out of the entire range of priorities, ruthlessly and with no qualms at all on having made the choice and sacrificing the rest.

Let me illustrate with an example that will resonate with all of you, dear readers, because this is a type of choice you have struggled with many times in your lives. When studying at the venerable Stella Maris in Chennai, I, like all the girls in the college, was compelled to pick a sport in the spirit of 'healthy bodies make healthy minds', which the dear alma mater propagated to all its disciples. I opted for hockey. Being a quirky mix of hugely unsporty yet highly competitive, my clear F1 for the whole endeavour was to make it to the college team. There was a requirement for a goalkeeper on the team and not very many takers for the same – probably because of how blue it left your ankles with all the hockey sticks you got hit with. (Back then in conservative Chennai, the social repercussions of this were potentially quite grave as it was the only skin that we girls got to display!) I tried for this position and, lo and behold, got picked for the team. What's more, I was fortunate that our college had the best team in the city circuit and our city the same in the state circuit. Since lazy selectors inevitably suffer from the bias of assuming that all players from the best teams must naturally be the best of all available options, before I knew it, I was playing for the Chennai and Tamil Nadu teams as well!

This is not only a brief story of my only claim to sporting success, but also a leadership lesson learnt early in life.

Simultaneously participating in the trials was a dear friend of mine, Leena. You should have seen her. A fine physical specimen she was: fast, lithe and powerful. On top of that, she had outstanding ball control and her stick moved as quick as lightning. If a person were to do a comparative analysis of the two of us, there would be no doubt as to who was more suitable for the hockey team. She however, wanted the glamorous role of the striker of the team. She believed that it was only this position that truly befitted her talent and skill. However, so did many other girls, and competition for the place was extremely stiff. Surely you can guess the moral of the story from here. Yes, she did not get selected for the team. A girl, clearly so capable, did not get into the college team, while another, comparatively much less skilled, not only got into the team but also progressed all the way to the state team. The only difference? The simple matter of priorities.

Now, I may be accused of compromising while Leena who did not make the team would be lauded for not being willing to settle for anything other than what she truly craved. After all, the most stellar heroines remain 'bloodied but unbowed' – there is great cinematic splendour in that. If indeed one has to fail, shouldn't it be in the pursuit of that singular happiness? I don't deny any of this. Neither do I want the generation of today, raised on a diet of self-assurance and intransigence, to compromise their lofty ambitions and not chase their heart's desire. But before you make that judgement and look down your snooty nose at me, the question you need to ask is, what was the first priority or F1 for Leena and me? In both cases the categorical answer was playing for the college team. Seen from that lens, it becomes obvious that she missed out only because she didn't make an informed choice between being on the hockey team at any cost, or playing only if she got the striker role. Either her F1 should have been different or her actions.

That being said, in today's dynamic age, when whole industries can be revolutionised and organisations made redundant in the blink of an eye, one can question whether steadfast adherence to an F1 is good for leaders or not. Doesn't that make them not 'agile', a term considered paramount for organisations to survive today? I would argue otherwise, primarily because prioritising between goals is the domain of strategy and not execution. The latter is performed by multiple teams across organisations and due to the innate entropy of the market, requires flexibility, creative thinking and constant innovation. The former however, is the prerogative of the leadership team and requires focus and a come-what-may rigidity, especially in the short-to-mid-term and especially when everything else is so dynamic. Goals must remain steadfast so that despite the mayhem surrounding them, teams strive towards one end purpose. In heaving seas, if a leader constantly switches between ports of landing, it will inevitably befuddle those under her and the ship will remain at sea forever. Just imagine this scenario: Your CEO communicates that the new focus for the organisation must be bottom-line expansion through cost-cutting measures, even though for the past six months the whole organisation, under the guidance of the same person, had been working towards top-line growth. How will this leave you and the rest of the team? I'm sure you'd be absolutely tearing your hair out. Implementation of any strategy takes time and teams need one vision to follow – to be the most admired delivery firm, to be the best place to work, to have the most radio stations, to have the highest profit margins in the industry. It can be anything, but it cannot be everything. It is the leader's duty to pick this one vision as the F1 of the company or division or team, so that the employees have not only a defined purpose and direction but also clarity in the implementation path.

This very mindful selection of an F1 also helps leaders to remain focused when they are faced with choices during the accomplishment of their promised vision. It can and should act as a sieve through which they can pass all the grandiose ideas they come up with during the course of the year. The failure to ensure this alignment can result in a reality that has nothing to do with the desired vision. Our own prime minister, Mr Narendra Modi, is an important case in this regard. When he ran for office in 2014, his manifesto's vision was 'Sabka Vikas' (Prosperity for Everyone). In which case, the most appropriate F1 would have been economic betterment for everyone, whether rich or poor, in a country that has been struggling to move into a middle-income economy for the past two decades. But the most high-profile initiatives of his reign were demonetisation and GST implementation – the first a scheme to target the country's black money and the second to overhaul India's legacy tax systems. Did either of them have anything to do with improving the universal welfare of India's citizens as the F1? The answer is an unfortunate no. Demonetisation, while penalising black-money hoarders, actually resulted in a hellish period for the vast majority of lower-income individuals, many of them losing their livelihood. No amount of 'shot-in-the-arm for the cashless economy' spin could change that fact.

If he had clearly articulated his F1, demonetisation (democratic in the harm it did to the rich and the poor, the entrepreneurs and the daily wage earners) would certainly not have passed through the sieve.

So to all the current and future leaders reading this book, please do give due consideration to your F1s, not just at the workplace but in all walks of life. You will find it vital in determining the course of action for any major decision you take, and the solid foundation of logic it provides will prove helpful in personal situations as well. So, deciding on a career change or on getting married? What is the absolute non-negotiable you want in the new job? What is that F1 quality your spouse must have? What can be less than ideal?

I find F1 helps bring clarity not just in big decisions but even in small things. On a recent family trip, HD and I were able to wheedle our way out of the general-like manner in which our son was shepherding us from tourist place to tourist place by stressing that the F1 of the holiday was just to spend some relaxed family time together and not to maniacally burn our candles at both ends by hitting each of the items on his list. Given the steadfast preference for logic and structure that he has inherited from us, he had no choice but to agree! See? Having an F1 helps. Just make sure that once you decide what it is, both you and those around you hold on to it like limpets!

IN SHORT

- Targeting multiple goals and priorities is an inevitable part of an annual business strategy, and articulating them logically and clearly is important.
- Even more important is to prioritise between the focus areas. What will be your F_1 – the first and foremost goal, the non-negotiable aim for the year?
- As the dynamics of the environment can change mid-course, having decided the F_1 early on helps you remain focused should a choice need to be made on a course of action.
- The F_1 also helps you make the right call in decision-making processes.

Curiosity Makes the Leader

If you are curious, you'll find the puzzles around you. If you are determined, you will solve them.

—Erno Rubik

Picture the setting of a chocolate company. Alas, it is not the imagination-fueled Willy Wonka factory of our childhood dreams, but just an ordinary Indian FMCG firm. A relatively easy competitive environment and a highly accomplished leadership team have ensured that its brands have become trailblazers in the chocolate market, and indeed are often used as surrogates to define the category. Years of stupendous growth and their stellar market performance have given them a virtually monopolistic market share, but growth has started displaying signs of a slowdown in the past year or so. A new marketing head joins, tasked with rectifying the slump and placing the company back on its yesteryears' growth pedestal.

Into the office he strides. Chest puffed out, self-confident gait. A man who clearly knows what he wants to pull off. Water-cooler gossip starts immediately, a cautious sideways glance is cast. Are changes beckoning? Will there be a rocking of the boat that will throw people over the edge? Or will it just give them a mild queasiness? The eager beaver new brand managers plan to treat this as their opportunity to impress and win brownie points, while the old-schoolers dismiss the rumours, believing past success inoculates them from future pain.

A naturally confident leader he might be (years of witnessing subservience does make people like that, after all!). But there's a reason he is where he is. Behind the air of self-importance that most leaders carry lies a thoughtful and – most importantly – curious nature. Otherwise, this gentleman would not have reached the position he has. And that brings me to my next valuable lesson in leadership – good leaders are naturally curious. They question the status quo and look beneath the hood to see why the engine is working or why it is sputtering. They probe, they question endlessly and they are restless in their quest for more information and knowledge. You cannot be a great leader if your mind has stultified, either because it has become inflexible and refuses to learn new things or because you have decided that as the mistress of all you survey, you already know everything that needs to be known!

Sapiens, the tremendously insightful novel by Yuval Noah Harari, which I'm sure many of you have already read, makes a very relevant point on this front (On a quick personal side note, I take great pride in quoting Harari as I credit myself for having 'discovered' him and his uber-cute Israeli accent in a Coursera course that I had taken long before this book shot him to international stardom!).

In the section of his book where Harari talks about the scientific revolution and how the modern world changed irrevocably after the inventions and innovations of that age, he credits this to a few critical factors, chief among them being the 'willingness to admit ignorance.' Only then, he says, did modern science as we know it truly commence the radical journey of discovery it has been on these past few centuries.

We do not know everything. And more critically, nothing we already know cannot be proven wrong. All concepts, ideas and theories are open to critical challenge; nothing is sacrosanct. And only after having admitted this in the fifteenth century or thereabouts did humans, using their exemplary observation skills, inherent curiosity and the powers of mathematics, go on to build the world as we see it today.

Sadly, as we grow in the corporate world and increase in stature, we forget that what brought us thus far was our spirit of inquiry, our quest for learning, our unquenching thirst to understand and resolve new challenges. Instead, we become prone to thinking of ourselves as omniscient deities and god-like know-it-alls.

'Who can give input to me, a thirty-year industry veteran? I have created this industry let me tell you!'

'Pray tell me what exists that I have not already seen? Malcolm Gladwell said ten thousand hours of practice to attain expertise, yes? Well, I've put in sixty thousand. Now is there anything further you want to say?'

You catch the drift? And if you think I'm exaggerating, trust me, I'm not. All leaders might not act this way, but they very often think like this. As a result, they stop questioning the things around them, stop viewing issues with that critical eye that was earlier held in such regard. But once complacency sets in, the edifice starts to crumble. Even the best product, the best company, the most innovative idea has scope for improvement, but the moment leaders start accepting the status quo, they accept that nothing better is possible. And if you have already reached the peak, the next step after that is only downhill, is it not?

Now let's come back to the story – about the marketing head and the chocolate company. Since I happen to be married to the hero of the story, I am also privy to the next episode and the grand finale in the saga of the search for growth.

The day he walked in, HD decided to shake things up a bit and called for a review of the business without much ado. Now, the organisation was stuffed to the gills with a bunch of old hands who had begun their days as marketing trainees in the same organisation and now roamed its corridors with mighty managerial titles like GM or BM, accompanied by the other markers of corporate VIPism – cabins and personal secretaries. Along with the long association with the company, they had also been hugely successful in the output they had produced for it. So they could be forgiven if they believed that 'they on honeydew hath fed and drunk the milk of paradise', to quote the poem 'Kubla Khan'.

The day of the meeting dawned and the legacy team came in with a swagger and a smile, ready with a ton of data, detailed analysis and complex algorithms to present, prove and rest their case without much ado. They didn't anticipate too many headwinds from the newbie marketing head and the young bunch of new brand managers he had collected around him. Plans for a celebratory lunch, where they would gently indoctrinate the marketing head and his brand team into the easygoing culture of the organisation, had already been fixed for after what they thought would be a breezy exercise in a largely self-congratulatory strategic presentation.

'See, sir? This is the analysis. The chocolate industry is this large; number of premium households into <*educated*

Curiosity Makes the Leader | 149

guesstimate of percentage that sounds about right 1> and number of normal households into *<educated guesstimate of percentage that sounds about right 2>* makes the overall market size for chocolates. This is our share over the years, with growth at a stellar rate! It has slowed down in the past couple of years or so, but what can you expect? Just look at our market share! It is 70 per cent! You really can't expect better than that.' They smirked as they lolled about in their seats.

'And why has growth slowed down over the past couple of years or so?' queried HD.

'Sir, what to do? The chocolate market has only grown at this rate. And finally, we have 70 per cent market share, no? It's 70 per cent! A little bit we should also give competition, no?' they said in falsely obsequious tones. Much playful finger shooting ensued followed by a generous amount of back-slapping.

Now any normal manager would have stopped there. He had asked the first layer of questions after all. And things were going fine. Why upset the apple cart? The chocolate market, as the team rightly had pointed out, was after all only so big. There was nothing he needed to do to effect change there. Spun the right way, such an explanation would easily be good enough for most stakeholders involved. And he could get on with the easygoing task of supervising the highly acclaimed team while they continued with their single-digit growth. Only a light touch was required and that would also give him a bit more time for golf.

But then he wouldn't be the hero of this story, would he? His inherently curious nature and desire to get to the bottom of things through a comprehensive interrogation made him probe on.

'And why do you consider yourself a player only in the chocolate market?' he asked in dulcet tones.

The team, while bright, was not necessarily perceptive (and lunch was already beckoning to them spiritually). They continued, at the same time making mental notes that replacing the word 'buddha' with the word 'buddhu' in the song *Main Kya Karun Ram Mujhe*, would generate much laughter at the next office antakshari get together.

'Sir, chocolate company ... chocolate market, no?'

'Okay, so tell me this. Where and when are chocolates given and eaten?'

One of the new brand managers piped in excitedly, 'Sir when boyfriend gives girlfriend ... err celebrating something ... maybe when children pass exams.'

'Excellent!' said HD, glad to see that at least the new team realised what he was driving at. 'And therefore, if chocolate is given during times of celebration, doesn't that mean that we should compare ourselves not just with other chocolate companies, but with whatever is shared during moments of celebration in India, that is, the entire mithai (Indian sweetmeat) market?'

As sure as you have it, when viewed from that lens, the market share of the company in this larger competitive landscape precipitously fell down to sub-1-per-cent levels! Suddenly, instead of facing the difficult prospect of trying to grow beyond 70 per cent, the opportunity in front of the company became a vast untapped mithai market. The growth prospects for a hungry, talented company morphed from a minuscule sliver into a huge and unexpected goldmine.

And it was precisely this approach, built on the foundations of curiosity and a desire to ask questions and know more, that paved the way for the second great wave of this chocolate company's growth, for what I've outlined to you is a very real, albeit simplified case study seen from the front seat in the stalls.

High-quality leaders who continue to break records left, right and centre are the ones who continually ask questions, both of themselves and of those around them. Where are we going? Why are we doing what we are doing? How can this be improved further? Where is the next iceberg going to appear? This is what allows them to constantly push beyond the expected and the obvious, and shatter barriers that box in lesser men and women. Because remember ... curiosity may kill the cat. But it makes the leader!

IN SHORT

- Stagnation of thought is the worst disease a leader can suffer from.
- Constantly questioning the status quo, re-examining accepted practices and revisiting set norms ensures that both people and organisations evolve and grow.
- Why? Why? Why? Three levels of probing are often sufficient to unearth new artefacts of information.
- Learning through curiosity requires daily practice, an openness to accept ignorance and a willingness to change your own mind.

Scylla and Charybdis: You Have No Choice But to Choose!

When faced with two equally tough choices, most people choose the third choice – to not choose at all.

—Jarod Kintz

The aficionados of Greek mythology among you will no doubt know about the tale of Scylla and Charybdis. The Homeric legend goes that these two mythical sea monsters, Scylla manifesting herself as a six-headed sea creature with shark-like teeth and Charybdis as an all-consuming whirlpool, were maritime hazards on the Strait of Messina, located so close to one another that they posed an inevitable threat to passing ships. Veering away from Charybdis meant the risk of being captured and ferociously devoured by one of the monstrous heads of Scylla, while avoiding Scylla meant being stuck in the vortex of doom that was Charybdis. And this tight spot where a tough decision loomed is exactly where our hero Odysseus found himself, midway through his long and arduous journey home to Ithaca after the Trojan wars.

Making difficult choices on a daily basis is an inescapable requisite of leadership (along with the ulcers, and by the way, that's why you get paid so much though no one tells you that at the beginning). When your juniors, your organisation and the people around you are looking to you for guidance, a leader cannot afford to be the metaphorical deer stuck in headlights. You have to decide, take a call and move ahead.

Before I give you my personal take on such decision-making, let's see what our Greek hero, Odysseus, did when faced with the choice he had in front of him. On the one hand, he could steer the ship closer to Scylla, who would ravenously devour six of his best men. On the other hand, he could elect to take on Charybdis, that fearsome swirl of the sea, and risk losing his entire ship and everyone on board. On the one hand, a definite end – an almost willing sacrifice of some of his own crew, men who had loyally accompanied and served him on all his travels. On the other, risking the entire enterprise in an almost calamitous gamble, with only a sliver of hope of getting out of it in one piece. Sounds like a tough decision? You bet it is. But one that a leader often has to make.

I know we all have a rose-tinted impression of Greek heroes – Hercules, son of Zeus, with his God-given daring and strength and Achilles with his (almost complete) invincibility and Trojan-war exploits are only two of the swashbuckling characters that are part of the great legends. Heroes who were the very embodiment of courage, manliness and indomitability, ready and willing to brave any danger or obstacle to save their fellow men or (more often) women! We see them as mythological stars braving the toughest of odds with no more than a second's thought. However, Odysseus was more modern-age CEO than a Greek tragic hero, which is why he, not the other heroes, features in this great saga on leadership! He was shrewd and clever and had in abundance that one element lost on most leaders even today – pragmatism. He knew that if it could be helped, there was no sense in risking the entire ship and bringing an early end to the journey that had cost them so much and was still not over. He went for the well-being of the collective over the individual. Even if Scylla did devour six of his finest, Odysseus trusted the rest of his organisation (here, of course the ship) to survive that loss and for the others to step in and pull their weight accordingly.

I present this decision between Scylla and Charybdis to you today as one of the most important lessons for leaders to learn. One of the toughest jobs of being a leader is having to make constant choices between several equally valid courses of action. Unlike in fiction where everything is black or white, real life operates mostly in shades of grey. Therefore the choices are never between good and bad but mostly between good and better or bad and worse, which is why it's such a harsh task. Did Odysseus not question his own morality for willingly making a judgement that would lead to six of his men perishing in front of his eyes? Did that not trouble him and force him to revisit and question himself endlessly? And what if he had braved the whirlpool and lost? Would he not have castigated himself for the foolishly brazen risk that led to the loss of his entire enterprise (if at all he survived that encounter himself)? Wouldn't he have wished and prayed that when he had the chance, he had been a little more conservative? Or maybe after he passed through Scylla, he would actually conclude that he had miscalculated the odds of losing the entire ship and he should have taken the risk of going through Charybdis instead. The moral and philosophical quandaries are endless.

I'm harping on about this because it is important to stress that leaders invariably have to make decisions in the realm of uncertainty and ambiguity, using limited information. Coupled with that is the fact that in life, no decision is as clear as what good old Karan-Arjun faced – to or not to avenge their innocent father's murder by killing Amrish Puri's most unlikable avatar, spurred on by their overtly virtuous mother across an entire cycle of birth and rebirth.

A few years ago, while at Radio City, I had a top-performing sales manager hand in his resignation letter. Now, he was one of our finest ever sales managers, an individual who had far outstripped his targets year on year on year. And while the rest of the team was also very competent, he stood out as a cut above the rest, so naturally we were very reluctant to lose him. When asked why he was leaving, out came the response that he had received a 20-per-cent increment from elsewhere, which was proving far too tempting to resist. So what would it take for him to stay? Yes, you guessed right. A simple matching of the sums on the table.

You can see the two immensely difficult choices here. As a company, we had a very clear policy that increments would only be given on an annual basis, with no discussions entertained during interim periods. We simply could not afford otherwise. If I stuck to that policy, I risked not only losing one of my key performers but also demotivating his entire team and perpetuating the perception that we were not a company that was willing to pay top dollar for top talent. On the other hand, if I did cave in, what message was I sending? That I was willing to be held to ransom by any individual who felt entitled enough to demand an out-of-turn raise; that I was willing to bend the rules for those select few that I felt deserved it? Was that in any way fair to the rest of the team?

Despite huge pressure from the national sales head who felt his entire world (and target achievement) would collapse if we did not retain this particular manager, in the end, I chose not to give the sales manager the out-of-turn raise. And despite being counselled by HR and listening to their best efforts to retain him, he duly did leave us. The following months were difficult, but other team members stepped in to fill the void, collectively doing this with great enthusiasm and helping us achieve record growth in that station that year. More importantly this particular episode went a long way in reinforcing one of the most important cultural values, that of fairness, which we were trying to institutionalise at that time.

While with the gift of hindsight it's easy to validate the decision made and call it the correct one, should one always take such decisions, where the might of the collective is trusted over the skill of the individual? I'm not so sure. I had taken a risk on the targets and what if they had really not been reached? Would fairness have been seen as a worthy enough payback for non-achievement? I certainly think so, but maybe another leader would have a different point of view. There are no right or wrong answers. There are only choices to be made.

So the key point that I'm making here is that when presented with such choices, leaders in charge have really no choice but to make a decision, no matter how unpopular. However, more often than not, I find leaders are not willing to take a call and just elect to bury their heads in the sand, hoping that the problem will go away. The truth of the matter is that it will not. It will be buried in the subterranean regions of the organisation only to rear its head once more and this time with far more vigour, having fattened itself on the flesh of uncertainty and loose talk in the meanwhile!

Having to make constant choices and decisions on behalf of the organisation and its stakeholders is a recurring theme in a leader's life and we cannot run away from that responsibility. There are several decisions I have taken that have worked out. Equally there are some (only a few!) that haven't, but even those bad choices were better than no choice at all. At least we moved ahead, figured out the mistakes and changed our tactics instead of continuing to dribble near the goalpost and not even take a shot at scoring. Freezing like a deer caught in headlights is the worst thing a leader can do and we should consciously avoid that state of refrigeration.

Many times, taking no decision is far worse than taking the wrong decision, because as we saw with Odysseus, losing six men at least allowed him to continue his decade-long voyage home. Imagine if he had dithered about what to do! Homer would never have been able to get his hero home and the Odyssey, already at a formidable length of twelve thousand and one hundred lines, would have been twice as long!

IN SHORT

- Leaders constantly have to make choices and decisions with limited knowledge of the future and ambiguous fallouts. Only hindsight has a perfect twenty-twenty vision.
- Unlike fiction, choices in real life are never between good and bad, but between good and better, or bad and worse.
- However, making no choice at all will only delay, not delete the problems.
- The faster you resolve issues and move on, the less they will fester in the organisation.

Perseverance

For all things difficult to acquire, the intelligent man works with perseverance.

—Laozi

Sohan Lal Dwivedi was a brilliant and accomplished poet, a Gandhian and a freedom fighter. A Padma Shri awardee, he is also the author of one of my most beloved poems, *Koshish Karne Waalon Ki Haar Nahi Hoti*. As all good poems do, this one evokes an outburst of passionate feeling in the reader. And since it's about making her feel unconquerable and invincible, it leaves her with an enduring sense that indeed nothing is impossible to achieve in this world as long as one puts in enough effort.

In its spirit, the poem offers one of the most important lessons of leadership I have learnt, and that is perseverance. The poem's prime message is that 'those who try will not fail'. It is as definite as that. Those who try just will not fail. The poet uses two metaphors – one of a little ant trying and ultimately succeeding in her attempts to carry a grain up a wall and the other of a diver's indomitable spirit in repeatedly going to the bottom of the ocean till at last he comes back with a pearl in his hand. This is followed by a beautiful passage on several aspects of perseverance, teachings of timeless wisdom whispered in verse from generation to generation. A message of not giving up. Maintaining positivity in the face of failure. Never running away from the battlefield of hard work. Holding on until you see that inevitable light at the end of the tunnel.

Now, despite all of the poet's (and your elders' – it is after all a favourite parental mantra!) instructions to persevere, you may very well question its legitimacy. And you may be very right in doing so. A long-term relationship that is not going anywhere, a dead-end job, a phase where no one seems to be buying into the great online platform you have launched – all these are unfortunate places to be stuck. Prospects can seem bleak, defeats endless. When should you give up? When should you carry on? Each one of us at some stage of our life has questioned the need to continue with a project or give it up as a lost cause. At these junctures the word 'perseverance' almost sounds like a gimmick, a cliché that is trotted around a little too easily by pseudo-philosophers and pop psychologists.

I understand this viewpoint. Opportunity costs need to be weighed and knowing when to cut the cord is definitely a valuable trait in a leader. However, the world is littered with the carcasses of good ideas, bright initiatives and smart start-up projects, because the people who had created them gave up far too early and far too easily.

When simply as a human being it is so difficult to persevere through periods of hardship and stagnancy, as a leader it is infinitely more difficult to do so. After all, the challenges are all-pervading – an idea ahead of its time, a shrinking market, transitory clients, poor macro-policy decisions or insufficient resources. To add to these, the future is inevitably opaque, with capricious trends, dense and insufficient data and no end of the tunnel in sight! In this complexity, a leader is expected not just to get herself going, but also play cheerleader to the whole team! Does persevering then sound like a gargantuan task? Let's just call that a rhetorical question.

The hard truth however, is that the benefits of having a never-say-die spirit are so visible, the impact so clear, that there is a certain unavoidability in possessing it as a good leadership characteristic whatever the situation, the industry or the environment.

In a nascent industry like radio, for example, volatility in the competitive scenario is par for the course. I have witnessed situations at Radio City where in certain markets we could be doing fantastically, having taken first-mover advantage to establish ourselves as the super dogs for several years, but then the inevitable happens. Competition gets a whiff and moves in to grab a slice of the pie. Before you know it, there are eight other stations vying for the top spot, rates have dropped and the government has decided to come up with another hair-brained scheme a la demonetisation. The sales manager, previously bubblier than an over-the-top Bollywood bahu, now starts coming to work with a hangdog expression. I try to gear him up, get him ready for the fight ahead, but unfortunately what I see in front of me is a broken man, someone who has already given up before the fight. It is after all the far easier alternative; just look at all the unfortunate externalities plaguing the poor soul! Nonetheless, we try to do all we can – we change the product, we bring in new processes, we even change the environment of the office! Doors get moved because vastu decrees it, feng shui means that one wall turns purple, some bells and crystal balls make a surreptitious entry in the reception area. But still no change. It's because the virus has already spread within the entire team. The attitude of their leader, previously so positive but now so despondent, becomes that most unfortunate of self-fulfilling prophecies. He has given up and therefore the team has too.

At this critical juncture, there's only one course left to pursue. It is to remove that leader and bring in someone else who will show that one all-important trait – the will to keep going and not give up. In comes the new person, and with him the original setup of the doors returns, the wall colour changes back to its previous pearly white, and the bells and crystal balls beat a hasty retreat. Slowly, but surely, the numbers become better and the station does return to its former position of glory. It is not a magic elixir. It's not a one week, one month or even a one-quarter fix. It's a dogged and daily struggle that just takes patience and a lot of perseverance from the team.

The underlying theme in the poem is that both the ant and the diver try to achieve their aim multiple times. It's not just a second or even a third attempt. Rather, incessant resolve and tenacity are displayed. In real life unfortunately, all too often, we give up quickly. It could be the fear of judgement or criticism or the fear of time running out or boredom with repetitive tasks or even a slow erosion in belief when, despite best efforts, the results do not come. Especially in start-ups, after the initial series of quick wins that accompany a new launch, there is a period where nothing moves. After the first thousand downloads of the new app, the next thousand take double the time and twice the effort. That is the period when people give up, and that ironically is exactly when there is only one quality that will help you across the valley of death. You guessed it right. It's perseverance!

And if you're still sceptical, still of the belief that perseverance is not a notion worth investing in because it seems that I am just extolling basic, dull hard work, do take a minute more to – yes, persevere. Recently I read a wonderful book called *Thinking, Fast and Slow* by a Nobel Prize-winning psychologist called Daniel Kahneman. The book sheds light on the various ways in which our mind processes and internalises the things around us, from the biases that most of us tend to display to some of the mental shortcuts we inevitably take. While there were many fascinating takeaways for me from the book, there is a key one that I felt was particularly apt to quote here – the concept of regression to the mean.

The concept of regression to the mean is exactly as it sounds. If a person performing a task on a regular basis has a certain competency, on occasion she might perform the task better or worse than that particular level. However, despite these periodic peaks and troughs, her next performance will in all likelihood regress to the mean that is her standard competency. Dr Kahneman uses this concept to beautifully illustrate his research on how we perceive the impact of positive versus negative feedback.

In a study conducted with Israeli fighter pilots, he observes that air force commanders (falsely) believed that their negative comments to pilots for mistakes made during drills resulted in better performances the next time around. On the flip side, they equally falsely believed that the reverse was true. Any praise imparted to the pilots after a good performance resulted in the cocky bastards becoming complacent and as a result putting in a poorer shift the next time around. I know what you're thinking: what brutal hardliners! But I'm sure all of us have had one or two bosses or teachers who behaved quite in the same fashion. Dr Kahneman, though, explains that what the commanders had assumed about how their own feedback worked was in fact merely the pilots' performances regressing to the mean! An incredible learning indeed and it should certainly be quoted to all bosses who are masters of feedback!

But when I contemplate this concept further, I realise this tale is particularly apt for our current topic of perseverance.

My experience, and I'm sure yours as well, is that if you have invested time and effort in building a good team, with a little application, some sincerity and a lot of hard work, most people will do a capable job of any given task. As people go about their quotidian work, they all have ups and downs, victories and defeats, dollops of good and bad luck, the metaphorical drops of rain and pieces of sunshine. The vagaries of life will inevitably mean that there are times when we punch above our weight and others when we are underperformers. But we will inevitably converge to our mean. Because those are the people we really are! In light of that, what conclusions can we draw? That whether we are flying with the wind very much beneath our sails or whether we are walking into a gale, we just need to go on. The mean is inevitable. We will ultimately reach the consistent level of our competencies. And if that bar is reasonably high, the team and we will succeed.

Just like the ant and the diver in the poem, it is grit and determination that will help us reach our goals while lesser mortals are left by the wayside! The woman who wins in the end is not necessarily the most gifted or the most accomplished or the luckiest. She is the one who did not give up.

IN SHORT

- One of the key drivers of success in any venture is the perseverance of the team and its leaders.
- Many difficult situations can be overcome by doggedness and determination.
- A leader's enthusiasm and can-do spirit in and by itself is a powerful motivator and precursor of change.

Planning the Implementation

Strategy is a commodity; execution is an art.

—Peter Drucker

In the last thirty years, CEOs and business heads of various hues, shapes and sizes have meandered across my path and I have had several opportunities to examine them with microscopic precision. Having studied these fascinating creatures at such close quarters and over such an extended period of time, I can confidently tell you that nearly all, or at least 90 per cent of them, get their strategy and vision right; they are highly capable executives and reaching CEO-ship is not exactly a cakewalk after all. But equally most of them fail to execute correctly, so even a well-crafted strategy converts to barely half its potential in reality.

No way! I hear you say disbelievingly. But I maintain the aforesaid as God be my witness!

As I said before, there is no doubt in my mind that most CEOs are fairly good at creating a visionary strategy. They work extremely hard at analysing markets, innovating products, benchmarking the competition and disrupting their consumer touchpoints. All of this is exemplified by the intense brainstorming sessions and passionate debates that are part of the annual off-sites, conducted with great sincerity every year.

But as soon as they come back from these jamborees, the strategy gets locked away in the bottom drawer of the boardroom cupboard, and everyone gets down to the practical business of running the company. As a result, it soon gets forgotten and through the year the business is run around a series of activities and discrete initiatives with tenuous links to the strategy. Even if in the initial enthusiasm, a strategy starts getting converted to implementation in Q1, you can be sure that it gets booted out without a moment's hesitation, either at the first sign of the competition doing something different or at a tiny swing of the market in an unplanned direction!

Factually, most businesses and ideas fail not because there is anything wrong with the idea per se, or that a market opportunity doesn't exist for that business, but because after identifying the opportunity and creating the strategy, entrepreneurs fail to get their implementation right. There is a lovely graph about startups and new businesses floating around in Silicon Valley, which shows that after the initial triumph of launching a new proposition, the idea falls into a deep valley or trough. For an app, getting the next ten thousand downloads after the initial ten thousand is twice as difficult. Selling the next million units after the first million have been sold is more than double the effort. Most entrepreneurs struggle at this phase. If the idea has merit, it will only emerge from this 'valley of death' if the leader gets her implementation right!

I worked with a visionary entrepreneur once who was known for his remarkable capacity to envision what no person had dared imagine earlier. He was considered a pioneer and a revolutionary mogul, but fewer than half of his grand visions converted to reality and those that did mostly failed after a few hundred crores had been spent on them. The reason was simple. He had the incredible knack of coming up with a new dream whilst brushing his teeth every morning, so it was '*Naya din, naya khwab*' every single day for him. To keep up to speed with him, his teams mindlessly spun from executing one idea to another like a posse of demented trapeze artistes, till it made one dizzy just to watch them leaping from rope to rope. No wonder he remains a one-trick pony even to this day.

So why is it that even the creators of the strategy often fail to convert it into action? That's because most managers jump straight from the strategy into its execution. But between the two steps is another vital one, which is planning the implementation, and often business heads miss this crucial step completely!

An architect converts her vision of building an apartment block or an opera house by first drafting its design into a detailed plan, where her CADD drawings include a break-up of the structure and its technical specifications such as materials, dimensions and procedures. Similarly, good leaders first make an implementation road map before hastening to construct their personal edifice.

So what are the critical steps in creating the implementation map of a business?

The starting point of any map, as all of you intrepid travellers or Uber-hailers know, is to begin by pointing the pin at your final destination. And it has to be just a single goal. We discussed earlier the importance of getting the F1 among all the goals of your strategy right. Dozens of strategies I have seen seem to want to do everything all at once: scale up, become profitable, address all segments, have the best distribution network and the highest market share and do this with scarce resources, all within six months. When I ask an entrepreneur what her single-most important and primary goal is, she struggles to give me a one-phrase answer. While I understand that businesses are complex and it is not possible to answer this question succinctly, I also believe that if you cannot articulate the principal business objective in one sentence, you are doomed to non-achievement from the word go. If one part of your organisation is chasing growth, another is chasing margins and yet another is not even sure what you want them to do because of a lack of clarity, nothing will happen, I assure you.

Once you have your F1 in place, you then move to the next step, which is to break up the goal into discrete building blocks. Sometimes looking at a strategy in its entirety is overwhelming for the leadership team. Such a big ask and such little time or so few resources to make it happen. Even for the CEO the complexity is huge. It is horrendously complicated to work across a minimum of seven functions, multiple geographies, different business verticals and then get them to move together in one direction to deliver on a strategy that is constantly being hit by an eight-hundred-pound gorilla of external economic changes, competitive headwinds and the internal dynamics of functions pulling in opposite directions. But it can be done and leaders must not lose heart.

This stage (after taking a deep breath) entails breaking the goals into bite-size and edible pieces. For example, starting with sales targets broken up into tinier sub-divisions by geography, by category, by month. Suddenly instead of that big insurmountable wall, there are smaller fragments that can easily be handled one piece at a time! I remember a large MNC many years ago decided to break the annual targets not into twelve months but equal periods of four weeks each. Suddenly, the sales teams had their yearly target broken into thirteen opportunities, not twelve, and hey presto, the bite became even more swallow-able! So clever, no?

The third step after breaking the objectives into sub-goals is linking the processes, the organisation's development needs and the resources available back to the desired goals.

Now here's the problem – till you figure out not only WHAT to do but also HOW to do it as well, the team will find even the bite-sized pieces difficult to chew. A strategy needs to be converted to process targets as well, which will help achieve those goals. 'Thus I want ten million dollars of revenue, of which three million will come from yield improvement and seven million from more volume of units being sold' or 'If I want to increase the spend per walk-in at my apparel store that sells only jeans, I can do so by adding tops and shirts for which I require to build a competency in my team to understand upper wear, which I will do by …'

After drafting the design of the building into a detailed drawing of each of the parts of the structure, the good architect then sits down and plans what materials she requires, what type of labour she needs and how she will put the limited budget her client has given her to its best use. Only then does she get down to action lest, after building half a wall, she realises that she has no more bricks left! Thus this third step is extremely critical to match the resources available to the output expected.

Balanced scorecards and 'where to play/how to win' maps that link specific output goals to the specific inputs required are great ways to accomplish the above, and I would encourage all business leaders to learn and use these techniques.

Good managers work hard at thinking about a strategy and then they work even harder at creating an implementation diagram. Only then do they jump (or push their teams) into the fray. An organisation where the leader shows not only what needs to be done but also how to do it, is where intent truly matches action and then magic can be created! To cross the valley of death requires a bridge that is the implementation map, and good leaders definitely need to know how to build it.

IN SHORT

- Most strategies fail because of poor implementation.
- Just as leaders think about strategy in great depth, they need to think about implementation in equal detail before moving into execution.
- Planning and creating an implementation road map is a vital leadership technique, which most managers omit.
- An implementation road map consists of:
  - Clear priorities with the foremost priority (F1) clearly identified;
  - Goals/objectives broken into sub-segments; and
  - Most importantly a plan to link specific input targets, process requirements and resources available, back to the desired goals before setting off on the journey.

Measurement and Monitoring

People don't do what you expect but what you inspect.

—Louis V. Gerstner, Jr.

Running an organisation or managing a team is like being a charioteer. If you are lucky you have a bunch of high-bred stallions pulling your chariot ahead seamlessly and efficiently. As any charioteer would know (and if you don't, please watch *Ben Hur*, and no, *Chariots of Fire* is about athletics, not horse racing!), to make these excellent animals gallop satisfactorily, you need to hold the reins firmly yet lightly in your hands. Too strong a grip and they are likely to lose their enthusiasm and native desire to win and you end up being the one carrying the heavy burden of having to spur them on; too slack your hand on the reins and they are likely to run amuck.

Most managers do not understand this concept at all. And if they do figure out how to achieve this balance at a particular stage in their careers, the moment they get elevated to the next rung of the leadership ladder, they forget it all over again! And gloomily I watch them as they start from scratch yet again, either micro-managing and trying to do everything themselves, or abdicating their responsibilities totally and struggling to figure out the ideal median of delegation that comes right in the centre of the above two.

To be a skilful charioteer, every manager has to accept that in her hands rests the responsibility of winning the race, but equally the realisation that she is not the one running the race – it is her team of charging steeds that has to run swiftly towards the finishing line. And how she holds the reins will determine their success or failure.

So what is the trick in getting this balance right? Over several years of trial and error while working with different types of teams, some majestic chargers, some young ponies and some lame horses, I have figured out that the most important thing is getting the composition of the reins perfect. Once you have the ideal reins in your hand, holding them becomes that much easier and almost instinctive. Thus you don't have to struggle too hard to get the perfect sweet spot that doesn't chafe but gently controls all the same.

I see you look askance at me. Reins, you wonder. Huh? Up until now you thought this was yet another flight of fancy where I was using the analogy of steeds and charioteers as, yes, an analogy. So why am I now suddenly talking of reins not in the proverbial sense but in a tangible leather and weather manner? Hold your horses, dear lady boss, channelise your Fearless Nadia avatar and ride with me on this allegorical journey a wee bit longer.

To me, good quality reins that can help execute a project successfully or run a business well combine two things. The first is high-quality dashboards and regular reviews that have a cadence and momentum and are implemented with military-like rigour. Second and more important is the ability to get the measurement metrics right.

Managers normally understand the review mechanism because reviewing, after all, is their reason for existing and sometimes their only claim to being a leader. If they didn't have a review or two to conduct, what would their life be like? An empty wasteland, a desert with quarterly board meetings as intermittent oases to break the tedium! Many senior and well-respected leaders have made the review processes in their organisation its very *raison d'etre*. So organisations under their charge seemingly exist only for the purpose of being reviewed. One CEO in the media world used to have his reviews from 9 a.m. to 10 p.m. every Monday. For the teams to be ready for this detailed and intense review (every Monday, mind you), they had to start preparing for it the previous Thursday. Which essentially left only two days for the business of the organisation to be conducted. No wonder it was and continues to remain in dire straits!

But while over-indexing the review process, the same leaders don't focus too deeply on what is being measured and what the metrics of evaluation should be. Either they use the wrong parameters of measurement or incorrect data, or they speak in English when measurement should ideally be in Maths only. Doing any or all of the above is getting the entire business of rein-holding utterly wrong and the team is destined only to lose the race.

The erstwhile media CEO I just talked about did incredibly detailed reviews with inordinately poor quality data. So his business heads kept doing very high-level analysis on bad data, leading to the operation of the classic GIGO principle: Garbage In, Garbage Out. Sometimes this practice is not deliberate but becomes a matter of convenience because people analyse whatever is available and in front of their eyes, rather than burrow hard to look for fundamental data that could actually address the issue.

In his remarkable book *How Not to Be Wrong: The Hidden Maths of Everyday Life*, Jordan Ellenberg talks about Abraham Wald, a brilliant statistician working for the Statistical Research Group during the Second World War. The military came to SRG to help them figure out the best place to armour a plane, given that there could only be an optimum level of armouring to prevent the planes from becoming too heavy and hence un-manoeuvrable and fuel-inefficient. Their data showed that the planes that had come back damaged from skirmishes had the maximum number of holes in the fuselage area. This data seemed to suggest that the armour needed to be put in the fuselage. The military thought they had the place and came to Wald to ratify how much armour would be needed.

However, Wald was a genius and the smartest man in the room. He told them that the armour shouldn't go where the holes were, but ought to go where the holes weren't – on the engines. Ellenberg says that Wald's insight was simple. He asked not about the planes that came back, but about those that didn't. The planes that were hit in the engine never came back to base. Thus the engine area required the most armour and not the fuselage, which when hit at least had the capacity to come back to base. The data to look at wasn't that which was available (the planes in front of the analysts' eyes) but that which wasn't (the planes that didn't return). And that piece of information ended up becoming the most important part of the puzzle.

Yet another mistake managers make in measurement is to speak English when they should be speaking Maths. That is, when they should be talking with mathematical precision, they end up waffling in imprecise prose. Jamshed, a very dear friend and incredibly talented management guru, once explained to me how we get our measurements wrong when we do this. The example he used was that of a cook (no more animals lest you think I run a zoo or a farm at work!).

'When we hire a cook,' he elucidated, 'We start by telling him that our expectations are for him to be good at his work. The cook totally agrees and immediately goes about his business of cooking for us every day. Now, as an experienced cook, he understands what it takes to be a good cook; after all he has been working in several houses for so many years. Western, Chinese, Indian, he knows it all and more.' Jamshed smiled benignly while explaining this to me, no doubt carried away by vistas of a delectable buffet. He is a foodie, you see.

'But over a period of time we start getting annoyed with him, although he believes he is doing an exceptional job. This mismatch happens because his interpretation of a "good" cook includes: knowing all varieties of cooking and being a quick worker. Whereas our definition of "good" is using little oil and masala while cooking and coming to work on time and not taking frequent leaves. This discrepancy is because we didn't bother to explain to him what we meant by "good". We assumed it meant the same to him as it did to us.'

Similarly, managers repeatedly make the mistake of not defining the metrics of measurement specifically and particularly, leading to mismanaged expectations and thus wrong actions and disenchantment across the board. Often the pushback I get, especially since I am part of the creative business, is that creativity cannot be measured, that it has to be understood with emotions and a warmly beating heart. This last statement is frequently made by my programming heads, with trembling fingers accusingly pointed at me, the stone-hearted 'suit' with arctic feelings and sub-zero creative sense. Ably rising to the reputation of being emotionless, I retort that everything in the world is measurable and thus monitor-able – love, sex as well as dhoka – and go about proving it to them.

Indeed, among my most notable and successful cases in proving this algorithm true is a performance index score we worked out to measure each song we play on air, based on researching its recall, likeability and fatigue levels. So there!

But the most fundamental error in measurement is getting the metrics wrong themselves. Measuring the wrong things often drives the wrong behaviour and nothing explains this better than the disenchantment economists have recently been feeling over the use of the GDP as a measure of progress. After all, what is the GDP? It is the total value of all goods and services produced in a country and everyone from armchair economists to the most educated businesswoman is obsessed with it, using it as *the* marker of a nation's progress. In turn, all our nation's leaders become solely focused on that figure and orient their behaviour towards improving it the best they can.

But let's dig a bit deeper. Is that something we really want them to do? Will it really improve the health and well-being of our nation's people? The answer is grey at best. GDP does not consider an umpteen number of metrics that we would consider important criteria of well-being – clean air, unpolluted rivers, green spaces, community services, technological progress, stress levels of citizens, the efficiency of public-transport systems, the valuable time a parent spends rearing their child. All these are requirements of the Utopia we want and yet completely ignored in the calculation of the one data point that is supposed to be the single greatest indicator of a nation's progress! It is truly gasp-worthy.

Conversely, let's see all the things that do fit under the purview of GDP measurement – expensive healthcare for chronic diseases; military spend in preparation for war; the lakhs we spend to try and cure our obesity, shoddy stamina or psychiatric issues. Now, are these metrics really what we want our leaders to chase? Of course not. But it's precisely what they will!

I'm not saying that our leaders are cynical enough to wage a war or create societal problems just for political gains like a few basis point increases on the GDP (ahem ahem), but can we really blame them if they do? After all, they are just acting in accordance with what we – the media, the economists and the public – are measuring, and that's the GDP. Behaviour is a direct consequence of measurement and this is just a small glimpse of how actual behaviour can go off tangentially from what we truly want, just because the correct measurement metrics were not selected.

Creating specific, correct and measurable metrics for everything – processes, milestones, targets, the success of a project or a relationship or an organisation and then monitoring them with dedication and a preordained rhythm is the ideal way to hold the reins and drive an organisation to success. Otherwise all we will be left with is heartburn, because we either reached the finishing line too late or actually ran in the wrong race. Or the cook put too much masala in the food!

IN SHORT

- As managers move up the leadership ladder, many of them falter at getting delegation right and fail to achieve the desired balance between micro-management and complete abdication.
- A disciplined cadence of reviews and the right measurement metrics will help them achieve this balance effortlessly.
- To be useful, metrics have to be objective, specific and based on accurate data.
- Often information is not in the data in front of your eyes, but lies below the surface and has to be extracted.
- Everything in life is measurable; we just need to apply mathematical precision and rigour to selecting the right metrics.

Creating Winning Teams

*Talent wins games, but teamwork and intelligence
win championships.*

—Michael Jordan

The first time I became a business head in my career, I had to lead an all-new, all-male team. Naturally I chose to make an impression on my alpha underlings by bringing in an elaborately frosted cake garnished with icing and laden with pink rosebuds for our very first meeting together on a fine Monday morning.

All the Rambos in the room clustered around the table, staring with horror at the cake as if it would detonate any second. A few moments ago these testosterone-infused creatures had been sizing up their opponents and calculating how they would jump over each other's carcasses on their way up the corporate ladder. Now they were internally groaning at the luck of having a female boss who wanted to use them as participants for her kitty party.

I ignored their glowering looks as I brightly urged them to dig into the cake and began to quiz them about their weekend. They were eager to get started on presenting spreadsheets, tallying data and telling me of the revolutionary ideas they had thought of, which would catapult our small company into the big league overnight. But all I wanted to know was how their weekend had gone, what movies they had watched and what fun activities they had done with their friends and families.

With immense reluctance and much foot-dragging I was allowed a peek into the human beings that lay behind the sharp suits and hungry ambitions that populated the room.

Obviously it was not just friendly conversations and small talk and we did get to work eventually, much to the men's relief. But every Monday morning, without fail, there would be a cheerful fruity and flowery cake waiting at the table, signalling both the start of a hard working week and inviting a freewheeling chat to begin it with.

It took many weeks and awkward silences for my macho heroes to reveal their inner softies, but it did happen. The men in the room on that first Monday only saw strangers and competitors when they looked at each other. But over a period of time they started seeing each other as friends, confidants and teammates. The cake went from being an object of scorn to a symbol of community, friendship and togetherness.

Maya Angelou said, 'I've learned that people will forget what you said, people will forget what you did, but people will never forget how you made them feel.'

In the past three decades, many of the teams I've led have disbanded or evolved and changed. Yet my cake meetings have become the subject of folklore – filled with the nostalgia of memories of working together, some of the victories we achieved, the failures we encountered and the joys and conflicts we shared that powered us through both good and bad times.

Good teams do not happen by chance. It takes immense effort, patience and diplomacy to turn a group of individual stars into a bright galaxy. If done right, a collaborative team will not only light up the department and the organisation to which it belongs, but it will also enrich the lives of the people in it immeasurably.

But when done wrong, it backfires into a cascade of supernova that has far-reaching destructive consequences. Instead of uniting kindred spirits and encouraging comradeship, it festers jealousy, ego and single-minded goals of self-interest. And the leader spends more time managing internal conflicts than trying to fight the enemy outside. In my experiences as a leader, there are mistakes I've made and learnt from, those I've witnessed and sworn to avoid and those I am in the process of making. Here are three key lessons about good team-building that this journey has taught me.

The first and foremost rule in the team-building gamebook is to create trust among team members. Competent leaders work hard at securing extraordinary individuals for each of the functions their team must perform. But they stop there. They think that they've got great people in the finance, HR, marketing and supply-chain roles. They give directions to each of them, forgetting that there is an interplay that has to happen between them, which requires each player to have faith in the other.

A team isn't created automatically just because people work together in a shared environment. The belief that there is an auto-pilot that starts operating when you've got the right people in place is misguided. A manager needs to spend an inordinate amount of time ensuring that teammates interact with each other well. And trust is the foundation that builds a successful professional relationship.

Unfortunately, there's no medicine you can hand out with the guarantee that on popping the pills for seven days, trust will build. It takes time, something that as a leader under immense pressure to deliver, you might not have.

But you can fast track the process by getting your crew to spend time with each other. That's how individuals start recognising fellow teammates as human beings with strengths and weaknesses instead of automatons with whom they share breathing space. Understanding allows for connection and bonding, which then leads to trust.

A majority of leaders miss this non-negotiable aspect of team-building. The few who do understand it uphold it extraordinarily well. When they sit and discuss strategy and plans of action, when they do weekly dashboards, when they take people off-site for meetings, when they call them home for dinner and yes, when they serve them cake week after week – they force togetherness, a precursor to building trust.

The second and extremely powerful mechanism for building teams is to bind them together around a common goal or purpose. Clever leaders use different ploys to make that happen, including sometimes using a mutual enemy to achieve this aim. For all of those who have seen the movie *Chak De India*, there's a scene that aptly exemplifies this manoeuvre.

The ragtag group of awkwardly assembled hockey players are sitting at a restaurant despairing about their future because they are about to be disbanded. One of the reasons is that they have not been able to convert themselves into a synchronised team. At that moment a group of ruffians enters and begins harassing the Manipuri girls in the group. Immediately the women spring into action and take on the harassers with immense bravado and gusto. As satisfying as it is to watch them beat the ruffians into pulp, it's even more fulfilling to see how a team gets galvanised together when they identify a common target. That's the moment in the movie when things turn around for the hockey team and that's exactly how it happens in real life too!

Success in the business world depends on collaboration and teamwork and not the individual performance of the superstars, valuable as they may be. This brings us to the third lesson – you have to certainly make the members of your team feel special, but you have to do this while enforcing the belief that they're good not in isolation but only in the context of the team.

We may be lured to the halls by a Shah Rukh Khan or a Madhuri Dixit. But it's the behind the scenes team of director, producer, writer, cinematographer and so on who make the movie what it is. Not just the star who comes on screen in all her or his cinemascopic glory, reciting dialogue to much acclaim. As a society, however much we cherish the stories of lone rangers and all-powerful heroes who will save the day single-handedly with six guns blazing all at once (and are conditioned to emulate such narratives ourselves), in real life, good work is always powered by team effort. In the initial days of the radio renaissance in India, when competition suddenly burst onto the scene, we lost a couple of our prized RJs to new rivals in the market. One of them replicated the exact show he used to do for us on his new employer's channel. But it fell flat and that's when it dawned on him, and the rest of us, that while he may have been the star of the show, he didn't make the show what it was. It was a team of producers, music managers, sound engineers and the programming head who were together responsible for the magic.

As all of you, dear readers and leaders of tomorrow, climb the career ladder, I notice that women do a far better job than men in leading teams. That's because of the intricate ways women – irrespective of class, caste and privilege – need to navigate the world and relationships around them. This gives them a masterclass in dealing with the mercurial moods and assorted needs of team members. For example, women ace at conflict resolution, because that's what they have been doing all their lives.

Professional success inaccurately leads to an inflation of the ego, but women are thankfully insured against this particular trait. Men, who don't need to learn to see the world from any point of view other than their own in order to survive, have a narrower lens that tends to get more dictatorial as they ascend the hierarchy. He is the general. The employees are his troops. That's a good enough foundation to build a team. Most male leaders I've witnessed are comfortable with the notion that the common purpose to which the team members need to pledge their loyalty is them. That 'love me, admire me, adore me, follow me' is a good enough call to arms.

Women trained from birth to see everything from the world's gaze (sometimes at the cost of their own viewpoint) will actually put in the effort to collaborate, to develop the strengths of the team, to cajole and massage egos, to educate them and to scold them when necessary. It is true that there are plenty of bad women team leaders and extraordinarily good male team heads. But the rigorous social conditioning that both men and women are subject to from childhood makes such cases the exception rather than the rule.

The workplace is an infinitely better place when we are surrounded by friends we like, role models we admire and subordinates we enjoy mentoring. Given that we spend the majority of our lives at work, being in charge of a group of people is not a responsibility we should take lightly. Getting to build and maintain a great team filled with trust, bonhomie and camaraderie, a team that plays together in complete synchronisation with each other is one of the greatest privileges of that position and imperative to achieving victory. Ask any great sports coach or otherwise learn from Shah Rukh Khan as he takes his gaggle of women hockey players to victory in *Chak De*!

IN SHORT

- Building winning teams is a precursor to success as a leader.
- Just hiring talented individuals and getting them together is not team building.
- It requires creating trust among them, bonding them to a common purpose and then enforcing within them a code that says that the team is larger than any individual supernova.

Kehna Karna Nibhana: Consistent Commitment

Your consistency says a lot about your commitment.

—Rasheed Ogunlaru

'Didi!' my cousin chirps on the telephone.

'Yes, Anjali? How can I help you?' I respond, using my cold and stoic 'official' tone, hoping that it will ward her off a little quicker. I have been practising this technique with limited success on family members who call unexpectedly in the middle of a weekday, not because there is anything wanting in my stoicism or coldness but because most of them have become inured to my inherent grumpiness.

She continues, undeterred (I told you so). 'I'm in Delhi, Didi! For my neighbour Abha's niece's wedding. You remember her, don't you? Beautiful girl, you would've met her at my fiftieth birthday party. She's getting married to this rich Delhi guy, son of an industrialist of course, and I'm here for the wedding … fancy it is, let me tell you that, people are dressed to the heights, but I'll match them bling for bling, after all I have that solitaire necklace that we bought with aunty-ji last year … and remember that pink saree I had shown you that I was wearing for the wedding? Well, I changed that, because Abha's mother gave me such a pretty one, Sabyasachi's new collection that too ... said I reminded her exactly of herself when she was younger. Well, herself or her sister, I can't remember but she said one of the two definitely, and now ...'

Given that it's a Wednesday afternoon and I'm currently in the middle of a series of office crises, I try to usher her closer to the point.

'That's fascinating, sweetie. I'm so happy for you. But why have you called?'

'Oh, yes, yes, yes, of course. Well Didi, you remember that saree material you had liked so much when we went shopping last time? I found exactly the same one at this awesome little store here, even better quality if that's possible, just fabulous that material, feels so nice in your hand I can't even tell you. I also spoke to the store owner and he promised to give me a discount, at a friends-and-family level you know. And I thought to myself that I just have to buy it for you Didi, I just have to. It'll after all go so well with your whole look, good for office and after work as well. I know for a fact that you'll look very nice in it, so what say, tell me no, shall I?'

Awash like the Liril girl (people, especially males of my generation, may remember her) under this verbal onslaught, I paused for a moment of reflection. Now, my cousin is many things. As a trained socialite and shopaholic very much in the know, she is on intimate terms with every vendor from Crawford Market to the upper echelons of high-street fashion and has the uncanny knack to gauge the most excellent deals. Unfortunately, an abider of commitments she is not.

Nonetheless, unfailingly polite as always (and in a hurry to end the conversation), I tell her that bringing me the saree would be extremely nice of her and that I would greatly appreciate it if she did that, given of course that it didn't inconvenience her too much. I agree despite knowing precisely how the story will play out. Sure enough, as predicted, despite her initial enthusiasm Anjali fails to follow through with her commitment of getting me the saree.

At this juncture, let me introduce you to three words that I hold very dear, the ones that will form the bedrock of this chapter's leadership lesson. They are 'Kehna, Karna, Nibhana.' Allow me to define them for you very briefly below:

Kehna – To say

Karna – To do

Nibhana – To do always. Unfailingly and without question.

Unfortunately, there is no way to translate Kehna, Karna, Nibhana (KKN for future reference) into English without losing its essence. The term it would come closest to is 'consistent commitment'. In our busy worlds, where all of us look to become self-actualised souls at the earliest age possible, we tend to cram as much as possible into our daily lives. We want to work hard so we may be professionally successful and earn a lot of money, but we also want to help our ailing parents, dote on our children, tend to our gardens, gossip with our friends and indulge in the adolescent fantasies that all of us are still waiting to achieve – whether that is learning French or becoming professional musicians. And despite knowing somewhere in the deeper recesses of our mind that all is not achievable, we plunge on unabashedly and a tad arrogantly. As a consequence of this, apart from inevitable burnout, we leave behind a wasteland littered with broken and unfulfilled promises – to friends, to family, to colleagues and to ourselves.

This is where the philosophy of KKN supersedes the concept of a mere promise. Because the value system that is at the heart of KKN is one of careful and mindful thought. KKN says that whatever I commit to do, I will deliver. And I will deliver consistently and repeatedly. KKN can therefore never be a litany of half-hearted, casual promises. Rather, it has to be those carefully deliberated oaths you have made to yourself and to everyone around you, because you know you have to fulfil them each time and always. Constantly and consistently. To the best of your abilities. As a result you make sure that you don't make these promises either lightly or loosely because you have to keep them not just once or twice, but upon every given moment of asking.

Now, when Anjali promised to bring me that saree, it would quite possibly have been one of the several casual promises she made to various people over the course of that one day. Due to their inherently trivial nature, the fulfilment or non-fulfilment of these promises would have mattered very little to her. She would do (or not do) whatever happened to convenience her at that given time. As a result, she treated this 'promise' not as something that was second nature to her, a commitment she had to fulfil, but as a mere triviality that dissipated with the same bubbly enthusiasm with which it had arisen.

Now let us examine the alternative. The one that KKN extolls. As I've said before, it is about careful thought. Promises that you hold as an extension of the self, and therefore want to complete both now and in all the instances to come. KKN manifests itself in behaviour that others see as always holding true and steadfast, no matter what the circumstances. Regular readers of my blog will recall our family dog, Scamper, as being a steady source of inspiration in the way he lived his life. And here, he serves as one as well. From the day he entered our house to the day he unfortunately passed away, it was almost that he had made it his daily duty to bring as much happiness as he could to those around him – from my husband and I, to my son and mother, and even to our household help. Whoever needed a leg up, he was there to provide it with a lick, a nudging paw or a look of love in his large, innocent eyes. No matter what the circumstances were in his life, this commitment was second nature to him. And it was unfailingly adhered to whether he was happy or sad, healthy or ill, hungry or full-bellied. That is the very essence of KKN.

When KKN is done just for yourself, it makes you a powerful individual, one who has a very clear set of values and stands by them and can be relied upon as a trustworthy person who fulfils all her commitments. And that's a great thing – something for all of us to aspire towards. But when this attitude of KKN is extended to a whole organisation – that's where the magic really happens. Because at that level, it can lead to the construction of a powerful organisational culture. When an organisation promises something and then consistently delivers on that promise, it builds a culture of reliability and trust among all its stakeholders. And those are important adjectives for any business, in any industry. Trust and reliability.

Now, this doesn't happen easily. KKN is a challenging concept to understand and imbibe. I have worked tremendously hard to get this point across to my organisation and especially the ones in charge of helping establish the culture – the HR team. While today I can say that they have indeed passed with flying colours, the path hasn't been one devoid of roadblocks. HR professionals, even the best of them, are notoriously excitable. While well-intentioned, they often want to run a range of interventions without ever thinking them through entirely. And nothing excites them more than creating new policies for a company. It is with this enthusiasm that one day a senior HR professional at one of the businesses I manage came up to me.

'Ma'am! The team and I have been thinking a lot about the things that we can do to make our 'Great Place To Work' ranking even better next year. One of the things that we've thought about, and ratified through the employee survey, is that an open-plan policy where everyone is sitting together really makes employees believe that all of us are equal. It encourages bonding and transparency too. You always say, if we believe in something, we should really come out and champion it. Well, we believe in this. And we'll walk the talk too. During your town hall, we will announce that we are breaking down all the cabins and all of us will sit together and you will sit right in the centre …'

While she proceeded to list various activities intended to dismantle any real or imagined barriers between all one thousand employees, I was horror-struck and could only visualise a disastrous fishmarket kind of open area, with me sitting enthroned in the centre like some deity and everyone shouting hysterically around me (our organisation is slightly loud, by the way). I decided I had to nip the idea in the bud immediately, and it's not because I doubted that her research was correct. What she hadn't thought through was the fact that nothing irritates employees more or makes them quite as disillusioned as empty promises made by their company and especially their seniors. If a company professes that it'll drive transparency through openness for everyone, employees expect that it will jolly well do that for all concerned, without exception. That is precisely also the sentiment of KKN, which was a key value system at our organisation.

When it came to this situation, no matter which way I examined it, an open-plan office was not something we could adopt. Apart from the practicality, there was also the issue of private meetings and confidential discussions. I remembered visiting a client's office early in my career where I found the CEO, after launching a massive search operation, sitting behind three metres deep foliage resembling a verdant rain forest. When I enquired about his love for greenery, which seemed a bit excessive, he sheepishly told me that it was his way of getting around the open-plan policy his US headquarters had ordained be followed in all offices! I asked my HR head whether she was willing to hold her meetings in front of everyone and conduct hiring and firing discussions in an area resembling a fish-bowl. Now, given that HR teams think of recruitment as their particular domain secret and the holy grail that has to be kept hidden in a deep, dark vault twenty thousand leagues under the ocean, I had obviously touched a nerve and immediately she quailed at the thought, saying that for certain things we would obviously have to have cabins and private rooms. And that was where the philosophy of KKN broke down. Consistently doing what we said also meant doing it across the board for everyone, with no exceptions.

KKN is a very valuable lesson for all of us in life, as individuals, as managers, as family members and as leaders. If you commit to something, please honour the commitment however trivial it is – like reaching a meeting at a designated time or returning that phone call. And if you say you believe in punctuality, then please be punctual, unfailingly and without question. Kehna, Karna, Nibhana. And if you can't, don't bother making that initial promise. That's okay. No one will think any less of you.

As a leader, if you can create a culture that values KKN, I promise you, the organisation will run almost on its own, like a well-oiled machine with everyone delivering whatever they committed to. What more can a leader want?

Now let's just hope I get my saree someday.

IN SHORT

- Beyond walking the talk is another realm of leadership that says it's not just about walking the talk once in a while, but walking it always. Once you commit to something you must fulfil your promise always and consistently.

- Steadfastness in honouring the commitments you make, whether big or small, demonstrates your reliability as a leader.

- Exceptions and ad-hocism are the biggest reasons for mistrust in an organisation and are value-eroders of a culture.

- An organisation built on the principles of consistently delivering on its commitments can build trust and create immense value among all its stakeholders.

Culture Vulture

The culture of a workplace – an organisation's values, norms and practices – has a huge impact on our happiness and success.

—Adam Grant

'Sports is life in quick motion,' HD proclaimed, looking down his imperious nose at me as he sizzled with righteous wrath and indignation at a comment I'd just made. It so happened that the entire extended family had gathered around some cricket match on TV and they were exhibiting assorted levels of heartburn, starting with resentment and moving right up to red hot rage at an umpire's faulty decision. Amid this maelstrom of masculine feeling I had innocently (and rather charmingly, I thought) observed that most of the pot-bellied men who lost their minds at every sporting event on TV had themselves not entered a gym or engaged in any sporting activity in decades. So their devotion to this athleticism surprised and puzzled me with its intensity.

In a salutary tone that was meant to correct my profound ignorance and to protect his brethren from unfair criticism, HD launched into an impassioned speech: 'All the highs and lows of life – the travails, the failures, the success – happen in a one-day match or a ninety-minute game. Whatever takes place in the compressed duration of a game plays out in a longer format in real life too.' He continued reverentially, 'Because ultimately sport is a metaphor for life itself. That's why we connect with it so intensely!'

I normally pay very little attention to the lectures HD is prone to giving me every once in a while (Reminder on why this is so in chapters thirteen and fourteen on menopause and mid-life crisis.). But the fact that sport and life have a lot in common with each other resonated deeply with me, because there is certainly one portion at work where I have definitely applied lessons from sport, and that's in the process of organisational culture-building.

Arsenal fans the world over, whether in Delhi or Dubai or a pub in London, belong to one tribe, just as HD and assorted Mumbai Indians cricket fans across the globe belong to another. They are bound by fervent loyalty to the teams and to the players and fused to each other by an unimpeachable sense of brotherhood. Loyalty to a team or to a sport fuels a sense of belonging, which in turn gives rise to a strong sense of identity based on a shared set of values. This invisible sentiment of togetherness is the secret behind the legions of followers great sports teams build up. It is also the secret sauce that helps certain organisations manage to repeatedly attract and retain talented employees. Intelligent and far-sighted leaders recognise the importance of creating this spirit of belonging, which is why they work as hard at building the culture of the organisation as they do at crafting its strategy.

In the decades gone past however, workplace culture-building was never considered macho enough to be taken seriously. It was assumed that culture, with its touchy-feely connotations of warmth and bonhomie, had tenuous links to organisational performance and was thus unimportant.

CEOs were quick to talk about strategy, budget, profit, revenue targets. These muscular centres of success were accorded a prominent seat at the boardroom table while ethos and culture, in all their intangibility, remained shrinking violets in the work environment.

Of course the consequence of this was not that an organisational culture did not get built at all. It did, but surreptitiously and informally.

The truth is that if leaders don't build culture mindfully, it gets built based on the random behaviour of a few senior people. Since no standard expectations of behaviour have been set for team leaders, they behave as they deem fit. And the culture that emerges out of this equation becomes a hodgepodge of senior leadership styles till one fine day you wake up and realise that inadvertently, your organisation is now known for petty politics or average performance standards or sluggishness.

When we recruit people, we do so for their functional skills. We don't tell them the behavioural expectations the organisation has from them. We only tell them our expectations in terms of their performance. But there is also an attitudinal aspect we need to focus on if we want to ensure the creation of a well-thought-through culture. When we clearly define what we want to stand for – be it fairness, respect for individuals, prioritising teamwork, etc. – we also by default demarcate what we are not. Believing that culture can drive business results and then thoughtfully creating it based on the organisation's business exigencies is a critical first step in organisational building.

I strongly believe that the success of Radio City as a leader in its industry is primarily because of the culture we worked very hard to build in a purposeful and careful manner. Many years ago when we first started working on Radio City's go-to-market strategy, we realised that we would be competing with the big daddies of the radio industry. Be it Times of India or Sun TV, every major media house had a radio network. We were owned by an emerging private equity fund, an ownership structure that had a default perception of being cutthroat and short-term oriented. So why would people come and work for us?

Very early on we decided that it was our culture that was going to draw top talent to us. Today we are one of the leading radio networks in the country and among the top ten places to work not only in India but also in Asia. We competed against giants and won. From a small four-city boutique network, we grew to one of the largest and most profitable radio networks in the country, en-route going through an ownership change, one public market listing and headwinds that buffeted us so often that turbulence management became our default style. The only thing that kept us on course was the lodestar of our culture. We did many things based on it and refused to behave antithetical to our values. Over a period of time this consistency created a strong and palpable culture that ensured that many of the best people in the radio industry continued to be Radio-Cityzens in good times and in bad. Culture may be an invisible differentiator but when done right, it can become a massive deliverer of profit. And Radio City is a textbook example of this.

Fortunately, now there is empirical evidence that there is a direct link between culture and performance and results. As India's economy increasingly becomes services-centric, for many organisations the product they sell is their employees and the behaviour of these employees. What an

RJ says on-air or what song a music manager decides to play defines a radio station's product. Similarly, in a bank, how a teller behaves with you and how smoothly a bank manager resolves your problem – these are the products customers are dealing with. How well the Swiggy guy delivers your food and how hospitable the employees of a hotel or restaurant are, define the organisations' brand and are centred around human connection and interaction. And therefore, the company's culture directly influences not only its employees but also the product's perception in the market and thereby its results.

So apart from doing it mindfully, what else does it take to build a good culture? We have an unbelievably successful model to take pointers from when it comes to setting up culture at our workplace – religion. Be it the major faiths of the world or the little-known sects that command small but fanatical followings, religion has fine-tuned the art of using culture as a powerful binder to build communities and forge connections, establish moral codes of behaviour and offer sources of faith and support that are intimately personal and universal at the same time.

Religious cultures are created using rituals that people are supposed to follow, value systems they need to adopt and codes they need to adhere to. They are then propagated across the globe using stories that are told across generations.

In the recession of 2008-09, all our competitors had to resort to dismissing people in order to survive. We didn't do that. Instead, company seniors decided to take a pay cut in order to ensure that in tough times, none of our employees and teammates lost their jobs. The recession is now a decade old. It is history. Organisations and the world have moved beyond those dark days. But I make sure that this is a story that gets repeated and retold at every possible occasion. Lest people forget. Because this is a story that defines our empathetic culture.

What are the defining legends of your organisation, the ones that will galvanise employees into action?

Apart from mythology and storytelling, meaningful rituals are at the heart of a religion's pull for its followers. At Radio City, rewards and recognition have been an important aspect of creating pride among employees about the work they do. Over the years, many rituals have been created around this aspect, such as 'Cheers to Peers', a monthly gathering where people come together to thank someone publicly for some help they have been given or 'Ring A Loud', a ritual where, if a person believes that she has done something extraordinary, she comes and rings a bell to tell her colleagues about her achievement. Some years back, I had initiated a small ritual when someone moved into a cabin after a promotion – a sure sign that she'd moved up in life. I would give them a Bourneville chocolate. The chocolate was chosen for its occasion appropriate tagline: 'You don't buy a Bourneville. You earn it.'

When I moved to an expanded role in the organisation where Radio City was not under my direct purview, I stopped performing what I thought was an inconsequential ceremony but the employees did not forget it. A few months passed and then the HR team told me, 'Ma'am, the new GMs who have been promoted and have moved into cabins are feeling very bad because you have stopped giving the chocolates.' So, I sheepishly restarted the ritual.

In the larger scheme of things, giving a bar of chocolate may seem like a trifling gesture to an outsider. But it had become part of the folklore at Radio City and an important moment in our employees' career journey.

Employees are constantly on the lookout for a culture that calls to their sense of purpose and value systems. Many founders at startups today believe that they can capitalise on this zeitgeist through token actions. A newbie boss thinks, 'Oh, I've built a great culture because I've put a green couch in the storeroom for people to sleep on. Or because I've put a foosball table in the common room or because everyone can wear whatever they want to work.' And then wonders why he has such high attrition levels despite the free ice-cream.

The difference between token simulators of culture and the real thing is when a leader's actions in culture-building are based on authentic values that she truly believes in.

The 2016 animated Disney film *Coco* enchantingly explores the arc of little Miguel growing from a self-interested individual to a key player in his family's rituals. The Dia de Muertos or the Day of the Dead celebrations hold no meaning for Miguel until he travels to the land of the dead and understands the full import of the festival. He realises that our dear departed remain alive in another world because we remember them as part of the rituals during Dia de Muertos. They truly die only when they start being erased from our memory and we stop remembering them. So to keep them alive in the other world, we celebrate Dia De Muertos and that is the true import of the ritual.

Good cultures are built not on hollow rituals but on rites attached with deep significance. The chocolate that we give our new GMs is not an empty celebration; behind that lies a statement that says, you have earned it. It is a recognition that the person truly deserves to be where she is and she has worked hard to get there. Equally it conveys to all that unlike in other organisations, promotions at Radio

City are not a natural outcome of tenure alone. You have to work hard to get a cabin!

Such a small ritual, but such deep meaning – motivation, recognition and a meritocratic culture. The Bourneville conveys all of that and more.

People crave to be part of something bigger than themselves. If a good culture at the workplace can tap into that innate need, then you've got the road map to harness potential into productivity.

Philip Kotler once said, 'Culture eats strategy for breakfast,' and I think that is the most relevant advice the sage has ever given us to manage our businesses and create strong and sustainable organisations.

IN SHORT

- Culture is a critical, albeit invisible, differentiator of success and sustainability in an organisation, because it has the power to unite people around it.
- Leaders need to work purposefully towards creating an engaging culture lest it build unconsciously around undesirable values.
- Strongly upheld and practised values, storytelling and meaningful rituals are some powerful tools to build great organisational cultures.

Personal Accountability: I Am Because of Me

Whether you think you can or you think you can't, you're right!

—Henry Ford

As we bring our conversation on leadership to a close with this final chapter, my dear readers, in the spirit of the lessons we learnt about good communication, I would like us to take a few moments to reflect on the crucial and I hope implementable suggestions that have been made in this section of the book.

When we began our journey of understanding the art of leadership viewed from the battlefield, so to speak, we saw how much we could adapt from a role that many of us have already been playing for several years now, that of child rearers. As parents, we dole out discipline and love in equal measure to help our children become better individuals and while doing so we also teach them to deal with the big, bad world with courage and fortitude. These are valuable leadership lessons to manage teams too. We learnt of the power that comes with listening to those around us and how implementation can be facilitated and goals achieved by a truly clear mind that has its priorities set correctly. We discussed the importance of being curious and asking questions, of making hard choices and of persevering through the trying times that all of us have faced at some point or the other in our lives. We made note of some of the common biases that leaders fall for – a pro-strategy bias and a negative skew against implementation, and the dangers of subjective measurement metrics. Lastly, we spoke of clearly defining and sustaining values, promoting genuine trust among teams, unfailingly keeping commitments and using all these as building blocks to create empowering and engaging cultures.

Each of these lessons has helped me be better at my job, and I hope they will one day do the same for you. I am sure that all lady bosses, and even some of the gentlemen bosses out there, will be able to incorporate the lessons learnt here and use them for both personal and professional growth. But ultimately, all these suggestions and any additional advice that other leadership gurus might advocate become irrelevant if the one trait that binds them all is missing. And that king among kings, Shahenshah-e-Alam of all leadership traits is personal accountability.

It is the single-most important driver of leadership in my opinion. I say this loudly and vociferously because I have seen too many talented managers unable to evolve to great leaders only because this particular characteristic was missing in their make-up.

When a very young child loses her ball while playing, she comes to her mother and happily says, 'Mama, the ball is lost.' Note the use of words. The child believes that the ball lost itself all on its own. And consequently it doesn't upset her. She believes her mother will take care of the situation and indeed the doting parent rushes out to the play area, scrambling around for the lost ball, frantically calling husband/assistant/parents/employees to tell them to drop everything and look for a replacement. However, when this same child grows up a little bit and loses the same ball, she returns crying, 'Mama, I lost the ball.' It's a complete turnaround of both syntax and associated emotion. This time, not only does the child feel terrible about losing the ball, but also for the first time in her life admits that it was her fault that the ball got lost. Several studies on developmental psychology indicate that this is the point in the child's growth (usually around the age of six) when the transition to adulthood truly begins. Because that's the behaviour that adults are expected to demonstrate, to take responsibility for their actions and the consequences thereof! To whit – personal accountability. 'I lost the ball.' The ball didn't lose itself of its own volition. Neither did some malignant universal force direct its disappearance. It was me and only me.

The reason I am highlighting this issue of accountability so vigorously is that most people struggle to accept onus, especially in negative situations. Despite being grown-ups, they morph back into that preschooler who happily says the ball disappeared through no fault of hers. This fundamental attribution error makes us prone to patting ourselves on our backs when things go right (and men are a little more inclined to doing this than women are), but also just as swiftly blaming the external situation around us when things go wrong. Sales targets not met? Must be the bad economic conditions. Marriage failing? It was because our kundalis didn't match. Child turning out to be a brat? Surely it's all the company he's been keeping at school. And before we know it, we start blaming everything but ourselves for the shortcomings and disappointments that our lives are inevitably littered with. For it is the easier route to take and so much better at ensuring a good night's rest and certainly far more preferable than seeing our own errors reflected in the mirror of our benighted circumstances.

My friend, Saumya, one of India's supremely talented women CEOs, quotes an example here of how one of her childhood friends, Vibha, insists on launching into a tirade every time they meet, of how she was in fact the better student during their school days, the one who always came first in class and was told by all and sundry that she was destined for great things in life. Unfortunately, she was stifled by her mother-in-law who wanted her to have babies as soon as she got married, which is why she did not scale the heights expected of her when compared with Saumya. Vibha also makes pointed references to all the strokes of luck that she believes fell Saumya's way, which according to her is the only reason why Saumya became a leading light in the industry while Vibha was left an unhappy victim of circumstances.

If only one day someone would recite to Vibha that famous Ghalib couplet, '*Umre bhar Ghalib yahi bhool karta raha, dhool chehre pe thi, aur aina saaf karta raha!* (His whole life, Ghalib kept repeating one mistake, the dust was on his face, but he kept cleaning the mirror!)' And like a video on auto-play I see this same story that Vibha has convinced herself of, repeat itself time and time again on various occasions and in different circumstances.

Our annual sales conference is underway as the new financial year begins, and there is a palpable air of good cheer and optimism all around us. The year gone by has been analysed in great detail and, depending on the sales achievement percentage for the year, either lovingly wrapped in soft cloth like the zari saree mother gave us and put away in the cupboard or unlovingly dumped in old newspaper like a piece of rotting fish and consigned to the dustbin.

But it's a new year and an opportunity to start again with a clean slate, and to add further joy, a Bollywood sports film has just released with tremendous success at the box office, so we have a fresh sales anthem too! A bright and shining new dawn looms on the horizon of sales teams across the length and breadth of the country. Who wouldn't feel all roused and enthusiastic then? Especially if Shah Rukh Khan is personally exhorting everyone to chale-chalo?

As the conference ends, I ask the team, 'Are you comfortable with the targets?' 'YES WE ARE,' they scream. 'Are you confident of achieving them?' 'YES WE ARE,' they roar even more buoyantly. 'Who takes charge of these numbers?' I push further. 'EACH OF US DO!!!' And the conference ends with a victory cry.

Now fast-forward to the mid-year review. It's been a mixed bag in terms of results. Some hits, some misses and a stuttering economy have kept things pretty muted. I ask the sales team about their below-par performance, 'So what happened?' And out pours a litany of reasons, from 'HR didn't give me enough people to work with', to the fact that competition dropped rates to gain share, to the economy that was hit by oil prices and finally, an accusatory finger pointed firmly at climate change. And suddenly the accountability that the team had started the year with unaccountably disappears!

I see this happen all the time, every time. Inevitably people outsource their lives to their circumstances or to other people around them by refusing to take culpability for anything that happens to them. They are essentially admitting that not they, but someone else is responsible for their successes and failures.

The worst consequence of this behaviour is that not only do people never seek to improve their actions in whatever drama that is unfolding, but at some stage they also start feeling powerless to change their own destiny. They believe that their actions can have no discernable and definite impact on their lives and end up relying on externalities for restitution. They become either victims or bystanders of their own lives.

In contrast, the moment we start thinking that we lost the ball, finding it becomes our responsibility, our prerogative, and we automatically start thinking about solutions. We tell ourselves that this quagmire we are embroiled in is a consequence of the decisions we have taken, but that's okay, because we also have the ability and capability to find a way out of it. This is an extremely powerful message to the brain and it is exactly what good leaders do.

Great leaders take control of the destiny of not only their own lives but also the lives of the people and organisations around them. They solve problems and find solutions to the messes other people create and by doing so they become the heroes of the story and of the narrative, which they control. The hero strides into the story and saves the day with her strength, guile and intelligence, completely comfortable in the knowledge that she had the ability to do so from the very start. Meanwhile, the victim wanders about in a lost manner, waiting for one more villain to blame, and the bystander in the story lets others determine what the next course of action will be in her life.

Isn't the distinction between these roles only hinged on taking accountability for everything that happens in the tale? And that's both the beginning and the end of the leadership saga.

Amy Cuddy, a well-known social psychologist, has propagated the use of a bodily action called 'power poses' where a person stands in a powerful stance (such as upright with arms spread out or in the veerabhadra asana, which is the warrior pose in yoga) for a few minutes before any high-pressure task such as an interview or presentation. This is supposed to instil a feeling of self-belief and confidence, which in turn has a positive impact on performance. Similarly, when you're in front of a mirror, make it a point to talk to yourself about how everything that has happened in your life is a result and consequence of your actions and your actions alone. Question the occasions when you let others rule your life for you and then promise yourself that never again will you let it happen, because only you have the final lien on your life. The moment you do that you will see the power flowing within you and the ability to find your own solutions.

As W.E. Henley says in *Invictus*, 'It matters not how strait the gate, how charged with punishments the scroll, I am the master of my fate, I am the captain of my soul.'

And that master and captain is you, dear lady boss. No one else.

IN SHORT

- The ultimate trait of a leader is personal accountability, where she takes complete charge of her destiny and also the destinies of the people around her.
- Externalising problems is a negative emotion. While being a momentary salve, it conveys to the mind a sense of helplessness and failure.
- Only by accepting that we are responsible for both the good and the bad that happens around us will we move into a solution mindset and that feeling of control will help us resolve the issues facing us and our teams.
- We need to consciously work on owning responsibility for our actions and the consequences thereof, so that we can become effective leaders.

Epilogue

What is the measure of your ambition? Would you like to weigh your life against diamonds and pearls and other markers of wealth? Or would you prefer to measure it on a speedometer in terms of the number of activities completed in a day or a month, maybe the number of frequent flier points you collect as you whizz through 265 days of travel every year? Perhaps you would like to assess it in terms of the happiness you gave your family, in the nurturing of two lovely children and the loving care you took of your parents as they aged in front of your eyes? Will the fact that you gave up the rat race for the passion of teaching, travelling or writing be your epitaph? At the time of the final judgement, will you rest your case of being successful on the evidence of having built a fine organisation, or a boutique firm from scratch, or the number of close and lasting friendships you had?

To every one of us is given the choice of what scale we want to gauge our life against, and then decide how well we performed on it. This book is not a guide or lesson on whether the choices you made or the goals you sought were right or wrong, good or bad. I wrote this book to tell you that you and you alone should have the power and authority to make that choice. Without the baggage of expectations, without the affliction of being seen as a woman in a largely male-dominated world, without the conditioning that was injected in your veins and the veins of your mother and grandmother – only you should decide who you are and what you want to become.

And as you stand and look at yourself in the mirror and reclaim your agency to make that choice, this book, as all good catalysts do, tells you what to *stop, start* and *continue* doing.

So stop saying yes when you mean no. It is okay to say maybe too, when you are not sure. Stop being that patient listener of the pompous male voices around you. Stop putting everyone else's needs before yours. Stop jumping up to make the coffee when you are the only woman in the room. Stop rushing to agree with an opinion that you secretly believe is incorrect just for the sake of keeping the peace or because the person opposite has a loud voice or because he sounds far more confident than you do. Stop minimising your achievements and attributing them to luck rather than the hard work you have put in so far. And do stop looking at only your flaws and making them larger than they actually are.

Please continue to be aware that you are different and therein lies your biggest strength and your ability to bring change in the world around you. This realisation has finally dawned upon you a little later than I would have liked, but since we are finally there, celebrate your uniqueness and your ability to see differing points of view, a talent only the very wise have. Enjoy the fact that your nurturing abilities can turn not only your little babies into outstanding adults, but also your employees into great professionals. Look around yourself and see how much the world needs your clarity of thinking, practical good sense and implementation skills to make sense of the chaos we have created and to undo the damage we have wrought on our planet. Look no further than at some of the outstanding women leaders around you who have demonstrated the ability to take tough decisions, the empathy to create bonds with their people and the inspiring vocabulary to align them towards a common charter. You are one of that tribe too. So let out that curly hair from that oiled plait, un-layer that dusky skin from the industrial level coatings of the latest fairness cream and don't worry if you are the only soprano in a room full of baritones and basses. Revel in being different and owning your true self.

To bring about the changes you desire, you cannot continue using the current instruments of trade. Change will only happen if you change the tools, which need to be uniquely yours and different from the ones used thus far. Audre Lorde, the American writer and feminist said, 'The Master's tools will never dismantle the Master's house.' It is an imperative and a necessity to remain different, to not fall in the trap of moulding yourself into becoming one of the boys or the boys' plaything.

Finally, start standing straight and tall, talking loudly and laughing boisterously. The default background score in our public and private spaces is deafeningly male. You need to change that. Your invisibility and your silence have been your biggest weakness. You are wise, you are talented and bright, but you have not been bold and brave. It is time you stood up to be counted. Display your legs and cleavage at your will. And ask the gentleman sitting next to you not to peer down your neckline. If he can stare openly, you can tell him to not do so as openly too. If you disagree with your board members, say so in the boardroom itself and don't hide behind one-on-one chats. Start letting go of your children, the wounds in your past, the organisation that did not give you growth or paid you less than your male colleagues, and even your desire to feel needed or to get married if you don't want to!

You have the entire universe inside you, so why do you allow yourself to be condensed or minimised into a microcosm? As you practise, so will you become. So practise the swagger, practise being flamboyant and confident, practise walking with a sway of your hips, a song on your lips and laughter in your heart. Practise, practise, practise this. Henceforth and more!

And as you reclaim your true position on this planet, remember you are giving strength to other women too. When they watch you, they will learn; and when they learn, they will grow. That is the only way we will quicken the pace of change and begin to hold up half the sky that rightfully belongs to us, one woman holding up one corner of it at a time! The sisterhood coming together, in a shared culture of kindness, nurturing and support is the only way to dismantle the existing patriarchal norms and you cannot let your community down by remaining a passive bystander.

When you unleash the leader in you, I hope this book and the points I am leaving with you to reflect on will help you maximise your real potential in its highest and truest form and give you all that your heart desires, in whichever form or shape you have chosen to bring these yearnings alive.

From one sister to another – may the force be with you!

Acknowledgements

Rakhi Chakraborty and Siddharth Purohit – my research assistants. This book is as much theirs as it is mine.

Deepa Dave, Rachna Kanwar, Tinaz Nooshian, Aparna Vishwasrao, Swapnalekha Basak, Kiran Manral, Kanchan Purohit, Divya Oberoi, Sulekha Bajpai, Sarika Bhattacharyya, Sagorika Kantharia, Monica Chaudhari and all the other gutsy ladies I know, whose stories inspire me every day.

RKA – friend, colleague, thought provocateur and guide. Teachers need someone to teach them too.

Kanishka Gupta from Writer's Side, who wouldn't give up and incessantly kept telling me that I had another book in me.

Varsha Ojha, Priyanka Gupta, Mitali Jathar and Sonia Mansata along with Team Archetype for their passionate and ardent support of my work.

Sangeetha Kabadi and Jimmy Oza – life is easier and better with them around.

DU BAI

Travel with Marco Polo Insider Tips

INSIDER TIP
Your shortcut to a great experience

MARCO POLO TOP HIGHLIGHTS

DUBAI MUSEUM ★1
Take a journey back in time to old Dubai in the semi-darkness of the Al Fahidi Fort.

➤ p. 30

BASTAKIYA ★2
Oriental fairy-tale scenery, with houses featuring traditional wind towers, in this restored quarter.
📷 *Tip: After sunset, take a long exposure of the illuminated wind-tower houses and the moon above them.*

➤ p. 30

CROSSING THE CREEK ★3
Travel to the other bank of the creek, not over one of the bridges but on a chugging wooden barge.

➤ p. 34

BURJ KHALIFA ★4
Zoom up to the viewing terrace of the world's tallest building, and the whole of Dubai will be at your feet.
📷 *Tip: Take a picture of the Burj Khalifa from the Dubai Opera so that part of the Opera's glass façade appears in your photo at an angle.*

➤ p. 38

DUBAI MARINA ★5
Between skyscrapers and mega yachts: soak up the *dolce vita* in one of the world's largest harbours.
📷 *Tip: Wait at the Marina Mall until someone comes zip-lining towards you. Water and skyscrapers make a great backdrop.*

➤ p. 44

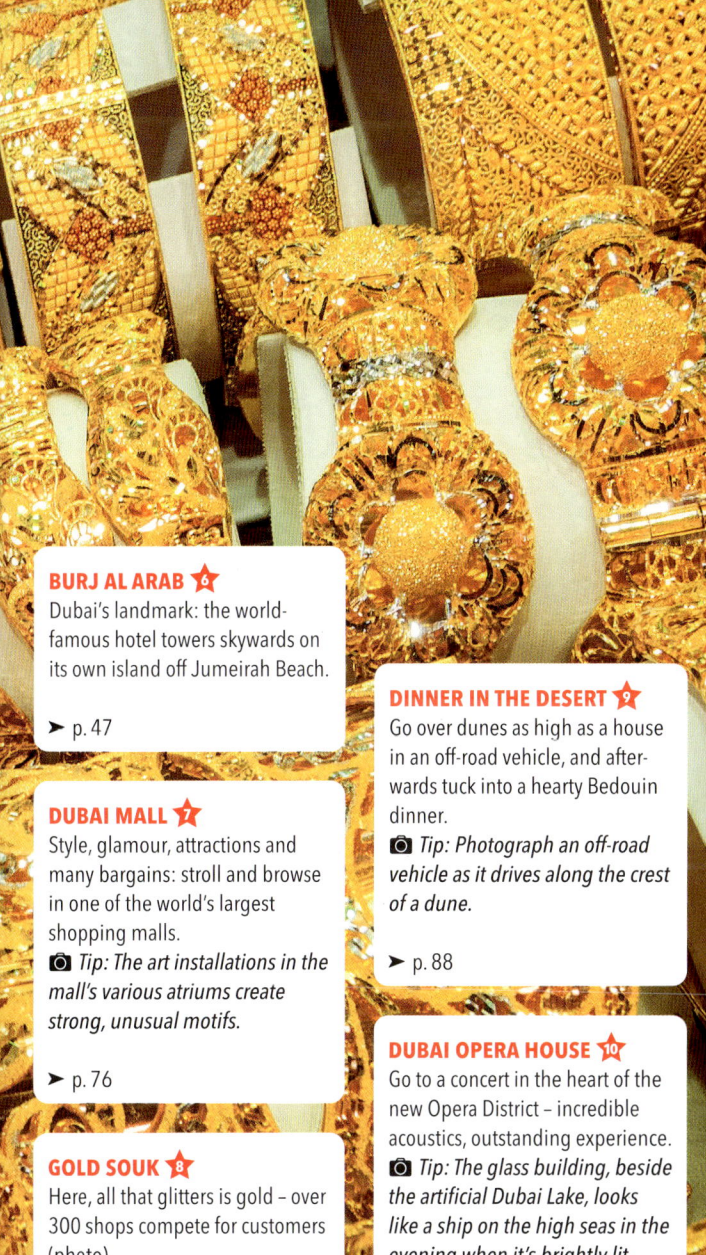

BURJ AL ARAB ⑥
Dubai's landmark: the world-famous hotel towers skywards on its own island off Jumeirah Beach.

➤ p. 47

DUBAI MALL ⑦
Style, glamour, attractions and many bargains: stroll and browse in one of the world's largest shopping malls.
📷 *Tip: The art installations in the mall's various atriums create strong, unusual motifs.*

➤ p. 76

GOLD SOUK ⑧
Here, all that glitters is gold – over 300 shops compete for customers (photo).

➤ p. 78

DINNER IN THE DESERT ⑨
Go over dunes as high as a house in an off-road vehicle, and afterwards tuck into a hearty Bedouin dinner.
📷 *Tip: Photograph an off-road vehicle as it drives along the crest of a dune.*

➤ p. 88

DUBAI OPERA HOUSE ⑩
Go to a concert in the heart of the new Opera District – incredible acoustics, outstanding experience.
📷 *Tip: The glass building, beside the artificial Dubai Lake, looks like a ship on the high seas in the evening when it's brightly lit.*

➤ p. 91

CONTENTS

- 🕐 Plan your visit
- £–£££ Price categories
- 🍴 Eating & drinking
- 🛍 Shopping
- 🍸 Nightlife
- 🌴 Top beaches
- 🌡 When it's hot
- 🐷 Budget activities
- 👨‍👩‍👧 Family activities
- 🚩 Classic experiences

(📖 A2) Refers to the removable pull-out map

CONTENTS

MARCO POLO TOP HIGHLIGHTS
2 Top 10 highlights

BEST OF DUBAI
8 ... when it's hot
9 ... on a budget
10 ... with children
11 ... classic experiences

GET TO KNOW DUBAI
14 Discover Dubai
17 At a glance
18 Understand Dubai
21 True or false?

24 SIGHTSEEING
28 Bur Dubai
34 Deira
38 Downtown Dubai
42 Jumeirah
49 Other sights

52 EATING & DRINKING

68 SHOPPING

80 NIGHTLIFE

ACTIVE & RELAXED
94 Sport & wellness
96 Festivals & events
98 Sleep well

DISCOVERY TOURS
104 Dubai at a glance
107 Enter the world of the souks
111 Between sea and wind towers
113 Beach life à la Dubai

GOOD TO KNOW

116 **HOLIDAY BASICS**
Arrival, Getting around, Emergencies, Essentials, Important information, Weather

124 **ARABIC WORDS & PHRASES**
Don't be lost for words

126 **HOLIDAY VIBES**
Books, films, music & blogs

128 **TRAVEL PURSUIT**
The MARCO POLO holiday quiz

130 **INDEX & CREDITS**

132 **DOS & DONT'S**
How to avoid slip-ups & blunders

BEST OF DUBAI

Inside the Burj Al Arab – one of the world's most luxurious hotels

BEST
WHEN IT'S HOT

SO COOL, EVEN IN THE HEAT

UNDERGROUND
On the basement floor of the *Dubai Museum* in *Al Fahidi Fort*, you are in semi-darkness, and it's a pleasantly cool spot to learn about aspects of everyday life in the Gulf in days gone by – like living in an oasis or doing business in an ancient souk.
➤ p. 30, Sightseeing

COOL ENTERTAINMENT
You simply can't get bored at the *Dubai Mall*. A whole day will fly by, thanks to an Olympic-size ice rink, the Dubai Aquarium, cinemas, indoor theme parks, and more than 160 cafés and restaurants.
➤ p. 39, Sightseeing

DOWNHILL OR ARMCHAIR SKIING
At *Ski Dubai* (photo) you can race down the slopes on skis or slide down in a tube. The lazy alternative is to watch the action through the windows of the St Moritz Café, while sipping hot almond milk by the fireplace.
➤ p. 48, Sightseeing

AIR-CONDITIONED SOUK SHOPPING
When the temperature gets to around 40°C and it's too hot to go to the Spice Souk or the Gold Souk, enjoy the bazaar atmosphere of the air-conditioned alleyways of the *Souk Al Bahar* and *Souk Khan Murjan*. Things might be a little pricier here, but the lanes are fragranced with oriental oils.
➤ p. 78, Shopping

CHILL OUT IN THE ICE BAR
Seats, tables, walls and the bar itself: in the *Chillout Ice Lounge* everything is made of ice. For protection against the sudden fall in temperature – you go from Dubai heat to -6°C – guests are given a padded jacket, scarf and gloves in the acclimatisation room.
➤ p. 85, Nightlife

BEST ON A BUDGET

FOR SMALLER WALLETS

FOUNTAINS ON DUBAI LAKE
What a sight! After sunset, when the illuminated *Dubai Fountain* system shoots its waters into the air to a height of well over 100m, accompanied by dramatic music, even the soaring Burj Khalifa behind the jets seems less significant.
➤ p. 39, Sightseeing

CITY TOURS FOR SHOPPERS
Dubai's shopping malls are not close together. Ask whether your hotel lies on the route of the free *shuttle buses* belonging to the Mall of Emirates, Dubai Mall or Deira City Centre Mall. And then climb aboard for a free tour of the city, with or without shopping.
➤ p. 40, Sightseeing, p. 77, Shopping

AQUARIUM XXL
It can't get any bigger than this: one of the attractions at the spectacular Dubai Mall is the 10-million litre (!) *Dubai Aquarium & Underwater Zoo* (photo). There's no admission charge to see the massive sharks, shoals of parrot fish and manta rays in this impressive underwater world.
➤ p. 40, Sightseeing

ARABIAN HORSES & ADRENALIN
You don't need to be a horse-lover to enjoy the atmosphere at the *Meydan Racecourse* between December and March, when it is *the* place to be for tremendous excitement and enjoyment. Best of all: access to part of the main grandstand is free.
➤ p. 50, Sightseeing

AUTHENTIC CUISINE
The restaurants in the *Karachi Darbar* chain serve great Pakistani and Indian meals at very low prices. After dark, tables at the Karama Mall branch are set up outside.
➤ p. 67, Eating & drinking

BEST WITH CHILDREN

FUN FOR YOUNG & OLD

CROSS THE DUBAI CREEK ON AN ABRA
Children enjoy *taking the little ferry boat across the creek*, the wind in their face, looking over the ferryman's shoulder and listening to the chugging of the engines.
➤ p. 34, Sightseeing

SLIDE INTO THE SHARK TANK
Dive among manta rays and glide from a pyramid towards the predatory fish in the depths: can there be a more exciting place anywhere in Dubai? Children who experience *Aquaventure*, the water park on Dubai's Palm Island, know the answer.
➤ p. 46, Sightseeing

BRICK MANIA
In the *Legoland Dubai* theme park, dreams of building and constructing with the iconic bricks come true. There's action on the Fire Dragon rollercoaster, thrills while taking the Lego driving test, and various themed countries to explore. Great fun all round.
➤ p. 50, Sightseeing

THE CALL OF THE DESERT
Just outside the city gates, sand dunes as high as mountains, called *Big Red* (photo) beckon. Just take your shoes off, and let the sand run golden yellow and fine as icing sugar over your toes. In this gigantic sandpit, the activities on offer – from camel rides and buggy rides to quadbike excursions – become almost secondary.
➤ p. 51, Sightseeing

BEACHLIFE À LA DUBAI
Children love *Kite Beach* and its adventure playground by the sea, romping on trampolines, watching the kitesurfers – and then ordering their favourite snack at one of the food trucks.
➤ p. 94, Sport & activities

BEST 🚩 CLASSIC EXPERIENCES

ONLY IN DUBAI

BASTAKIYA
Dubai's most historic quarter gets its character from its narrow alleyways, some of them shaded by roofs, and old merchants' houses that are now occupied by galleries, restaurants and cafés.
➤ p. 30, Sightseeing

GET TO THE TOP
Burj Khalifa is the world's tallest building. For a special thrill, visit the *"At the Top" viewing platform*, with outdoor terrace, on the 124th and 125th floors. The organised tour places Dubai at your feet.
➤ p. 38, Sightseeing

JUMEIRAH BEACH
Wealthy locals, expats and tourists flock to these miles of long sandy beach, with the Burj Al Arab on its own small island, the man-made *Palm Jumeirah* island, and beach clubs offering shishas and mocktails (photo).
➤ p. 42, Sightseeing

DINNER ON A DHOW
Old Arab trading ships as floating restaurants: as the last rays of the sun fall on the city, help yourself from the buffet and see Dubai from the water on a *dinner cruise*.
➤ p. 87, Nightlife

THE DUBAI DESERT
What would Dubai be without a trip to the desert? It's an integral part of the emirate, and a visit to the sand dunes that glow golden and copper is essential. Just a vast expanse of sand, as far as the eye can see – and a *Bedouin dinner* at a camp.
➤ p. 88, Nightlife

A FOUR-WEEK SHOPPING SPREE
Discounts, prize draws with millions to be won, fashion shows, charity galas and other events are the highlights of the glamorous *Dubai Shopping Festival*.
➤ p. 96, Festivals & events

GET TO KNOW DUBAI

A nostalgic adventure: *abra* ride on the Dubai Creek

DISCOVER DUBAI

Sheikh Zayed Road in the evening light

Dubai – you have to see it for yourself. Spectacular luxury hotels, mega-malls and huge, utopian construction projects have turned a small Arab trading port into a global destination measured in superlatives. The world's tallest building and largest man-made waterway; artificial islands that are visible from space; the biggest airport. And new ventures are announced all the time, with buildings rising up in record speed.

BEGINNING OF THE BOOM

The opening of the seven-star Burj Al Arab hotel in 1999 was just the beginning; within a few years, Dubai had become a sought-after destination for short breaks, a kind of eighth wonder of the world at the start of the 21st century. The emirate, one of seven making up the United Arab Emirates, draws visitors to the Arabian Gulf like a magnet, with its sunshine, beaches and awe-inspiring man-made

1793	1833	1870	1966	1971	1979
The Bedouin tribe of Bani Yas settles in Abu Dhabi	Sheikh Maktoum settles at the Creek and declares Dubai's independence	Dubai is the most important harbour in the Gulf region	First oil discoveries in the Fateh field	Foundation of the United Arab Emirates (UAE); opening of Dubai International Airport	Inauguration of World Trade Centre, Dubai's first skyscraper

GET TO KNOW DUBAI

sights. Seen from the observation deck of the 828m-tall Burj Khalifa, the world's tallest building, the city and beyond stretches to the horizon. From up there, even the nearby skyscrapers seem like cute toy houses. At the foot of the tower is Downtown Dubai, with arabesque modern villas made to look like historic desert palaces, the huge, gleaming Dubai Mall and a striking glass opera house shaped like a dhow.

A DESERTLESS CITY IN THE DESERT

Dubai is pushing the desert back ever further. Some 25km away from the historic souks and wind-tower houses of the Bastakiya district lies Dubai Marina: artificial harbours filled with mega-yachts, lined by palm trees and extraordinary skyscrapers. One reason for the rapid development of this mega-city is that the oil reserves are being depleted. In 15 to 30 years, it is forecast, no more oil will be extracted in Dubai. Dubai planned ahead for this by opening itself to international tourism, which now brings the emirate more than 25 per cent of its revenue. Sunshine all year round and clean, light-coloured sand make a winter beach holiday in the emirate a pleasure for many. There are also outstanding architectural highlights and traditional souks to experience. The dazzling emirate is a place of constant growth and action around the clock. The motto here is "nothing is impossible".

IT'S ALL A MATTER OF OPINION

Dubai polarises opinion: while some people see it as the most modern and vibrant city anywhere and are intoxicated by the dizzying speed of its

1985	Foundation of the national airline Emirates
1999	Opening of the Burj Al Arab, the world's first seven-star hotel
2002	Foreigners can acquire private property in Dubai
2006	Sheikh Mohammed bin Rashid Al Maktoum becomes head of government
2010	Inauguration of the Burj Khalifa, the tallest building in the world
2025	Planned completion of Dubai Creek Tower, over 1,000m tall

development, others are put off by its aura of excess and feel that the extravagant luxury and consumption that is normal here are ostentatious and trivial. If you speak to the many foreigners who live in Dubai, you get a different picture. For them, the most important things are not the size and superlatives behind the frenzied growth in Dubai, but the quality of life that is on offer. Europeans who work here enjoy the enormous opportunities available to them: the dynamic lifestyle, the countless leisure facilities, and the permanent sunshine. They say you can get used to the summer months, when it is hot as hell, the water in swimming pools has to be cooled, the city heats up like a huge oven and public life becomes more and more lethargic: "We simply compare the temperatures of over 40°C, which make it impossible to live outdoors, with the icy winter months in Europe. We don't want to leave the house when it's freezing either," one explained.

THE IMPACT OF OIL

Dubai is the second largest of the seven emirates that make up the United Arab Emirates. A huge construction boom drives the dynamic economy and brings people here from all corners of the world. The real estate and service sectors have been growing for decades. "Only a very small part of my visions for Dubai have been realised", Sheikh Mohammed bin Rashid Al Maktoum, head of government and the most important stakeholder in the emirate, is reported to have said. But, until the 1960s, Dubai was an insignificant Bedouin settlement by the sea with a population of a few thousand people, who made their living by oasis agriculture and fishing. It was the discovery and export of oil that began the whole region's meteoric rise. Today, as a business and tourism hub, Dubai has its finger on the fast-forward button. The locals have become a minority in their own country, making up just 17 per cent of the population. Nevertheless, world records, luxury and the pursuit of profit are only one side of Dubai. While champagne flows in the bars and clubs, the Quran is still the basis of parts of the legal system and the everyday and family life of local people is guided by Islam.

LIMITLESS GROWTH

Dubai is growing seemingly without limits – ever faster, ever higher, ever bigger. In La Mer, the new beachfront district of Jumeirah that was created around 2020, you'll be reminded of California. It's young, hip and even (slightly) sustainable. Between palm trees, street art, boutiques and restaurants, there is a chilled beach atmosphere. You can swim and relax here. The Dubai Water Canal, a project worth billions, has transformed the emirate into a lagoon city. The Dubai Creek Tower is scheduled for completion by 2025 in a completely new district. It will be over 1,000m tall, pushing the Burj Khalifa into second place among the skyscrapers. You may think you know Dubai, but the city is still growing and changing every second. Change is the essence.

GET TO KNOW DUBAI

AT A GLANCE

30.1 YEARS
Average age

United Kingdom: 40.2 years

"27,321"
Name of the most expensive cocktail, costing 27,321 dirhams (approx. £5,500) in the Burj Al Arab

100 LITRES
Average annual rainfall

United Kingdom: approx. 1,300 litres

828m
Tallest building: Burj Khalifa

The Shard, London: 310m

POPULATION
3.43 MILLION

London: 9.5 million

WARMEST MONTH
AUGUST
54°C

Peak temperature

BILLIONAIRES
14

and rising

BOOMING TRADE

40 per cent of the world's gold sales take place in Dubai

0%

Tax deductions: in Dubai gross salaries equal net salaries!

CRIME: ALMOST ZERO BECAUSE PLAIN-CLOTHES POLICE OFFICERS AND CAMERAS ARE EVERYWHERE

THE POLICE DRIVE FERRARIS, LAMBORGHINIS AND ROLLS-ROYCES

UNDERSTAND DUBAI

DEMOCRACY IS RELATIVE

At least, that's the opinion of Sheikh Mohammed, for whom personal freedom, security and stability are the key features of true democracy. Political parties? No way. Instead, there's the *majlis*, a reception room where selected locals can appear before a sheikh with their ideas, criticism and wishes. If he likes them and considers them good for the country and the people, and they are also in accordance with Islam, then new laws can be drawn up and passed, sometimes in less than a day!

LUXURY CARS

Nowhere in the world are high-value limousines as thick on the ground as in the emirate. At weekends, Hummers, Porsches and Maybachs queue up outside the foyers of luxury hotels for valet parking. The object of desire of the Dubai rich is the Bugatti Veyron, the most expensive and the fastest sports car in the world, which costs over a million dollars. A racing car licensed for normal road traffic, it has over 1,001hp and can reach speeds above 400km per hour. One in five of these Bugattis is registered in the UAE. Luxury car manufacturers have their largest and most extravagantly designed showrooms in Dubai. And bargaining over the price is a matter of course here – whether it's for a limousine or a high-quality racing camel.

Falconry is a traditional hobby and falcons are a status symbol

GET TO KNOW DUBAI

FALCONS

Not dogs and cats, but camels and falcons are the favourite animals of the people of Dubai. The birds of prey are trained for several months by experienced falconers. When the bird has got used to humans and is fully trained, it goes to its new owner. Out in the desert a falcon will take off from an outstretched arm and plummet down when it has seen its prey, waiting there motionless for its master. The most valuable falcons have a price tag of up to one million dirhams and sometimes accompany their owners abroad for hunting trips. Hunting with falcons is an ancient passion of the Gulf Arabs that foreigners rarely get to see, though falcons are on show at the Al-Maha and Bab Al-Shams hotels, and sometimes they can be seen at an organised "Bedouin dinner".

ESOTERIC HAPPINESS

With 365 days of sun a year, and shopping and clubbing until you drop, it's understandable that sooner or later you may want to find something that brings a deeper kind of happiness. Many European residents have discovered the delights of yoga, meditation and Far Eastern philosophies. Tucked away in unassuming shopping centres and top locations, there are sessions with favoured teachers and gurus, who are either resident in Dubai or flown in regularly from India. From yoga in the desert at full moon to Zen yoga, and even underwater yoga, the offer is colourful and varied.

REMOTE-CONTROLLED CAMELS

It's not rude to call someone a camel in Dubai. Not only does every single person love and revere the desert animals, but racing camels are as precious as gold. As well as the internationally renowned, highly lucrative horse races, camel racing is a big deal here. The rulers of the emirates and their ministers and entourages of (male) locals meet at camel race tracks between October and April. The excitement peaks when the best animals from each of the seven emirates race each other. The jockeys? They're lightweight racing robots that are remote-controlled by the camels' owners; they've been in use since child jockeys were banned. Owners drive alongside the racing camels in their all-terrain vehicles, activating a tiny whip at the touch of a button that is designed to spur the animals on. And of course there's plenty of shouting and cheering, sounding of horns and accelerating of engines, so that the whole spectacle is quickly engulfed in a huge cloud of sand. For the winners there are prizes and prestige, while the delicate camels are pampered with wild honey and goat's milk.

HENNA

To this day, hands and feet painted with complex patterns in henna paste are part of the ideal of beauty for an Emirati woman, and henna is particularly popular for special occasions such as weddings. The powder, which is made from the leaves of the henna plant, is mixed with aromatic oils and lime juice to make a paste that is

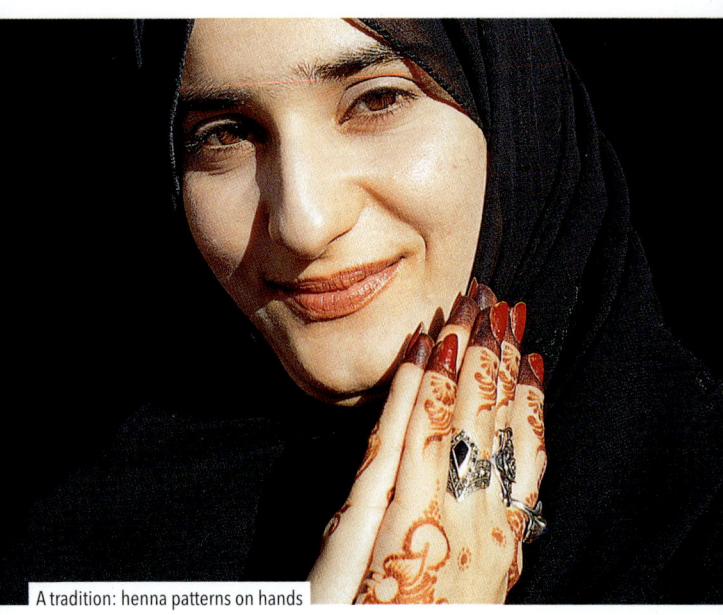

A tradition: henna patterns on hands

applied to the skin. The red-brown colouring lasts for several weeks before fading. In Dubai a range of beauty salons offer henna decoration to tourists.

ART

Dubai may not be the first place that comes to mind when you think of art, but the desert metropolis has become home to internationally renowned galleries over the last few years. Although there is no particular district known for its art scene in Dubai, those who are interested in contemporary Arab art know just where to go. For example, local art dealers are to be found on Alserkal Avenue in the Al-Quoz quarter, where the galleries offer a large selection and international curators mingle with tourists. The showroom of highly successful gallery *The Third Line* (see p. 74), owned by Iranian Sunny Rahbar, is located nearby. The Dubai International Financial Centre (DIFC) is also a major hub for galleries. After browsing through the many exhibits, you can check out the dozens of good cafés and restaurants in the centre.

WOMEN TAXI DRIVERS

Haddis, originally from Ethiopia, is instructed to leave men standing by the roadside. She is out and about driving one of the taxis with a pink roof and seats, known as "ladies' taxis", which only carry female passengers and children (although they may also accept married couples). Haddis enjoys her work and says that many women passengers prefer a woman driver. Apart from personal safety concerns, this could also be because they realise that women drivers tend to be more relaxed at the wheel and don't drive as fast as their male colleagues.

RAIN

The sun shines for about 360 days a year in Dubai. On the remaining five days when it rains, there is chaos: cars form tailbacks miles long and the city is gridlocked. The next day news reports highlight the disruption that came in the rain's wake. The chaos is caused by Dubai's rudimentary drainage system. Water cannot run off and so it quickly pools and levels rise. A simple downpour can cause floods and tankers have to be brought in to pump off the water. But soon the sun is shining again and life returns to normal.

SHEIKH & EMIR

"Sheikh" is a title traditionally given to the leader of a Bedouin tribe. As a spiritual as well as temporal head, sheikhs are said to be part of an unbroken lineage that goes back to the Prophet Mohammed. This is why some sheikhs are still revered with devotion long after their death. The concept of a sheikh is historically different to that of an emir, who has governmental authority and command over a group of soldiers (in Arabic *"amir"* means "commander"). However, in Dubai today, "sheikh" is also the official title of the head of government. In personal conversations, the correct and respectful way to refer to Sheikh Mohammed is "His Highness".

TRUE OR FALSE?

THE WORLD IS NOT ENOUGH

As you come into land at Dubai, you can see a group of small, white islands off the coast that look like a map of the world. In addition to the already-realised Palm Jumeirah, "The World" is a particularly wacky project, even by Dubai standards. Three hundred artificial islands, visible from the moon, have been created from heaped-up sand off the coast to represent continents. Construction was halted by the 2008 financial crisis and much of the project remains incomplete, but "South America" was completed in 2022, and "Heart of Europe" is also finished. You can stay in luxury hotels and villas here. So, yes, the world is not enough in Dubai!

WOMEN ARE AIMING HIGH

Uneducated and dependent? Dubai's local women are certainly not that. Young mechanical engineer Nura Al-Matruschi applied to NASA in 2021, went through a multi-stage selection process and is now being trained as an astronaut. There are more and more like her: businesswomen, professors and artists. In addition, women are making strides in government, among them Mariam Al-Mheiri, now serving as head of the Office of International Affairs in the Presidential Court.

CALLIGRAPHY

Your name in Arabic script? The *XVA Gallery* (see p. 74) is one place where a skilled calligrapher can write your name in ink on handmade paper. Names might be Arabised (Michael becomes Miichaa'iil, Liliane, Liliiaan) – and the Arabic letters are turned into sweeping arcs. The aesthetic appeal is more important than legibility, which is why the artist may also interlace some of the letters with each other. This art of beautiful calligraphy originated from the birth of Islam. The aim was to achieve harmony between the spoken and written word, which arose from the responsibility attached to writing down the words of the Prophet. To this day, calligraphy is most often used to write verses from the Quran, which is why this particular art form is still viewed with tremendous prestige in Dubai.

SHISHAS

Strawberry, banana or latte macchiato? The flavours of tobacco smoked in shisha cafés change according to the season. Even though word has now got around that smoking is bad for your health, an increasing number of establishments where a shisha, or water-cooled pipe, can be ordered have sprung up in recent years. And what used to be the preserve of Bedouin men is now increasingly finding favour with women, especially foreign women. It seems that despite health risks, the relaxing bubbling of the pipe – which is, after all, also known as a hubbly-bubbly – is still seen as a way of chilling out. As a low-cost souvenir, shishas can be found everywhere in Dubai. The cheapest ones are in the shops in the Old Souk in Deira.

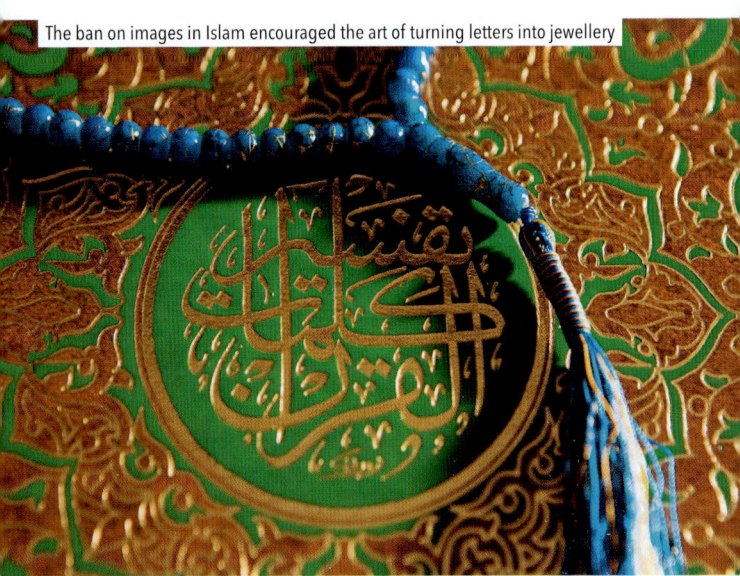

The ban on images in Islam encouraged the art of turning letters into jewellery

GET TO KNOW DUBAI

WATER & DESERT

The United Arab Emirates is situated in one of the earth's dry zones, on the edge of the Rub Al Khali Desert. Great technical efforts are being made to prevent the desert from spreading further, as water – in contrast to oil – is a scarce commodity in the region. In Dubai, a bottle of water sometimes costs more than a litre of petrol. However, millions of shrubs, trees and flowers are artificially irrigated in the emirate. In spite of the meagre resources of groundwater, which is brought to the surface from deep boreholes, Dubai's water consumption is among the highest in the world. It is also one of the biggest wasters of water, according to a list compiled by the World Wide Fund for Nature (WWF). More than 80 per cent of the emirate's water is supplied from seawater desalination plants, which are energy-intensive and operated using a great deal of oil or natural gas, and pumped into the city or through long pipelines to golf courses and settlements in the desert. The emirate will have to be more careful in its use of this resource, but this will probably only happen gradually.

Well-irrigated flower gardens are a common sight in Dubai

CHARITY

When Dubai hosts trade fairs, more often than not they involve the luxury or consumer goods sectors. But for over ten years, the emirate has organised the International Humanitarian Aid and Development Fair (DIHAD). In collaboration with the United Nations and the International Red Cross, participants from around 20 countries meet each year at this fair for panels, workshops and discussions concerned with humanitarian aid in developing countries and areas affected by catastrophes, as well as other charitable projects. Dubai Cares *(dubaicares.ae)* is a state organisation with the stated aim of enabling every child on earth to attend school. It builds schools and libraries in locations including Africa and Asia, and arranges meals for schoolchildren.

SIGHT SEEING

Sure, showing off and bragging are part and parcel of this metropolis of superlatives: the largest aquarium, the best clubs, the tallest building. It's all ultra-modern and exciting. But near the Creek, in the souks of Bur Dubai and Deira, things remain down to earth.

The Burj Khalifa is visible from everywhere. The gleaming silver wonder of the world gives every visitor to its viewing terrace the uplifting assurance of being in the tallest building on earth. Downtown Dubai was built at its feet: the huge Dubai Mall beckons

Steel and glass, light and water: ingredients for the futuristic Dubai Marina

and the light is reflected in the glass Dubai Opera. Jumeirah is the place to go kitesurfing and chill out in one of the beach clubs. From there, you can go shopping and eating in the nearby Dubai Marina, where – in typical Dubai fashion – the whole world has been incorporated in the design, and you can expect southern French lightness combined with a Manhattan-style skyline. And as you fly in, you'll get a good view of the man-made islands that form the shape of a giant palm. Only in Dubai …

> You'll find all the venues in this chapter on the pull-out map

NEIGHBOURHOOD OVERVIEW

MARCO POLO HIGHLIGHTS

★ **DUBAI MUSEUM**
A historic fort is home to the city's largest and most interesting museum
➤ p. 30

★ **BASTAKIYA**
Where it began: the original settlement, between the fort and the Dubai Creek
➤ p. 30

★ **CROSSING THE CREEK**
Enjoy a crossing on a traditional *abra* and experience Dubai from the water
➤ p. 34

★ **AL KHOR CORNICHE**
Dhows put into Dubai Creek here. Once they carried goods; now they're mainly used for tours ➤ p. 37

★ **BURJ KHALIFA**
The tallest building in the world ➤ p. 38

★ **DUBAI FOUNTAIN**
Early evening on Dubai Lake: a spectacular show with dancing water
➤ p. 38

★ **DUBAI AQUARIUM & UNDERWATER ZOO**
Fascinating underwater worlds across three floors ➤ p. 40

★ **DUBAI WATER CANAL**
Now the Creek flows through the entire city ➤ p. 41

★ **DUBAI MARINA**
Huge harbour, impressive yachts, skyscrapers and cafés ➤ p. 44

★ **ATLANTIS**
"Only" a hotel – but you simply have to see it ➤ p. 45

★ **BURJ AL ARAB**
The design of Dubai's iconic tower was based on a dhow sail ➤ p. 47

JUMEIRAH p. 42
Hip, luxurious and gigantic: beach life in Dubai

BUR DUBAI

The history of the emirate began in the 18th century in Bur Dubai ("Dubai-side") at the southwestern end of the Creek, when a branch of the Baniyas Bedouin tribe from Abu Dhabi settled there.

The historic wind-tower houses in Bastakiya are still crowded together in narrow lanes. Hardly any Dubai locals live here now: the houses have been restored at great cost and now accommodate offices, cafés and shops. The centre of Bur Dubai, around the old fort, is lively and multicultural. People from Afghanistan and India, Sri Lanka and the Philippines live and work here. Indian sari stores, cheap Pakistani restaurants, and the colours, sounds and smells of every part of Asia accompany a stroll around the district. From here, it's only a few steps to the banks of the Creek and the historic Shindagha district, with the fabulous palace of Sheikh Saeed Al-Maktoum, grandfather of Sheikh Mohammed. Afterwards, take a seat in one of the cafés: this atmospheric old Creekside quarter has been perfectly restored and invites you to linger.

1 SHEIKH SAEED AL MAKTOUM HOUSE

Wind towers as air conditioning, carpets instead of light-reflecting marble: this is where Sheikh Saeed, grandfather of the current ruler, reigned over his small, then not so well-known desert emirate. For almost 50 years, state guests were received in the palace, built in 1896, and strategic plans were hatched here. There are all kinds of historical drawings, photos and valuable hand-carved furniture on display. However, the palace itself remains the real attraction, a complete work of art from the past, although perhaps a little too perfectly restored for some tastes. *Sat–Thu 8am–8.30pm, Fri 3–9.30pm | admission 15 Dh | Shindagha | Metro Green Line: Al Ghubaiba | ⊙ 45 mins | ⎕ V4*

2 AL SHINDAGHA MUSEUM

Replicas of old palaces on the banks of the Creek serve as a venue for exciting, ultra-modern presentation technology. Two pavilions, the *Perfume House* and the *Creek House* showcase the world of oriental perfume oils and the history of the Dubai Creek. *Wed–Sun 10am–6pm, Fri 2.30–9pm | Shindagha | alshindagha.dubaiculture.gov.ae*

WHERE TO START?

If you want to see **old Dubai**, the best place to start is the **Al Fahidi** metro station (Green Line). From here, head for the restored historic **Bastakiya quarter**. Then it's not far to the banks of the Creek, at the heart of the original settlement, and to the Dubai Museum in the old Al Fahidi fort. To explore the modern district of **Downtown Dubai** – including the towering Burj Khalifa, the colossal Dubai Mall and the man-made Dubai Lake – it's best to start from the **Dubai Mall** station (Red Line).

SIGHTSEEING

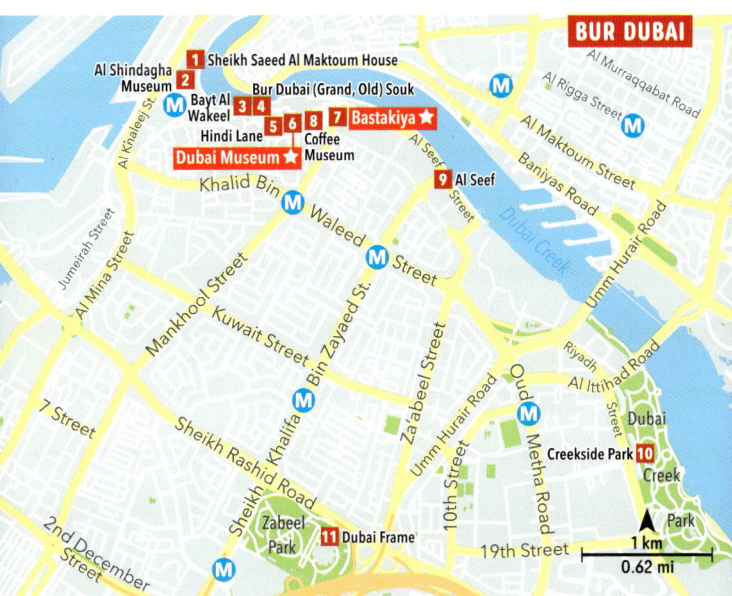

Metro Green Line: Al Ghubaiba | 60 mins | V4

3 BAYT AL WAKEEL

Soak in the atmosphere on the wooden café terrace of this traditional commercial building ("House of the Agent") dating from 1934, with its two-storey arcades directly above the Creek. Watch the ceaseless activity on the water, with the coming and going of *abra* passengers, and the dhow and water taxi traffic, and take in the view of the high-rises in Deira. *Bur Dubai Souk | between the two abra stops | Metro Green Line: Al-Ghubaiba | V4*

4 BUR DUBAI (GRAND, OLD) SOUK

Either smile and walk by the insistent sellers waiting outside the shops, or else haggle cheerfully with them until you reach a price that suits both of you. All along the covered, pleasantly shady souk, which has two heavy wooden doors at the end, are rows of shops selling pashminas, colourful T-shirts with prints of Dubai sights and camels (from 5 Dh), as well as oriental trousers and wonderful pouf cushions. There is a tremendous selection of fabrics, although the quality and prices vary widely. *Between the abra stops | Metro Green Line: Al Ghubaiba | V4*

INSIDER TIP: Dubai T-shirts

5 HINDI LANE

Little India in Dubai – the Indian presence is more evident in Bur Dubai and around the Meena Bazaar than anywhere else in the emirate. As well

BUR DUBAI

as establishing shops and Indian pubs, the Indian community also lives out its spirituality, as visitors can witness on "Hindi Lane", in particular. That's the name given to this little alleyway, where people come for devotional objects before visiting the temple. The air smells of patchouli, and you'll see lots of Indian women in colourful saris. One of the shops not only sells king coconuts for a few dirhams, which are cut open and drunk there and then, but also all sorts of offerings for the gods, including small pictures of Ganesh and Vishnu. Behind the Grand Mosque in Bur Dubai are a number of Hindu temples, located unobtrusively on the second floors of simple town houses. Visitors are admitted when they have left their shoes on one of the shoe racks on the street. Pujas are held on special days (which can include full moons), involving praying, recitals and meditation, and offerings are also brought here. *Between Ali Bin Abi Taleb Street and Dubai Creek | ⏱ 30 mins | 📖 V4*

> **INSIDER TIP**
> **Coconut instead of Coca-Cola**

6 DUBAI MUSEUM ★

Climb down into the basement of *Al Fahidi Fort*: as the oldest building in Dubai (it dates back to 1787), this has long been a national monument, and as such is of great significance to locals. The best time to come is around noon, when it's too hot to be outside. As you immerse yourself in the bustle of the replica of a souk, the atmosphere becomes pleasantly cool and semi-dark – exactly as it would have been for real in the Dubai of a few decades ago. Isn't that a blacksmith working by the fire? At first glance, the life-size, moving puppets acting as traders and buyers are deceptively real; there are animated conversations on tape, you can hear the fire blazing and the hammer striking.

> **INSIDER TIP**
> **Cool history**

Other departments are dedicated to pearl fishing and crafts, and transport you into a fishing settlement with basic huts and into the desert, where an artificial starry sky is the only source of light. *Closed for renovation at the time of writing | admission 3 Dh | Al Fahidi Fort | Al Fahidi Street | Metro Green Line: Al Sharaf | ⏱ 90 mins | 📖 V4*

7 BASTAKIYA ★ ⚑

At noon, the old heart of the town (the Al Fahidi Historical Neighbourhood) is deserted, and therefore quite sterile. However, the alleyways, small galleries, museums, shops and cafés start to fill with people at sundown – which is the best time to enjoy Bastakiya. The historic old quarter is clearly laid out. It consists of around 50 houses made of clay and coral limestone, built around 1890 by wealthy Persian merchants. The traditional Arab-style houses are usually original, and have been restored and refurbished – after many plans to tear them down were thwarted – and are now listed. Look out for the large wind towers: Dubai's earliest air-conditioning, and entirely without electricity.

30

SIGHTSEEING

The *XVA Gallery* (see p. 74) is a hotel in the old arabesque style, gallery and café-restaurant in one. Enjoy a drink in the courtyard here, surrounded by modern art. Then ask the way to the little *Coffee Museum* (see below) a few alleyways away inside a wind-tower house.

Traffic-free Bastakiya is next to the Creek, and *Al Fahidi Fort*, Dubai's oldest building, is nearby.

INSIDER TIP — Get to know Bastakiya
It's worth experiencing Bastakiya behind the scenes on a great walk guided by local people.

Guided tours can be booked at the *Sheikh Mohammed Centre for Cultural Understanding (Tue, Thu 10.30am–noon, Sat 9–10.30am | fee 100 Dh | Historic Building, 26 Al Musallah Road | Al Fahidi Historical Neigbourhood | tel. 03 53 66 66 | cultures.ae). Metro Green Line: Al Sharaf | V4*

8 COFFEE MUSEUM

The smell of coffee seeps through the open doors of the two-storey, old Emirati villa. Each of the total of 12 rooms in this little private museum tells a different story. In the midst of ancient, fascinating coffee machines, collected in Arab and European countries, different coffee varieties are offered to visitors to sample, and you can also browse around the coffee and gift shop. *Sat–Thu 9am–5pm | admission 10 Dh | House 44 | Al Fahidi Historical Neighbourhood | coffeemuseum.ae | Metro Green Line: Al Sharaf | 30 mins | V4*

Indian migrant workers have formed their own neighbourhoods in Bur Dubai

BUR DUBAI

A must for all lovers of the black bean drink: the Coffee Museum

9 AL SEEF

Great for a stroll in the evening, this area is historic and trendy at the same time! In a prime location on the Creek and adjacent to the Al Fahidi Historical Neighbourhood, the heart of old Dubai, Al Seef is a new car-free hotspot that catapults you right into the past of Dubai while also – of course – offering plenty of opportunities for shopping and dining. In beautifully rebuilt clay buildings with wind towers (great photo opportunities!) that take you back to pre-oil Dubai, the creators of Al Seef have paid homage to the past on a site parallel to the banks of the Creek, confidently referencing the emirate's rich tradition as a centre of pearl diving.

The inclusion of modern design elements such as palm tree promenades and wooden walkways on the waterfront, as well as a marina for private yachts (still under construction), has been a particular success. While the northern part is historic, the southern part of Al Seef is home to shops, cafés and restaurants in colourfully styled shipping containers – a new face for the old quarter. *Businesses and shops daily 10am–10pm and midnight respectively | Metro Green Line: Al Sharaf | V5*

10 CREEKSIDE PARK

A whole 2.5km-long park stretching beside the Dubai Creek! With huge palms, exotic trees, shrubs and themed gardens, this is one of the loveliest parks in Dubai. It's a fabulous spot for photos of the Creek and its skyline as well as for enjoying some time away from the city with a picnic. It also includes the *Children's City (Mon–Fri 9am–7pm, Sat/Sun 2–8pm | admission 15 Dh, children 10 Dh, plus park admission 5 Dh | Creekside Park/Gate 1 | childrencity.ae | Metro Green Line: Healthcare City)*, where youngsters can experience the world of adults through play. It features interactive play stations In themed areas such as "Human Body" and "Natural Wonders".

The park is busier at weekends, when the smell of barbecues fills the

SIGHTSEEING

air. A tip: stock up on sandwiches, drinks and fruit and spend your siesta under a shady tree among Sri Lankan maids and children playing badminton. *Daily 8am–11pm | admission 5 Dh | between Garhoud Bridge and Maktoum Bridge | Umm Hurair | Metro Green Line: Healthcare City |* V6

11 DUBAI FRAME

What's that supposed to be? A huge golden picture frame in the park? No – it's two 150m-high, interconnected towers from which you can experience Dubai from a completely new, unfamiliar perspective. Take the lift to the top of the "frame" and the 93m-long connecting bridge.

The walk over the abyss can give you a queasy feeling in your stomach, but dare to walk across the glass floor at a height of 150m: the view is, of course, absolutely amazing.  You can see the Creek and the dhows, the souks and the skyscrapers of modern Dubai. On the ground floor, you can expect audio and video presentations showing how the city was created. Then it's off through a "time travel tunnel" into the visionary future of the city. *Daily 9am–9pm | admission 50 Dh | Zabeel Park | thedubaiframe.com | Metro Red Line: Al Jafiliya |* 90 mins | U5

INSIDER TIP — Better than bungee jumping

In the Al Seef quarter, the historic becomes the backdrop for the modern

DEIRA

The souks of Deira give you a first impression of the importance of Dubai as a historic trading port and the culture of its people.

Spices and gold, electronics and clothing – shops line the lanes and streets of this buzzing quarter. Back in the 19th century, local and Iranian traders set up in Deira and founded the largest souk on the whole Gulf coast here, at the tip of land by the Creek known as *Al Ras*. In Deira the merchants' Dubai of days gone by is still alive and well, and goods are offered for sale until late in the evening; the Indian and Pakistani restaurants stay open late too. Things get going later on Fridays, with many stalls remaining closed until the afternoon following Friday prayers. Modern high-rises with striking designs put their stamp on the Baniyas waterfront road, where dozens of traditional wooden dhows are moored.

Crossing the Creek on an *abra*

🔴 CROSSING THE CREEK ★

The ultra-modern skyscraper architecture of the Deira waterfront and the historic, honey-coloured buildings of the Bastakiya quarter are divided by the city's lifeline, the sluggishly flowing Creek. It can be crossed using the Shindagha Tunnel and four bridges. However, the best way to get across is a 👫 trip across the Creek on one of the open wooden boats known as *abras*, which can take about 20 passengers. The boats, which are often moored four-deep, make the crossing around the clock as soon as enough passengers have, which usually takes only a few minutes. This enjoyable trip costs just 1 Dh. During the ten-minute crossing you have a panoramic view of the city skyline and the traditional Bastakiya quarter. The boats depart in Deira and opposite on the Bur-Dubai bank from two abra docks each side. Hire your own *abra* for the one-hour trip to the Floating Bridge and back for about 120 Dh. *V4*

🔴 AL AHMADIYA SCHOOL 🐦 👫

Arcades, courtyards and a 7m-tall wind tower: Dubai's first school, dating from 1912, has had a thorough

SIGHTSEEING

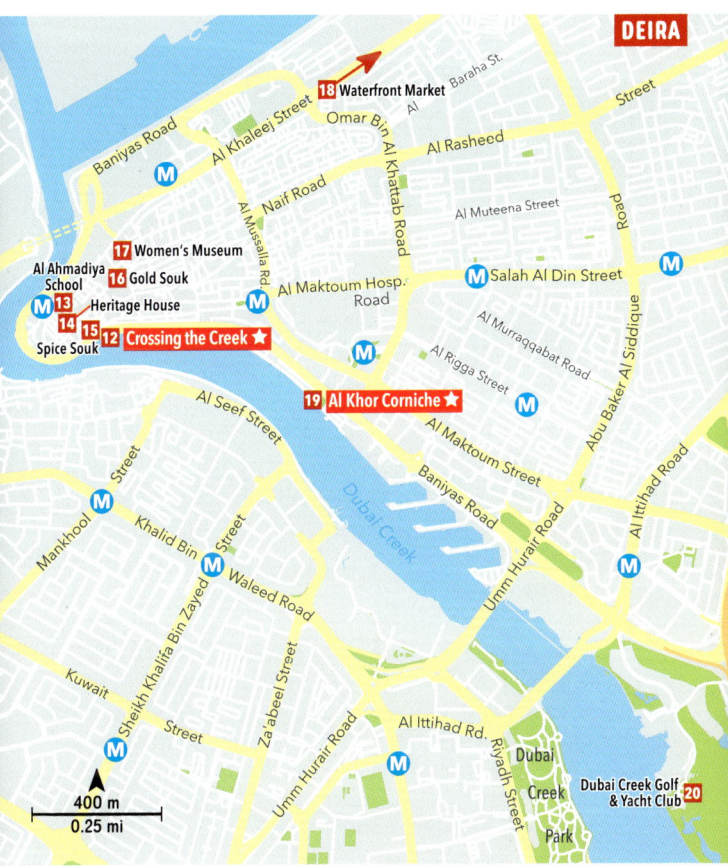

restoration. Lettering in relief with verses from the Quran decorates the high-ceilinged rooms. The school was originally intended for adult men, and another 20 years passed before the sons of the ruling family and of rich merchants were educated here. *Sat–Thu 8.30am–8.30pm, Fri 2–8.30pm | admission free | 15a Sikka Street | Metro Green Line: Al Ras | 30 mins | V4*

14 HERITAGE HOUSE

This museum lets you look behind the scenes of middle-class life in Dubai in the early 20th century. This house, built in 1890 in the traditional Arab style, was extended to a size of over 900m² in 1910 by the owner of the day. From the courtyard you have access to a *majlis*, a reception and assembly room for men, adorned with verses from the Quran and weapons. The sparsely furnished rooms, the

DEIRA

Smell, taste and listen to the traders: the Spice Souk is a feast for the senses

modest number of personal possessions, most of them functional, handmade and of a high aesthetic standard, create an impression of timeless beauty. *Sat–Thu 8am–7.30pm, Fri 2.30–7.30pm | admission free | Al Ahmadiya Street | short.travel/dub14 | Metro Green Line: Al Ras | 20 mins | V4*

15 SPICE SOUK

Little shops are crowded together in the narrow lanes of the Spice Souk. There is a delicious smell of cardamom, cloves and coriander, and traders from Pakistan sell cinnamon sticks, peppercorns and henna from jute sacks. Coffee and tea, nuts, almonds and pistachios, saffron and dried fruit are also on offer. *Sat–Thu 8am–1pm and 4–10pm, Fri 4–10pm | Al Ras Street | next to the Gold Souk | Metro Green Line: Al Ras | V4*

16 GOLD SOUK

Not just a place for shopping, but also one of the city's sights: the Gold Souk has more than 300 stores where gold jewellery is sold, almost exclusively, by weight. Arab, Asian and Europeans all come here – some to look, others to buy. Dubai is known around the world as an important centre of the gold trade, and the sign reading "City of Gold" at the entrance to the souk is actually a fitting description of the city as a whole. Here in the souk, most of the jewellery that's traded is 24-carat gold, and the shops and the way the jewellery is sold have changed little since the days before oil. Around 10 tonnes of gold are said to

SIGHTSEEING

be stored here – after sunset, the sparkling displays are truly spectacular. **INSIDER TIP – All that glistens**: The small camels, palm trees or beaked coffee pots in 333 or 585 (9 or 14 carat) gold, for necklaces or charm bracelets, are inexpensive and make lovely souvenirs. *Daily 9.30am–1pm and 4–10pm | Sikkat Al Khail Street | Metro Green Line: Al Ras | 60–90 mins | V4*

17 WOMEN'S MUSEUM

Artistic, private, authentic – and hidden away inside a narrow town house. A visit to this museum offers insight into a world that can seem mysterious and alien to many Europeans. Old (worn) burqas; the first passports for women, some of them even without photographs; the deep, moving voice of a long-dead writer, who never wanted to appear in public, reading from her works; portraits and pictures, as well as art installations, are shown in this interesting museum. It also has a café and a small souvenir shop where you can buy bags, T-shirts and so on. *Sat–Thu 10am–7pm | admission 20 Dh | Al Dhaghaya | behind the Gold Souk | womenmuseumuae.com | Metro Green Line: Al Ras | 60 mins | V4*

18 WATERFRONT MARKET

Sure, there are lots of dead fish lying around, which is why the UAE's largest fish and seafood market smells a little pungent. But there is plenty to see, photograph and eat here. Omani prawns, sea bream and angelfish from the Arabian Gulf are piled up on countless stalls. It's worth coming here in the morning when the new catch is unloaded and auctioned off; you'll find a big crowd here. **INSIDER TIP – Best fish in town**: Several restaurants in the fish market will fry your catch of the day or prepare everything expertly to your liking. Tastes simply delicious! Of course, there are also typical small cafés and restaurants. *Fish market daily 24 hrs | Deira Corniche, corner Al Khaleej and Abu Hail Street | waterfrontmarket.ae | Metro Green Line: Palm Deira | X4*

19 AL KHOR CORNICHE ★ ⚑

The smell of the salty sea mingles with the aroma of spices and diesel fumes: Al Khor Corniche, on Baniyas Road on the banks of the Creek, presents a refreshing contrast to the glamour and materialism that mark Dubai today. For decades fat-bellied, heavily laden dhows have anchored three and four deep by the quay walls of the Dubai Creek, with boxes and sacks, mattresses and bolts of fabric, car tyres and much more unloaded onto the shore. Today dhows are often used for tourist tours. *Baniyas Road | between Al Maktoum Bridge and Al Ras | Metro Green Line: Baniyas Square | V4*

20 DUBAI CREEK GOLF & YACHT CLUB

A fabulous sight. On the one hand, the landscaping – rich, luscious greens and little lakes, set against the skyline of the city and the Creek. On the other hand, the club house, with its

DOWNTOWN DUBAI

fabulous concrete sails, so reminiscent of an Arabian dhow and one of the unmistakeable symbols of New Dubai. *The Boardwalk (Sun–Thu noon–midnight, Fri, Sat 8am–midnight | ££)*, built on wooden stilts over the Creek, is the most beautiful restaurant in the golf club and has been an institution in Dubai for over 25 years. The atmosphere here is simply perfect and it's worth taking a seat on the terrace, whether for brunch at the weekend (book a few days in advance!) or a drink at sunset. *Al Garhoud | opposite Deira City Centre | tel. (restaurants) 02 95 60 00 | dubaigolf.com | Metro Red Line: Deira City Centre | V6*

DOWNTOWN DUBAI

It makes every other skyscraper look small: the 828m-high Burj Khalifa is the tallest building in the world, and can be seen from almost every part of Dubai. It is also the centre of dynamic Downtown Dubai and a must-see for visitors.

People shop in Dubai Mall at the feet of the architectural icon, delight in the Dubai Fountain and walk along the new Dubai Water Canal, an extension of the Creek that continues to the sea. Typical of Downtown Dubai is the exciting mix of the hyper-modern and the traditional. Luxury hotels such as the Palace, as well as apartments blocks, have been built here in a lavish oriental desert style.

21 BURJ KHALIFA ★

Be at the very top for once – it's possible here and the whole of Dubai is at your feet. The landmark rises 828m into the sky, its unique and gleaming silver aluminium façade tapering several times towards the top. There are 163 floors and 57 lifts, and floors 1 to 8 and 38 to 39 are occupied by the Armani design hotel. The Burj is the city's most prestigious address for international companies, luxury flats and restaurants. The ⚑ viewing platform on the 124th and 125th floors (At the Top) and another (At the Top SKY) on the 148th VIP floor (at 555m), where drinks and sweets are also served, are open to the public. A breathtaking experience! You should book tickets online to avoid queuing, secure your preferred time and head to the world's fastest lift. You can also buy tickets in the Dubai Mall (lower ground floor) at the "At the Top" counter. *At the Top: Mon–Fri 7am–3.30pm and 7–11pm 179 Dh, 3–6.30pm 259 Dh. At the Top SKY: daily 9am–6pm 553 Dh, from 7pm 399 Dh | Financial Centre Road, 1st Interchange | burjkhalifa.ae | Metro Red Line: Dubai Mall | ⏱ 90 mins | S5*

INSIDER TIP: In the fast lane

22 DUBAI FOUNTAIN ★

An artificial lake with a fountain? Although it might not sound very exciting, Dubai has really pushed the boat out here, and created a huge experience. After all, the Dubai Fountain cost over £176 million. As the sun goes down, loud music is broadcast

SIGHTSEEING

– classical favourites as well as pop and world sounds. And the delicate fountains, constantly bathed in different colours, shoot water high into the night sky in graceful formations and rhythmic movements to the sounds of, say, Whitney Houston's "I Will Always Love You". Kitschy? 🐷 Maybe, but this is a truly impressive, free music event, which most of the thousands of visitors find rather moving. *Sat–Thu 1–1.30pm, Fri 1.30–2pm, daily 6–11pm (every 30 mins) | Dubai Lake | Metro Red Line: Dubai Mall | S5*

23 DUBAI MALL

Shopping mall and leisure complex with around 1,200 shops, the *Dubai Aquarium & Underwater Zoo* (see p. 40), a gold souk, a huge cinema complex, and 160 cafés and restaurants.

Children love the huge *Dubai Ice Rink* on the ground floor. The air temperature in the rink is 20°C, so you'll need a jumper or light jacket. Children also enjoy a visit to *Kidzania (daily 10am–10pm | admission 80 Dh, children up to 16 years 195 Dh | kidzania. ae)*, where they can play at being grown-ups. Here, little ones drive cars, pilot aeroplanes, act as doctors or shop assistants – it's great fun that is taken seriously by the participants. Another unmissable attraction is the 155-million-year-old *Diplodocus longus* from the Jurassic period, known

DOWNTOWN DUBAI

as the "Dubai dinosaur". The skeleton is 24m long and 7.6m high and has found a place among the boutiques and cafés *(Souk Dome/Grand Atrium, ground floor)*. The dinosaur was flown in, in parts, from Wyoming, where it was discovered in 2008. The skeleton is 90 per cent original and intact!

The Dubai Mall operates 12 free shuttle bus routes from all parts of the city to the mall. They run between individual hotels and the bus stop in the Dubai Mall, where timetables are available, and they also work as a free "city tour". *Sun–Wed 10am–midnight, Thu–Sat 10am–1am | Financial Centre Road | from Sheikh Zayed Road, 1st Interchange | thedubaimall.com | Metro Red Line: Dubai Mall | S5*

A futuristic coffee bar in the Dubai Mall

24 DUBAI AQUARIUM & UNDERWATER ZOO ★

Fascinating: watch over 30,000 marine animals, including 400 sharks and rays, in Dubai's aquarium, with its 33x8m viewing window. Visitors walk through a glass tunnel and find themselves surrounded by fluorescent jellyfish, sea anemones and many rare fish. In the *Underwater Zoo* on the second floor you will find exhibitions and smaller aquariums, for example with fish, otters and seals. *Mon–Thu 10am–10pm, Fri Sun 10am–midnight | admission from 169 Dh, children up to 2 years free | Dubai Mall | Sheikh Zayed Road | thedubaiaquarium.com | Metro Red Line: Dubai Mall | S5*

25 GATE VILLAGE

Olive trees and cacti on the plazas and in small gardens within the Dubai Stock Exchange, with shade provided by ten residential towers. The area is all set on a raised platform and is a traffic-free zone. A number of galleries and boutiques have opened their doors here, and people meet in the cafés and restaurants, all with their own outdoor tables, and enjoy the almost Mediterranean flair. The highlight is the Art Deco-style Ritz Carlton

SIGHTSEEING

DIFC. "Work hard, party even harder" seems to be the rule for bankers and stock exchange executives, who meet at the Sunken Garden for a drink by candlelight. Here you can sit outdoors between palm trees and bamboo and enjoy a shisha. *Sheikh Zayed Road | Dubai International Financial Centre (DIFC) | Metro Red Line: Financial Centre | 🚇 S-T5*

INSIDER TIP Evening relaxation

26 JUMEIRAH MOSQUE

The city's largest mosque, and considered by many to be most beautiful when seen from outside, is a domed building that was built from ivory-coloured limestone in 1983. It is flanked by two minarets, and columns bear the weight of the great domed roof. The prayer niche *(mihrab)* is, as everywhere, oriented to Mecca, and to its right is the pulpit *(mimbar)*. The doors of mosques in the emirate normally remain closed to non-believers, but the Jumeirah Mosque is an exception. Here, you can ask anything you want to know about Islam and religious customs in Dubai. *The Sheikh Mohammed Centre for Cultural Understanding* (see p. 31) offers interesting, hour-long guided tours of the mosque *(meeting point Sat–Thu 10am and 2pm in front of the mosque | registration 20 Dh, 30 mins beforehand)*. Men may not wear shorts, and women will be given a black robe *(abaya)* and headscarf. *Jumeirah Road | cultures.ae | Metro Red Line: Trade Centre | ⏱ 60 mins | 🚇 T4*

INSIDER TIP Learn all about Islam

27 ETIHAD MUSEUM

Etihad means unification, and this futuristically styled museum takes you on a journey to the origins of the emirates. The many interactive presentations, with sounds and music, are fascinating. The seven rulers of the individual sheikhdoms are portrayed and some of their personal belongings are also on display. *Daily 10am–8pm | admission 25 Dh | 1 Jumeirah Street | short.travel/dub11 | Metro Red Line: Max | 🚇 T4*

28 DUBAI WATER CANAL ★

Get your trainers out! Following the opening of the Dubai Water Canal and the Boardwalk that runs along both sides of it for use by pedestrians, joggers and cyclists, you can experience the architectural icons and all the dynamics of the city up close.

The 3.2km-long canal – an impressive 80–120m wide and 4–6m deep – links the Business Bay with the Arabian Gulf (Jumeirah Beach). It was the missing link in the 9km-long extension of the Dubai Creek that was completed in earlier years, creating a semicircle of waterway that runs uninterrupted from the Creek through the city to the coast. The *Dubai Ferry (dubai-ferry.com)* stops at nine stations along the Canal and its extension! Even by Dubai's standards, it's almost impossible to beat the views you can see from the ferry – such as the skyline of Downtown Dubai at sunrise.

Are you out and about after sunset? Then look out for the waterfall that descends from Sheikh Zayed Bridge

JUMEIRAH

into the canal and glows in every colour. Incidentally, in addition to several urban motorways, the seawater-filled canal is also crossed by three suspension bridges, marvels of construction, which – sign of the new Dubai! – are also reserved for pedestrians. ▯ *Q–V 4–7*

JUMEIRAH

This is where Dubai makes dreams of sunny beach holidays come true. Several luxurious and beautiful hotels adorn the sandy miles of ⚐ Jumeirah Beach, and the world-famous Burj Al Arab spreads its sail here too.

If you drive south on the long Jumeirah Road, the sea is on your right. In between, concealed in dense greenery and behind palm trees, lie the fine residences of wealthy locals and the palaces of the ruling family. Jumeirah is not only the place of choice to live but also the leisure and pleasure strip for Dubai society: quays for yachts, parks, resorts and hotels whose architecture, furnishings and room prices aim to break records line up next to one another here. And the view offshore is a showcase for Dubai's huge projects: The Palm Jumeirah and The World, man-made islands that create a fantasy Caribbean or South Seas feeling in an Arab city. In Jumeirah no-one gets around on foot: you take a taxi or a tour coach. Luxury limousines queue in front of the Royal Mirage Hotel. Male Dubai residents in white *dishdashas* stroll to the entrance accompanied by their elegant and beautiful wives: the hotels of Jumeirah Beach are popular

The modern Etihad Museum traces the emirates' history

SIGHTSEEING

with some of the richest Emiratis, who are rarely spotted in their home country but can be seen here if anywhere.

29 THE WALK AT JBR

For many Emiratis, this is the hottest promenade in the city. Every evening, the popular strip outside the massive ochre apartment and hotel site of the Jumeirah Beach Residence (JBR) by the sea, fills up with tourists, locals and expats, while others drive up in brand-new Porsches and Ferraris. It's not hard to get rid of your money here: the 1.7km-long walk is flanked by 200 boutiques, cafés and restaurants, all shaded by luscious date palms. Even closer to the sea are the café-restaurants and shops of *The Beach at JBR*, all housed in elegantly designed, hyper-modern and consistently low buildings. A place with a high chill factor: from the soft-as-butter jogging route (special surface coating!) to yoga sessions on the lawn behind the snowy white Jumeirah Beach, you can see a wholly relaxed Dubai here – a real beach metropolis. *Between The Palm Jumeirah and Dubai Marina | Metro Red Line: DMCC | J3*

30 AIN DUBAI

Yet another record! Ain Dubai, the world's highest Ferris wheel at an incredible 260m, can accommodate

JUMEIRAH

This fountain at the Dubai Marina features the obligatory skyscraper backdrop

up to 1,750 passengers in its 48 cars, each being 30m² and glazed all round. It goes without saying that you have a fantastic 360-degree panoramic view of the sea and Dubai from up here. The Ferris wheel stands on its own man-made island, built at the same time, called *Bluewaters Island*, which is connected to the mainland by a bridge. Construction is ongoing, but restaurants and hotels have already opened, as well as a new, ultra-cool lifestyle and shopping district called *The Wharf*. Patio courtyards and walkways, plus an old-style souk, invite you to stroll around, and there are also great views of the Arabian Gulf and the coast. *Temporarily closed at the time of going to print | admission from 130 Dh | next to Palm Jumeirah | aindubai.com | Metro Red Line: DMCC |* J3

31 DUBAI MARINA ★ ▐

Skyscrapers, crazy high-rise buildings, a 4km-long man-made estuary and several yacht harbours: not all of the approximately 200 mega buildings of Dubai Marina have yet been completed, but everyone loves the vibe there. It's the cool combination of water, (mega) yachts and the high-rise skyline. It's brilliant to walk around here in the evening, as the sun goes down, together with people from all over the world – peaceful and

SIGHTSEEING

spectacular. You can get out onto the water from Dubai Marina Promenade (outside the smart Marina Mall), either by Dubai Ferry *(dubai-ferry. com)* or the reasonably priced *Waterbus* (see p. 119). The skyline sparkles in the light, while the water flows in gentle waves.

> **INSIDER TIP**
> **Hubbly-bubbly by the water**
> And finally, you simply must try a shisha outside one of the many terraced cafés.

From October to April the *Marina Market (Wed 10am–10pm, Thu–Sat 10am–11pm)*, with crafts and souvenirs on sale, takes place on the Dubai Marina Mall Promenade. The Dubai Marina is situated – with a direct connection to Sheikh Zayed Road – approx. 25km southwest of the city centre. *Interchange 5 | Metro Red Line: DMCC and Damac |* 📖 *J4*

32 THE PALM JUMEIRAH

The man-made island opposite Jumeirah Beach is in the shape of a palm tree and consists of a "trunk" just over a mile long and 17 "palm fronds", in addition to a breakwater surrounding the island that is known as The Crescent. The fronds house villas costing millions, some of them nevertheless set very close together. Along the trunk is a huge marina with 600 moorings for yachts. Beyond the fronds and just before it reaches The Crescent, the road descends into a tunnel and emerges into daylight again at the luxurious Hotel Atlantis. This is also the last stop of the *Palm Monorail (20 Dh, return 30 Dh | palm-monorail.com)*, which runs from the Gateway Station *(Al Sufouh Road | Metro Red Line: Nakheel)* on the coast by the Royal Mirage Hotel across The Palm Jumeirah to the Crescent.

The ★ *Atlantis (1,539 rooms | £££)* on the Crescent is an opulent pink palace with towers and turrets. The interior is a crazy sight: columns as high as towers are adorned with reliefs of shells, the door handles have the shape of sea horses and dolphins, pictures of octopuses, corals and sea anemones cover the walls. Sadly, admission is reserved to hotel guests. The aquarium *The Lost Chambers (Crescent Road | admission 100 Dh | atlantisthepalm.com)* is populated by fluorescent jellyfish, enormous rays and majestic groupers. Non-residents can visit the *Lost Chambers* – so-called because the aquarium is decorated with ruins as a reminder of the legendary lost city of Atlantis – in a system of tunnels. The hotel also boasts 20 restaurants and *The Aquaventure* water park (see p. 46).

Not afraid of heights? *The View (daily 9am–10pm, last admission 9pm | admission 100 Dh, 4.30–7pm 158 Dh | Nakheel Mall | theviewpalm.ae |* 📖 *K3)*, the glass viewing terrace on the 57th floor of the St Regis Hotel on the Palm's trunk, is better than a helicopter ride: from a height of 240m, you can enjoy a fantastic panoramic view of the island.

Afterwards, it's worth visiting *The Point*, an entertainment district at the tip of the trunk, opposite the Crescent, with plenty of stylish cafés, restaurants and a mile-long stretch of beach. After sunset, you can see the lavishly

JUMEIRAH

Dubai style: sunglasses and the Burj Al Arab

**INSIDER TIP
Fabulous setting**

illuminated water fountains of *The Palm Fountain*, with the Atlantis Hotel behind it, lit up like a fantasy fairy-tale castle. A real dream vision that is hard to beat, even in Dubai.
K–L 1–3

33 AQUAVENTURE

One of the largest and most beautiful water parks in the world, the *Aquaventure* has a fantastic location next to the Atlantis Resort. The slides here are aesthetically styled works of art that ensure big thrills and lots of action. Seven of them start at the top of a 30m-high Mesopotamian-style ziggurat pyramid and some race down a glass tunnel through a shark tank. The Shark Safari (separate ticket) is a top attraction because kids can don oxygen masks and walk on the sea bed between sharks. Younger children love to touch the tame rays in the lagoon at the "cownose feeding". *Daily 10am–6pm | admission (online) from 299 Dh, children from 249 Dh | Crescent Road/Jumeirah Road, Atlantis Resort | The Palm Jumeirah | atlantisthepalm.com | Metro Red Line: Nakheel | 1 day | L1*

34 MADINAT JUMEIRAH

Seen from the air, it looks like a mixture of an Arab village and the city of Venice: large multistorey buildings, but in the traditional Arab style and the colour of brown clay, with added wind towers, delicate wooden balcony grilles, arcades and terraces, bordered by broad watercourses on which electrically powered *abras* glide to and fro.

Madinat Jumeirah (Jumeirah City) is just an illusion. On entering the

SIGHTSEEING

area, you can see there is nothing old and weathered here, and two hotels have been inserted into these artificially created surroundings. Nevertheless, these huge cod-Arabian palaces are well worth seeing and provide a contrast to the rest of Dubai's skyscraper architecture. There is also a replica of a traditional souk, a meeting place for locals to shop and dine at weekends. You can enjoy a great atmosphere in the restaurants and cafés located here, the most beautiful of which have open terraces facing Little Venice, as the development is known. *Jumeirah Road | jumeirah.com | Metro Red Line: Mall of the Emirates | M4*

35 BURJ AL ARAB ★

Raspberry red morphs into grass green and pale turquoise: after dark the Teflon-coated sail of the Burj Al Arab hotel shimmers like a tropical bird and changes colour every 15 minutes. When it opened in 1999, this hotel brought worldwide publicity to Dubai and marked its rise to a top-class holiday destination. The "Arab Tower", which cost around $1.2 billion, was built in the sea on a man-made island 300m from the beach. A self-proclaimed seven-star hotel (officially there are only five categories), it features 202 suites, ranging in size from 169m² to 780m². It is the emblem of the emirate, designed as a stylised dhow sail filled by the wind. The circular platform on the 28th floor is a helipad. Next to the escalators leading from the ground floor into the hotel foyer, jets of water spurt 30m high from the floor, a light show in all the colours of the rainbow lending a

The Aquaventure park also features water landscapes without animals or slides

JUMEIRAH

dazzling aspect to the fountain. If you want to enter the hotel, you need a reservation in one of the restaurants, cafés or bars. For lunch, perhaps, at the *Al Mahara* (the huge aquarium provides a great underwater atmosphere) or the *Al Muntaha*, the "Heavenly View" restaurant at a height of 200m, with a fantastic view of Dubai and the beach. You make a booking by credit card and receive a reservation number to show at the entrance. Or you can book a city tour including a visit to Burj Al Arab or even a special Burj Al Arab tour at a travel agent. *Jumeirah Road | tel. 04 3 01 76 00, 04 3 01 77 77 | jumeirah.com | Metro Red Line: FGB | N3*

36 SKI DUBAI

Some 6,000 tons of snow were used to convert an area the size of three football fields into an indoor skiing arena. With a temperature of -2°C, it's a setting for winter sports fans to enjoy themselves on five downhill slopes. There are tow-lifts and even a proper cabin lift to take visitors back to the top. At a maximum of 400m, the slopes are not particularly long, but the level of difficulty varies. Every night, 30 tons of artificial snow are added, and the meltwater is used to cool the shopping mall where it's located. *Mon–Fri 10am–midnight, Sat/Sun 9am–midnight | admission from 175 Dh incl. skiing suit, from 275 Dh also incl. cabin lift and gloves | Mall of the Emirates | Sheikh Zayed Road, 4th Interchange | theplaymania.com/skidubai | Metro Red Line: Mall of the Emirates | M5*

37 SAFA PARK

The green oasis in the centre of the city is great for jogging – or daydreaming. And since the Dubai Water Canal was created, running through the huge 64-hectare landscaped park, it has undergone a major upgrade, even if there is still some construction work going on. At weekends, expats meet here to play sports or enjoy a barbecue with friends and family. *Sun–Wed 8am–10pm, Thu–Sat until 11pm | admission 3 Dh | Sheikh Zayed Road | Al Safa | Metro Red Line: Business Bay | Q–R 4–5*

38 LA MER

A relaxed beach atmosphere in the style of a 1950s Californian town. In the two bays and along the golden, 2.5km-long sandy beach, you can hire

SIGHTSEEING

sunbeds and parasols. In between, there are plenty of nicely styled shops, restaurants, cafés and food trucks. For children, there is the dune-shaped *Hawa-Hawa* adventure playground. *Sun–Thur 10am–10pm, 10am–midnight Fri/Sat | Jumeirah Beach Road | between Pearl Jumeirah and Darla Island | lamerdubai.ae | Metro: Business Bay | S-T 3-4*

Nevertheless, you don't have to drive far to get the desert feeling. Sand and dusty shrubs fringe the multi-lane roads that lead into the desert. The best way to experience it is to take a taxi, which is not expensive and stress-free, to hire a car, or to book a complete day trip. Among other interesting experiences, you can see the locals' passion for horses demonstrated with a visit to the Meydan Racecourse.

OTHER SIGHTS

From the air it is plain to see that Dubai is a metropolis surrounded by desert. However, within the city limits there is little evidence of this.

39 RAS AL KHOR WILDLIFE & WATERBIRD SANCTUARY

7km from the Dubai Mall / 10 mins by taxi

An area of 6km² at the inland end of the Creek has been established as a nature reserve to protect and preserve the habitat of migratory birds and

Winter sport in the desert at Ski Dubai

OTHER SIGHTS

some species that permanently live here, including a large colony of flamingos and herons. This is one of the few opportunities to enjoy nature in Dubai. Three observation towers were built especially for this purpose; a permanently installed Leica telescope provides unforgettable impressions and a ranger (who is usually present) can answer your questions. With a bit of luck, you might even spot a rare kingfisher! *Sat–Thu 9am–4pm | admission free | Ras Al Khor | Metro Green Line: Creek or Healthcare City (plus a 5km taxi drive) | T7*

40 MEYDAN RACECOURSE

10km from the Dubai Mall / 14 mins by taxi

When there are no races, you can explore this for free. No other racecourse anywhere in the world can match it for its sheer impressiveness and luxury: the grandstand is a vast, ultra-modern construction with space for 60,000 spectators, a five-star hotel, restaurants, an IMAX cinema and a museum (all about horse racing, of course).

INSIDER TIP — Stable tour

Be sure to take part in one of the interesting stable tours. They start with a breakfast buffet at the Meydan Hotel, and then you go to see the horses and their wellness facilities, which include swimming pools and treatment rooms. You'll also get to see the horses training on the racecourse and enter areas that are normally only open to the jockeys. You'll probably be keen to come back for one of the weekly races – that is, of course, unless you can make it to the prestigious Dubai World Cup. *Horse races Nov–Mar Thu/Fri 7pm | admission from 40 Dh | Al Meydan Street | Nad Al Sheba | meydan.ae | 2½ hrs | R7–8*

41 LEGOLAND DUBAI

45km from the Dubai Mall / 30 mins by taxi

Lego has long been a cult in Dubai. This leisure park, which opened in 2016, offers 60 million of the coloured building bricks, various themed "lands" and endless fun for fans of all ages. As the park is aimed at two- to 12-year-olds, the carousels and rides are somewhat on the tame side. *Daily 10am–6pm | admission 295 Dh, children 250 Dh | Sheikh Zayed Road | Jebel Ali | legoland.com/dubai | 0*

42 SHARJAH OLD TOWN

28km from the Dubai Mall / 30 mins by taxi

Not far from the superlatives of Dubai is the UNESCO-protected old town of Sharjah, capital of the conservative neighbouring emirate of the same name (no alcohol is served anywhere in Sharjah). The restored wind-tower houses and palaces of the car-free *Heritage and Arts Area* are home to around two dozen great museums *(sharjahmuseums.com)*, all of which can be visited for just a few dirhams. The *Sharjah Calligraphy Museum (Sun–Thu 8am–8pm, Fri 4–8pm | admission 10 Dh | between Al Boorj Av. and Corniche Road)* and the *Sharjah Art Museum (Sat–Thu 8am–8pm, Fri 4–8pm | admission free)* in the impressive Bait Al Serkal in the Arts Area are

SIGHTSEEING

well worth a visit. Also outstanding is the *Museum of Islamic Civilization (Sat–Thu 10am–6pm | admission 10 Dh | Majarrah Waterfront)*, where the exhibits, some of which are thousands of years old, are complemented by extremely stylish presentation.

> **INSIDER TIP**
> **Time for a chai**
>
> You'll feel like you're in a time capsule in the coffee house in Souk Al Arsah, which is bathed in semi-darkness. In this meeting place, where old men come to chat, black tea is served with cardamom, milk and sugar.

After your refreshment, let the books, quirky antiques, kaftans and pashmina scarves tempt you into the small shops. You can bargain here, sometimes getting a third off the original price. 🕮 0

43 BIG RED

60km from Downtown Dubai / 45 mins by car on the E44

The last rays of the sun bathe the 100m-high desert dunes of Al Hamar in shades of gold and deep red. Late afternoon is a great time of day to visit, but don't come expecting a peaceful desert atmosphere. There's usually a lot going on here at any time of day: a range of hire companies have quad bikes, motorbikes with huge, balloon-like tyres on which you can race through the sand and up and down the dunes (½ hr for approx. 100 Dh). A camel ride is more leisurely, more environmentally sound and cheaper, too. Make sure that you agree the price before you get on the camel (½ hr for approx. 50 Dh). 🕮 0

If you don't fancy this, you can also explore Big Red on a camel

EATING & DRINKING

Go out for a meal in Dubai, and you'll have the whole world at your feet, because the restaurant scene here is probably more diverse than anywhere else on the globe. It's also highly creative, exciting and innovative.

Dubai has long been the culinary hotspot of the region, a paradise for food lovers; it's hardly surprising in a city where over 100 nations live check by jowl. This is where cardamom meets coriander, French crêpes meet sushi, and Kentucky steaks meet Indian dahl. In Dubai, cooking traditions from all over the world come together.

> You'll find all the venues in this chapter on the pull-out map 🗺

When it comes to food, you'll be spoilt for choice in Dubai

Hungry? You can eat here around the clock, and on wildly different budgets. You can dine in upmarket hotel restaurants or temples of gastronomy managed by star chefs, and you can even experience local cuisine in a desert tent. Or you can eat at fast-food outlets in shopping malls and small Indian and Arab restaurants run by expats, or in the cluster of little spots in Bastakiya, Dubai's old quarter near the Creek.

WHERE TO EAT IN DUBAI

MARCO POLO HIGHLIGHTS

★ **AYAMNA**
Arabic *meze* on a palm tree-lined terrace at the iconic Atlantis, the Palm Hotel
➤ p. 60

★ **BAYT AL WAKEEL**
Watch the *abras* go by as you enjoy Arabic dishes on a terrace overlooking the Creek ➤ p. 29, p. 61

★ **PIERCHIC**
The perfect spot for a proposal: a romantic location on a terrace on stilts set in the sea ➤ p. 64

★ **FRYING PAN ADVENTURES**
Discover culinary highlights on this tour through Dubai's alleyways and avenues ➤ p. 67

MADINAT JUMEIRAH
Stylish speciality restaurants and cafés in Dubai's Little Venice

JBR WALK
Expats meet in fashionable locations by the beach to enjoy Mediterranean food

THE WORLD

Ayamna ★

ARABIAN GULF

THE PALM JUMEIRAH

Pierchic ★

AL SUFOUH

Sharaf DG Ⓜ

King Salman Bin Abdulaziz Al Saud Street

DUBAI INTERNET CITY

DUBAI MARINA

Ⓜ DMCC

EMIRATES HILLS

JUMEIRAH ISLANDS

Sheikh Zayed Road

Garn Al Sabkha Street

CAFÉS

Ever tried a camelcino? Admittedly, a cappuccino made with camel's milk may not be to everybody's taste, but it is supposed to be healthy. And that is why you will now find camel's milk and camel's milk yoghurt in every supermarket today – and included in breakfast buffets everywhere.

When it comes to new culinary trends, Dubai is right out in front. As well as street food and a growing number of vegetarian establishments, Emiratis and Western expats alike are increasingly seeking out restaurants that use organic products and fair-trade ingredients. And customers like it if any perishable food that is left at the end of the day is passed on to charitable organisations.

There are numerous Indian restaurants in Dubai, and they rarely disappoint. Everyone thinks they know dahl, but prepared Dubai-style – cooked for hours with coconut milk and freshly crushed spices – and served with tandoori chicken, it's heavenly.

There are many Arab restaurants too – usually serving Lebanese cuisine – of every price category. The ones in Deira and Bur Dubai are also often visited by migrant workers from other Arab countries.

Can you find local Emirati cuisine in melting pot Dubai? You might have to search around, but it's worth the effort, and when *khameer*, the traditional bread that is made with date syrup rather than sugar and which is served with herbs and melted cheese, is on the menu, then you simply have to go for it. The high-calorie desserts, flavoured with saffron, rose water and plenty of nuts, are also notable.

Don't miss out on the national snack *shawarma*, thinly sliced chicken or beef from a rotating grill, stuffed into pitta bread with salad and tomatoes like a kebab and sold everywhere. However, the traditional *shawarma* stalls now have competition: locals queue up at the silver Airstream bus on Kite Beach to buy miniburgers from SALT. And a vintage Citroen H draws crowds when *Ghaf Kitchen (ghafkitchen.com)* offers finger sandwiches and British party food at festivals and events. Mexican tacos from a brightly coloured bus are sold by *Calle Tacos (calletacos.ae)*, which is constantly changing its location. There is no need to worry about eating from street stalls in Dubai, as all the restaurants and snack stalls are run along hygienic lines and meet basic standards. So the good news is that in Dubai you can have a good dinner for 10 Dh or, if you prefer, for 1,000 Dh.

> **INSIDER TIP: Star cuisine at half price**
>
> Even in upmarket restaurants, you only pay half price (or a little more) if you use online coupons for "special deals", whether for lunch or dinner, seafood buffets, Friday brunch or dining events, which give 30 to 50 per cent discounts *(groupon.ae/coupons/dubai/restaurants)*.

CAFÉS

1 LEVEL 43 SKY LOUNGE

Unforgettable: here, at a height of 155m, you can enjoy a "Sky-High Tea"

EATING & DRINKING

A huge variety of drinks is on offer at the Level 43 Sky Lounge

with sandwiches, cake, tea and a glass of champagne – plus, of course, the fabulous views. When you book, please remember to ask for the "Downtown Dubai view" if you want to see the Burj Khalifa and the Opera House. *Sky-High Tea daily noon–6pm, lounge until 2am Hotel Four Points by Sheraton Sheikh Zayed Road | tel. 056 4 14 22 13| level43lounge.com | Metro Red Line: Financial Centre | ££ | Jumeirah | T5*

2 BRUNCH & CAKE
Refresh yourself after a swim with delicious cheesecake and doughnuts with raspberry and cream filling, plus a wide selection of speciality coffees and teas – while looking out over the pink Atlantis Hotel! *Daily 9am–11pm | The Pointe | Palm Jumeirah Road, Palm Jumeirah | tel. 04 5 80 04 37 | £ | Jumeirah | L2*

3 EMPORIO ARMANI CAFFÈ
After shopping in the luxury boutiques of the Mall of the Emirates, you can meet here under the glass dome for a chai latte or a quick espresso, or something to eat. The cappuccino foam comes with a golden Armani logo, but the pasta dishes taste like they do in Tuscany. *Daily 10am–2am | Mall of the Emirates | Fashion Avenue | Metro Red Line: Mall of the Emirates | ££ | Al-Barsha | M5*

4 KEVENTERS
A hit in India since 1920 and now also in the trendy beach quarter of La Mer. This small shop is one of the best places for ice cream, with the butterscotch milkshake and the Sundae Dark Conspiracy being big hits. *Daily 10am–midnight | Unit 207, La Mer Central | keventers.ae | Metro Red Line: Business Bay 7 | Jumeirah | T4*

CAFÉS

Coffee, prepared the Arabic way

5 LIME TREE CAFÉ
The front terrace of this villa is a rendezvous for Europeans who meet here for a breakfast-time latte macchiato with crispy croissants, or the lunchtime snacks, salads, cakes and soups. There is a huge choice of freshly pressed juices. *Daily 7.30am–6pm | Jumeirah Road | near the Jumeirah Mosque | tel. 04 3 25 63 25 | thelimetreecafe.com | Metro Red Line: Emirates Towers | Downtown Dubai | ▭ T4*

6 KAVA & CHAI
If you just want a coffee you can go elsewhere. In the Mall of the Emirates branch of this small chain with just three cafés, you'll have to pull out your mobile phone: with this degree of styling, the Instagram account is as happy about your cool photos as the caffe mocha is about the dark chocolate. Various teas, creatively topped croissants and chic salads round off the menu. *Daily 8am–midnight | Sheikh Zayed Road | kavaandchai.com | Metro Red Line: Mall of the Emirates | Al Barsha | ▭ M5*

7 ARABIAN TEA HOUSE
A typical Arabic café-restaurant with a patio, located in an old, lavishly refurbished wind-tower house. Lovely decorations, benches, flowering bougainvillea and attentive service create a cosy atmosphere. ==Take a break here during the lunchtime heat when life slows down. The atmosphere is cosy and chilled, the prices are moderate.== Order lamb, houmous and oriental salads. The small adjoining shop sells individual jewellery and art. *Daily 7.30am–10pm | 63 Al Fahidi Street | tel. 04 3 53 50 71 | Metro Green Line: Al Sharaf | Bastakiya | ▭ V4*

INSIDER TIP Siesta under an awning

8 RAW COFFEE COMPANY
Everything is about coffee here, and – naturally – you'll find it hard to get a better coffee anywhere else. But in addition to that, all sorts of expat groups gather here among the sacks of coffee and sales counters, which will leave you feeling less like a tourist, and instead (almost) as if you belonged in the city. *Mon–Fri 7.30am–7pm, Sat/Sun 7am–8.30pm | Warehouse 10 | 7a Street, corner 4a*

EATING & DRINKING

TODAY'S SPECIALS

Starters

FATTOUSH
A green salad with toasted pitta-bread croutons

ACHAR
Vegetables marinated in vinegar and garlic: cauliflower, olives, onions, peppers

BABAGANOUSH
Purée of aubergine and tomato, with onions, parsley, salt and sesame oil

MOUTABEL
Baked puréed aubergines with sesame paste and olive oil

Main courses

THEREEF LAHM
Lamb with vegetables and potatoes

FOUL MESDAMES
Fava beans in a spicy tomato sauce with onions and vegetables, served with warm pitta bread *(khoubiz)*

MAKBUS
Fried lamb with rice

HAMMOUR
Bass from the Arabian Gulf (grilled or fried)

SHISH TAWOUK
Marinated chicken pieces grilled on a skewer

Desserts

MEHALABIYA
Pistachio milk custard

BAKLAVA
Dessert of flaky pastry, almonds, pistachios and cardamom, soaked in honey

MUHAMMAR
Sweet rice with raisins, cardamom, rose water and almonds

Mocktails

G&J
Freshly pressed grapefruit juice with mineral water, lemon, palm sugar and a pinch of sea salt

BLACK CINNAMON MOJITO
Lime juice, water, mint leaves and fresh blackcurrants, served with a cinnamon stick

MILK & HONEY
Fresh pineapple juice, cardamom syrup, coconut milk and honey on crushed ice

Street | tel. 04 3 39 54 74 | rawcoffeecompany.com | Metro Red Line: Noor Bank | £ | *Al Manara, Al Quoz* | 📖 *05*

🟩 TOM & SERG

Loft atmosphere and industrial chic. Many say the espresso at Al Quoz is better than anywhere else, and so is the all-day brunch. Try caramel French toast, Cubano sandwich or tuna tacos: the food served by Tom from Australia and Serg from Spain is just fabulous. *Mon–Fri 8am–4pm, Sat/Sun 8am–6pm | Al Joud Center | 15A Street, Al Quoz Industrial Area | tel. 056 4 74 68 12 | tomandserg.com | Metro Red Line: Noor Bank | £ | Al Quoz | 📖 O5*

ARABIC

🟩 AL BAIT AL QADEEM

After strolling through the souks, head for this historic town house a few blocks away. The Arabic-style rooms and large inner courtyard with an awning only fill up at a late hour.

INSIDER TIP — Some like it hot

Be careful when ordering: "spicy" means *really* hot here. The menu includes kebabs and classics of Lebanese-Persian cuisine as well as chicken biryani and fish curry. Fresh king coconut water and pomegranate juice are served as an aperitif. *Daily 8am–10pm | Al Ahmadiya Street | tel. 04 2 25 61 11 | albaitalqadeem.com | Metro Green Line: Al Ras | £ | Deira | 📖 V4*

🟩 AWTAR

Hot and cold meze dishes – rich and delicious, and best shared – are served here. Follow your meze selection with meat dishes. The kebabs grilled at the table and served with delicious flatbread warm from the oven are particularly recommended.

INSIDER TIP — For night owls

Don't book too early because the atmosphere doesn't really hot up until after midnight, when the musicians have tuned up and the belly dancer really gets going. *Tue–Sun 7.30pm–3am | Grand Hyatt | Al Qataiyat Road | tel. 04 3 17 22 22 | hyattrestaurants.com | Metro Green Line: Al Jadaf | ££ | Umm Hurair 2 | 📖 U6*

🟩 AYAMNA ⭐

The most romantic of Dubai's many Lebanese restaurants. Inside it is all exotic Arabian glamour, with the special ambience of the Atlantis Hotel. Flickering lanterns and rustling palm fronds conjure up an irresistible atmosphere on the terrace. Excellent red wines and oriental pastries. *Daily 6–11pm | The Palm Atlantis | tel. 04 4 26 26 26 | atlantisthepalm.com | £££ | The Palm Jumeirah | 📖 K-L1*

🟩 ASHWAQ CAFETERIA 🚩

Dubai without *shawarma* is like London without sandwiches! Here you can get these tasty and cheap snacks in crispy flatbread, with a well-seasoned yoghurt sauce and hearty meat for on the go. The mutton sandwiches, and chicken and prawn paninis (5–7 Dh) also taste great. *Daily 11am–midnight | Sikkat Al Khail Road | opposite the Deira Palace*

EATING & DRINKING

Hotel | tel. 04 2 26 11 64 | Metro Green Line: Al Ras | £ | Deira | 🕮 V4

14 BAYT AL WAKEEL ⭐ 🚩
This traditional merchant's house with its two-storey arcades serves snacks and Arabic dishes, including delicious fish specialities, on a large wooden terrace above the Creek. *Daily noon–midnight | Bur Dubai Souk (between the abra docks) | Bur Dubai | tel. 04 3 53 05 30 | Metro Green Line: Al Ghubaiba | ££ | Bastakiya | 🕮 V4*

15 LOCAL HOUSE
Dishes from the emirates are the strength of this restaurant, which serves authentic regional cuisine. There's even a camel burger on the menu. *Daily noon–11pm | 65 Al Fahidi Street | tel. 04 3 54 07 05 | Metro Green Line: Al Fahidi | ££ | Bastakiya | 🕮 V4*

16 AL NAFOORAH
Al-Nafoorah is still regarded as the best Lebanese restaurant in Dubai thanks to its excellent cooking and large array of warm and cold starters *(meze)*. The classic dish here is *kibbeh nayyehi*, minced lamb with bulgur wheat and mint. The styling of the restaurant is also great, transporting you to the palace of an Ottoman sultan. Arabian Nights à la Dubai! *Daily 1–11pm | Jumeirah Zabeel Saray/Crescent Road | tel. 04 4 53 04 44 | jumeirah.com | Metro Red Line: Nakheel | £££ | The Palm Jumeirah | 🕮 J3*

17 RAVI 🐷
Whether you come here for breakfast and order potato paratha and chai, or for dinner and try the chicken biryani, you'll find authentically Pakistani dishes, delicious and excellent value!

At the Ashwaq cafeteria they cook up delicious and inexpensive food on the rotary grill

FISH RESTAURANTS

Daily 5am–2am | Al Dhiyafa Road | tel. 04 3 31 53 53 | Metro Red Line: Trade Centre | £ | Al Satwa | T4

18 SHABESTAN
The best Persian restaurant in the city: opulent furnishings and traditional Iranian cuisine with live music in the background. For a starter try houmous and pitta bread, then rice flavoured with raisins and saffron to go with tender lamb, followed by ice cream perfumed with rose water. *Daily 12.30–3.15pm and 7.30–11.30pm | Hotel Radisson Blu, 2nd floor | Baniyas Road | tel. 04 2 05 70 33 | short.travel/dub6 | Metro Green Line, Red Line: Union | £££ | Deira | V4*

19 SHEIKH MOHAMMED CENTRE FOR CULTURAL UNDERSTANDING

INSIDER TIP Authentic breakfast

The centre in Bastakiya serves typical delicacies that you won't get in any hotel: *lugimat* (balls of dough with date syrup), *bilaleet* (sweet noodles), *houmous nakki* (chickpea soup) and *kobs khameer* (bread). At the *Cultural Lunch (Mon–Thu 1pm | 130 Dh)*, spicy chicken, fish and rice specialities are on the menu. *Tel. 03 53 66 66 | cultures.ae | Al Musallah Street | Metro Green Line: Al Fahidi | Bastakiya | V4*

FISH RESTAURANTS

20 BU QTAIR
This basic fish restaurant near the Burj Al Arab looks like a slightly shabby

---

HOMEMADE

LOCALLY GROWN
Raspberries from Perigord and mineral water from Tuscany? No longer necessary. The Europeans who work here are not alone in thinking that it's better and more environmentally friendly to eat local produce rather than food imported from abroad. The Emiratis are also changing their thinking, and realising that local, organically grown fruit and vegetables are always better than products that are flown in. People come to one of the three weekly *Ripe Markets (ripeme.com)* for excellent organic, farm-fresh products, and also to listen to local musicians, meet artists and artisans, and interact with others.

EATING & DRINKING

container. Don't be too quick to judge, but join the queue, choose fish or prawns and wait to be shown to an outdoor table. It's not every day that you'll be served something so delicious, and certainly not in such a relaxed and friendly atmosphere! *Daily 11.30am–11.30pm | 79 2b Street | Jumeirah 5 (off Jumeirah Road) | tel. 055 7 05 21 30 | Metro Red Line: Noor Bank | £–££) |* Umm Suqeim *| ⌘ O4*

21 THE FISH MARKET

This fish restaurant has been renowned in Dubai for three decades, and it has a simple recipe for success: diners choose the tiger prawns, fish steaks or langoustines displayed on an open counter between bamboo and orchids themselves, then select the vegetables and the method of cooking (wok, grilled or fried). Then they wait for the meal to be prepared while enjoying a view of the Creek and a Thai cocktail. *Daily noon–11pm | Hotel Radisson Blu, 2nd floor | Baniyas Road | tel. 04 2 05 70 33 | short.travel/dub7 | Metro Green Line, Red Line: Union | £££ |* Deira *| ⌘ V4*

22 GOLDEN FISH

A seafood platter or *hammour* (grouper), plus Arabic *fatoush* salad! Take a seat right beside the Creek and watch the passing *abras* and "water buses". This is the original and lively Dubai, rather than the glamorous version. *Daily 10am–1am | 3A Street | tel. 04 3 27 73 55 | Metro Green Line: Al Ghubaiba | £ |* Bur Dubai *| ⌘ V4*

Sheikh Mohammed Centre: get to know the local food culture

FOOD TRUCKS

23 PIERCHIC ★

The most romantic place to eat sea bass or prawns is beneath the stars: a wooden jetty leads to a terrace built on stilts in the middle of the sea, with a stunning view of the illuminated Burj Al Arab and Madinat Jumeirah. *Daily 12.30–3pm and 6.30–11.30pm | Madinat Jumeirah | Jumeirah Road | tel. 04 3 66 67 05 | jumeirah.com | Metro Red Line: FGB | £££ | Pierchic | M4*

24 SALMONTINI

You're probably more likely to eat salmon on a Norwegian fjord than on the Arabian Gulf. Nevertheless, it's worth coming here for smoked heart of salmon, salmon tartar or salmon with pesto – the name of the restaurant tells you what to expect. For dessert try the apple pie or pomegranate sorbet. The entertainment while you eat is a view of the indoor ski hall. *Daily noon–10.30pm | The Mall of the Emirates, Level 1 (West End) | tel. 04 341 02 22 | salmontini.com | Metro Red Line: Mall of the Emirates | £££ | Al Barsha | M5*

FOOD TRUCKS

25 LAST EXIT

Last exit E11! ==A dozen historic trucks and Airstreams create an atmosphere that is just like 1960s USA.==  **INSIDER TIP: A 1960s feast** Whether they've ordered Tex-Mex, Thai prawns or pistachio ice cream, people sit on picnic benches to eat their food and chat to other guests. *Sheikh Zayed Road E11/Interchange 11 | tel. 04 3 17 39 99 | lastexit.ae | £ | Jebel Ali Hills | 0*

At the Pierchic, the views may overshadow your food

EATING & DRINKING

FUSION FOOD

26 AL DAWAAR

If you get a table by the window, all of Dubai is at your feet, as this restaurant on the 25th floor of the Hyatt Regency Hotel rotates 360° every hour. The Arabic and European buffet is so exquisite that you will need at least two full rotations to try all you want. À la carte orders are also taken. It's highly recommended to book a window table! *Daily 6.30–11.30pm, Sat/Sun also 12.30–4pm | Hyatt Regency Hotel | Al Khaleej Road | tel. 04 2 09 69 14 | short.travel/dub8 | Metro Green Line: Palm Deira | £££ | Deira | ⌑ W4*

Fine fish at Al Dawaar

27 THE CROFT

Beef Wellington, gratinated cheese on toast with pears, or a classic

Indian-British curry: expats and locals alike meet here to enjoy a beer on the modern-style terrace overlooking Dubai Marina. The dishes, which are mainly made with organically grown ingredients, are extremely varied and hail from locations ranging from Barbados to Australia. The diversity of Commonwealth cuisine inspires the buffet at the Brunch Nation Evening every Saturday. *Daily 4–11pm, Sun from 12.30pm | Dubai Marriott Harbour Hotel | King Salman Bin Abdulaziz Al Saud Street | tel. 04 3 19 40 00 | marriottharbourdubai dining.com | £ | Dubai Marina | ⌑ K4*

28 KYO

Sushi and sashimi, wagyu and Angus steaks: the cooking here is ambitious, and there's the added attraction of a view of the Atlantis opposite; you can see the water fountains dancing after sunset, too. The lounge serves great cocktails, accompanied by house and electro music. *Daily 3pm–midnight |*

INDIAN & CHINESE

Arva Ahmed's Frying Pan Adventures promises you culinary discoveries

The Pointe West Marina 04 | tel. 04 5 57 51 82 | kyorestaurant.com | Monorail Atlantis Aquaventure | ££ | The Palm Jumeirah | ▥ K1–2

29 MANHATTAN GRILL
Business people meet here at lunchtime for the three-course set menu, which is very reasonably priced. Fish and lamb specialities feature heavily on the menu. Strawberry crème brûlée is recommended for dessert. *Sun–Fri 12.30–3pm and 7–11.30pm | Grand Hyatt Hotel | Trade Centre Road | tel. 04 3 17 22 21 | hyattrestaurants.com | Metro Green Line: Healthcare City | ££–£££ | Bur Dubai | ▥ U–V6*

30 SHAKESPEARE & CO.
The "Victorian elegance", as the owners describe the style of furnishing here, is a wonderful mix of the fantasy worlds of *Mary Poppins* and *Alice in Wonderland*. The café serves coffee and cakes as well as salads and sandwiches, with shisha service outdoors. *Daily 7am–midnight | Sheikh Zayed Road | Al Saqr Business Tower | tel. 04 3 31 17 57 | shakespeare-and-co.com | Metro Red Line: Emirates Towers | £–££ | Trade Centre | ▥ S–T5*

INDIAN & CHINESE

31 AAPPA KADAI
Typical southern Indian *appams* (pancakes shaped like bowls) are served here with veggie masalas and different curries as a set lunch, but you'll also find north Indian tandoori dishes and specialities from the Malabar coast such as beef coconut fry and fried pomfrets. *Daily 9am–midnight | 16 Street | tel. 05 3 74 75 00 | Metro Green Line: Gold Souq | £ | Deira | ▥ W4*

32 ASHA'S
Located for over two decades in the elegant Wafi Centre (as well as in the Mall of the Emirates), Asha's is part of an internationally successful restaurant group that celebrates "contemporary Indian cooking". Delights include *amritsari machli* (fried grouper bites) as a starter, followed by kebabs from the clay oven and a vegetarian biryani rice dish. *Sat–Thu noon–11pm, Fri 2-11pm | Pyramids, Wafi City | tel. 04 3 24 41 00 | ashasrestaurants.com/*

EATING & DRINKING

dubai | Metro Green Line: Healthcare City | ££ | Oud Metha | U6

33 GOVINDA'S
All-vegetarian dishes, including excellent dhal (lentil curry) with spinach; freshly pressed juices are the perfect accompaniment. *Sat–Thu noon–3pm and 7pm–midnight, Fri from 1.30pm | Trade Centre Road, behind the Regent Palace Hotel | tel. 04 3 96 00 88 | mygovindas.com | Metro Red Line: ADCB | £ | Al Karama | V5*

34 KARACHI DARBAR
This restaurant, which is frequented by Asian migrant workers, serves up Pakistani and Indian meals at very low prices. After dark the tables are set up outside. *Daily 5am–2am | Karama Shopping Complex | tel. 04 334 72 72 | karachidarbargroup.com | Metro Red Line: ADCB | £ | Al Karama | U5*

35 SHANG PALACE
If it's too hot to go outside, you can enjoy authentic Cantonese cuisine in elegantly styled surroundings. The large selection of dim sum, including Chinese dumplings filled with shrimps and meat, steamed or deep-fried, is impressive. Follow it by Peking duck with your choice of ingredients and sauces. *Daily noon–3pm and 7pm–midnight | Hotel Shangri-La | Sheikh Zayed Road | tel. 04 4 05 27 03 | Metro Red Line: Financial Centre | ££ | Downtown Dubai | S5*

INSIDER TIP Dumpling heaven

36 SIND PUNJAB
Windows are decorated with fairy lights and plastic flowers: it might look kitsch on the outside, but in culinary terms, this place is the tops. The Indian-Pakistani restaurant is excellent value, and every single dish is delicious. A good idea (if there are two of you) is to order several vegetarian curries, plus chapatis or butter naan, and a bowl of raita. Or simply point to the dishes that the Indian families at other tables are eating. *Daily 8am–11pm | Bukaz Building | Al Esbij Street (off Fahidi Street) | tel. 04 3 52 50 58 | Metro Green Line: Al Ghubaiba or Al Fahidi | £ | Meena Bazar, Bur Dubai | V4*

TOURS

37 FRYING PAN ADVENTURES ★
Are you curious and do you enjoy making culinary discoveries? If so, this tour is for you. Enjoying walking is also helpful because sisters Arva and Farina Ahmed take their guests through the back streets of Old Dubai. You'll walk around 4km, stopping at little tea shops and tiny exotic restaurants to sample Yemeni, Lebanese or north Indian finger food (usually standing up). It's stimulating, delicious and exciting. Just book online and be at the meeting place on time! *Middle Eastern Food Pilgrimage | 425 Dh | meeting point: bicycle racks by exit 2 of the Al Rigga Metro station, Al Rigga Road, opposite the Diva Gents beauty salon | tel. 056 4 71 82 44 | fryingpanadventures.com | Al Rigga | W5*

SHOPPING

Shopping in Dubai is a mixture of seduction, exaggeration and illusion. In fact, those in the know call this place "Do Buy". In this glittering city, advertising is taken to extremes, as is the range of goods on offer. But from the traditional souks to the mega-malls, it's great fun to shop here and max out your credit cards.

Dubai's "nothing is impossible" ethos is ever-present in the world of shopping. Shopping malls? Here, they're veritable temples of consumption, created as a kind of wonder of the world that have

You'll find all the venues in this chapter on the pull-out map

You can spend a whole holiday in the Mall of the Emirates

now achieved the status of tourist attractions in their own right. Variety and entertainment are guaranteed in the spectacular malls. In the booming early years, people were amazed by the real palm trees and man-made water courses, or an Olympic-sized ice-skating rink. Today, it takes a ten-million-litre aquarium or an integrated ski slope and toboggan run to impress visitors. Very different but just as much of an attraction is the world's biggest gold bazaar, where trade is carried on much as it has been since the early 1900s.

WHERE TO SHOP IN DUBAI

MARCO POLO HIGHLIGHTS

★ **DUBAI MALL**
The world's second-largest mall draws customers with luxury shops and the Dubai Aquarium ➤ p. 76

★ **GOLD SOUK**
All that glitters here really is gold. You can buy high-quality jewellery at low prices in Dubai ➤ p. 78

★ **SOUK AL BAHAR**
Arab design in an unrivalled location. Come here for high-class souvenirs
➤ p. 78

THE WORLD

ARABIAN GULF

MALL OF THE EMIRATES
Prepare to be amazed – and with integrated ski slopes, too

THE PALM JUMEIRAH

AL SUFOUH

King Salman Bin Abdulaziz Al Saud Street

DUBAI INTERNET CITY

JBR WALK
Dubai's equivalent of Miami's Ocean Drive: elegant and hip

DUBAI MARINA   EMIRATES HILLS

Ⓜ DMCC

JUMEIRAH ISLANDS

Sheikh Zayed Road

Garn Al Sabkha Street

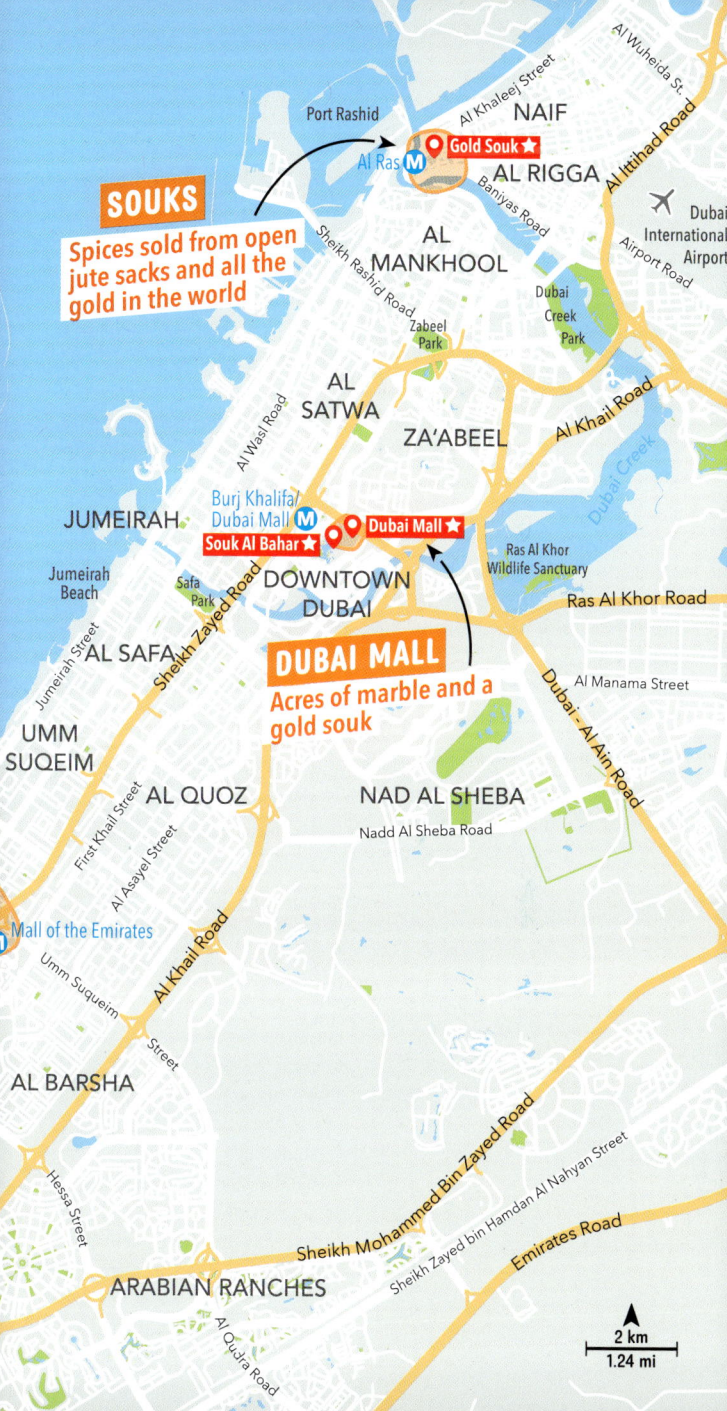

BOOKS

There is even an annual festival dedicated to shopping: the legendary *Dubai Shopping Festival (Jan/Feb | mydsf.ae, see p. 96)* goes on for a whole month. Feels like an end-of-season sale? Not at all – more like a euphoric shopping marathon, with almost all of the city's shops and boutiques enticing visitors with discounts of up to 70 per cent. The charged mood is further enhanced by a fabulous cultural programme of music, fashion shows and fireworks.

Dubai's souks are an entirely different kind of experience. The rule in the alleyways and streets of the traditional bazaars is that you have to haggle! One gram of the finest saffron and the vanilla pods for 50 Dh? Smile, and name a smaller amount. And before you take your leave, the seller will have thrown in some fragranced oil as well.

However, please be aware that, although the whole world comes to Dubai to shop, and even though the emirate does not levy any taxes on goods, branded goods are now more expensive than in Europe, partly due to the exchange rate.

BOOKS

1 KINOKUNIYA

Nothing but books? Far from it. Founded by a Japanese company, this bookstore in the *Dubai Mall* (see p. 76) has a selection that is simply amazing. There are the most beautiful picture and art books on Dubai and the desert, as well as really affordable paperbacks, international magazines and amusing souvenirs. It also has its own café. *Sun–Thu 10am–6.30pm | Level 2, Dubai Mall | Metro Red Line: Dubai Mall | Downtown Dubai | ☲ S5*

DESIGN & FASHION

2 CITY WALK

This new, elegantly styled pedestrian zone, which stretches over several blocks, is home to a huge range of fashion boutiques. Alongside the usual suspects in the middle and upper price segments (Diane von Furstenberg, Hilfiger, Armani Exchange, and so on), you'll find young, unconventional labels such as Demobaza (futuristic designer goods) and Being Human, the fashion label of the charitable Khan Foundation founded by Bollywood star Salman

---

WHERE TO START?

The shops selling the famous designers are situated on Fashion Avenue in the **Dubai Mall**, the world's second-largest mall, which you can reach by taking the Metro to the Dubai Mall stop (Red Line). In this modern shopping nirvana you will also find electronic goods and the latest young fashion. For an Eastern bazaar atmosphere try the **Souk Al Bahar** opposite, where high-quality Arab souvenirs are sold. If you enjoy browsing in traditional markets, the **Bur Dubai Souk** between the *abra* stops on Creek Bur Dubai is also a good option.

SHOPPING

Come to look: it doesn't get much more luxurious than on Fashion Avenue

Khan. *Daily 10am–10pm | Al Safa Street | citywalk.ae | Metro Red Line: Dubai Mall | Downtown Dubai | S4*

3 FASHION AVENUE

What do Hermes and Cavalli, Marc Jacobs and D&G, Blumarine and Gucci all have in common? A flagship store on Fashion Avenue, the most exclusive area of the *Dubai Mall* (see p. 39, p. 76). With around 80 luxury stores, even just window shopping here is exciting. Then there's the high-end styling, making billionaires from everywhere from Korea to Mongolia feel completely at home. *Ground & First Floor, Dubai Mall | Metro Red Line: Dubai Mall | Downtown Dubai | S5*

4 GARDEROBE

Blazers by Chanel and D&G, a Balenciaga bag, a Hermès Birkin bag: everything that owner Micha Maatouk has on display in her second-hand boutique, among the leather sofas and Baroque mirrors of her villa, has class. And there are always bargains to be found, such as Chanel ballerinas for only US$170 and a vintage Mulberry bag for under US$220. It's worth browsing online: the website shows what's currently on offer, ideal for planning your visit here. And if you buy several items, there's an even bigger discount. *Daily 10am–7pm | Villa 1224, Al Wasl Road | Umm Suqeim 1 | garderobe.ae | Metro Red Line: Noor Bank | Jumeirah | P4*

INSIDER TIP: Be prepared

5 KARAMA MARKET

"Ugg" boots for 80 Dh, a "Ralph Lauren" shirt for 100 Dh: there is a wide range of fake designer T-shirts, jeans, leather bags and imitation wristwatches on offer here. Of course, this is not legal in Dubai either, but you can have a

ART

look! The usual luxury brands are represented, although some of the copies are not particularly convincing. *Sat–Thu 9am–10pm, Fri 9am–11am and 4–10pm | Metro Red Line: ADCB |* Bur Dubai *|* ▥ *U5*

ART

6 MAJLIS GALLERY

Lithographs, photographs, paintings, sculptures and much more. Here you'll find changing displays of works by local artists and international painters who have some artistic connection to the region. *Sat–Thu 10am–6pm | 67 Al Fahidi Street | themajlisgallery.com | Metro Green Line: Al Fahidi |* Bur Dubai *|* ▥ *V4*

7 THE THIRD LINE

Dubai's most famous gallery, in a plain-looking building, represents contemporary Arab and Iranian artists. The star of the local scene is Iranian artist Farhad Moshiri, whose works seem to viewers like a synthesis of Arab calligraphy and the neo-Baroque. *Sat–Thu 10am–7pm | Warehouse H78 & H80, Street 8/Alserkal Av., Sheikh Zayed Road, Exit 43 | Al Quoz 1 | the thirdline.com | Metro Red Line: FGB |* Al Quoz *|* ▥ *O5*

8 XVA GALLERY

In this renovated house with a wind tower, most of the changing exhibitions show works by modern Arab artists. Shop and café attached. *Daily 7am–10pm | Al Fahidi Street, behind Majlis Gallery | xvagallery.com | Metro Green Line: Al Fahidi |* Bastakiya *|* ▥ *V4*

MARKETS

9 DUBAI FLEA MARKET

You can get hold of shishas for half price, second-hand books, pre-loved designer clothes and English china if you are out and about early. Unfortunately, the flea market only takes place during the winter months. Locations and dates can be found on the website – locations include Zabeel Park. *Oct–April, 1st Sat of the month 8am–3pm | admission 5 Dh | Zabeel Park, Gate 1, 2, 3 | dubai-fleamarket. com | Metro Red Line: Trade Centre or Al Jafiliya |* Zabeel *|* ▥ *U5*

FASHION FROM THE EMIRATES

Pieces by local designers can be reminiscent of a tropical garden. Lemon yellow, bright green and pink are the predominant colours, along with artistic embroidery and appliqué – sometimes with a touch of irony. Billowing, expensive fabrics and intoxicating colours for kaftans and tunics are the trademark of *Royal Rickshaw (royalrickshaw.com)*. Their creations are available at *Tiger Lily* in the Wafi Mall (Oud Metha Road). Matching accessories can be found at *Accessori* in the Dubai Mall and at *Aldo Accessories* in the Mall of the Emirates.

SHOPPING

Majlis Gallery sells paintings that represent the region

10 RIPE MARKET

For over ten years, these popular open-air markets for organic fruit and vegetables, plus art and bric-a-brac, have been part of the shopping experience in Dubai. People meet at nicely styled food trucks, and sometimes there are great street performances with artists and musicians. Ripe Markets take place at different locations, sometimes only during the colder months of the year (October to April). Check the website for information on current locations. *Sat/Sun 3–10pm | ripeevents.com | M4*

TAILORS

11 PARMAR TAILORS

Parmar Tailors is the top address for made-to-measure suits and business outfits for men and women, and has been guaranteeing its quality since 1956. *Sat–Thu 10am–8pm | Almas Tower, Jumeirah Lake Towers | parmartailors.com | Metro Red Line: DMCC | Jumeirah Lake Towers | J4*

12 TEXTILE SOUK

Bales of Indian cotton fabric, brocade and silk, one more gloriously coloured than the next, are just waiting to be made into Bollywood-style blouses and dresses, baggy Indian trousers and knee-length kaftans. There are numerous skilful and inexpensive Indian tailors in the covered Textile Souk in the *Souk Al Khabeer* at Bur Dubai. And any one of the businesses will also be able to copy your favourite designer dress for you.

INSIDER TIP: Be your own fashion designer
The tailors will also skilfully and quickly turn your own ideas for an unusual dress or a skirt into reality in bright and cheerful sari fabric! *Bur Dubai | V4*

SHOPPING MALLS

SHOPPING MALLS

Dubai has taken the idea of the shopping mall to extremes. There are almost 50 of them and they are shopping centres and theme parks wrapped up into one. People don't go to a mall just to go shopping, but to be entertained as well. Cinemas, aquariums, ski slopes, ice rinks and an overwhelming number of cafés and restaurants pull in the crowds. The other factor is Dubai's climate: from May to September life is only bearable in air-conditioned spaces.

13 DUBAI DUTY FREE

The last temptation before your onward flight or return home: this retail space of almost 10,000m² in the Sheikh Rashid Terminal, which has been extended several times to the point where shoppers can get lost, turns over US$1 billion per year in a host of little boutiques and larger stores that sell designer fashion, gold jewellery, leather goods, cosmetics, toys, sports equipment and electronic goods from all over the world – some of it at attractive prices. Look out for sales! *dubaidutyfree.com* | *Metro Red Line: Airport, Terminal 3* | *Al Garhoud* | *W7*

14 DUBAI MALL ★

Luxury and opulence – these are the hallmarks of Dubai's biggest mall, which is the world's second largest. Galleries, arcades, floors inlaid with shining marble and granite, works of

Visitors stroll through distant lands in the Ibn Battuta Mall: this is the Chinese area

SHOPPING

art, splashing fountains and effects with light and water are the framework for a retail area of more than 220,000m². You can't get lost here: interactive information screens make it easy to find your way around. Over 1,200 shops cater for your every wish. At various information counters you will find a list of all the shops and, of course, information on where you can buy the labels you want. The lower floor harbours the *Gold Souk*, where some 300 exquisite jewellers' shops twinkle beneath a starry dome. From the balcony of the large *Apple Store*, which extends over two floors, you have a great view of the Burj Khalifa and the evening show on Dubai Lake. But this mall's biggest attraction is the *Dubai Aquarium* (see p. 40), which extends over three floors, so you can watch piranhas and zebra sharks while you shop. *Daily 10am–midnight | Financial Centre Road, off Sheikh Zayed Road, 1st Interchange | thedubaimall.com | Metro Red Line: Dubai Mall | Downtown Dubai | S5*

INSIDER TIP Fabulous tower views

15 IBN BATTUTA MALL

What distinguishes this mall from the others in Dubai are the elaborate illusions of its architecture: visitors stroll through the lands that the great Arab seafarer Ibn Battuta saw on his travels in the 14th century: Persia, India, China, Egypt. Entire arcades are dedicated to these countries and kitted out in the style of village streets and squares, with rows of houses in the local style, including domed buildings, mosaic-clad walls and huge, antique-looking sailing ships. Few of the 290 shops are in the hands of designer brands, but there is a good assortment of local crafts.

There is also, of course, a food court that takes care of the culinary side. A recommended eatery is the *Soy* restaurant *(tel. 04 3 68 54 74 | ££)*, serving Southeast Asian cuisine in *The Gardens* area. *Sun–Wed 10am–10pm, Thu–Sat 10am–midnight | Sheikh Zayed Road, between Interchanges 5 and 6 | Jebel Ali | ibnbattutamall.com | Metro Red Line: Ibn Battuta | The Gardens | G4*

16 MALL OF THE EMIRATES

The operators of this huge mall describe it as a "shopping resort", because you can not only buy things here but can also stay – right next door at the *Kempinski Hotel*, which is designed in the style of a Swiss ski resort. Not only that, but this mall is connected to *Ski Dubai* (see p. 48). In the area by the front entrance you can get a glimpse of the ski slopes through a window and plan your visit to the mall over a glass of tea.

INSIDER TIP Admire the snow in the desert

Among the approximately 500 shops is a branch of London's upmarket Harvey Nichols department store, selling trendy and luxury goods. You'll find dozens of cafés and restaurants here, and for older children and teenagers there are rides such as dodgems in the *Magic Planet* indoor amusement park. At regular intervals 🐾 free shuttle buses fetch customers from

SOUKS

luxury hotels (for example, the Ritz-Carlton and Royal Mirage on Jumeirah Beach). *Sun-Wed 10am-1opm, Thu-Sat 10am-midnight | Sheikh Zayed Road, between Interchanges 4 and 5 | malloftheemirates.com | Metro Red Line: Mall of the Emirates | Al Barsha | ⌘ M5*

SOUKS

17 GOLD & DIAMOND PARK

For those who like gold jewellery and want to know how it's made, this modern gold mall, with the expected levels of glitter and glamour, is home to a museum that presents details of working methods, and also exhibits precious items of Arab and Indian design. *Sat-Thu 10am-10pm, Fri 4-10pm | Sheikh Zayed Road | Interchange 4 | Al Quoz | goldanddiamondpark.com | Metro Red Line: FGB | Umm Al Sheif | ⌘ N5*

18 GOLD SOUK ★

As much a part of Dubai as the desert sand. Welcome to the famous Gold Souk, where covered alleys host around 300 gold jewellery shops cheek by jowl! The prices are based solely on weight and the daily rate for one gram (of 24-carat or 21-carat) gold, processing included. The offer is more or less the same everywhere, as is the procedure: you choose what you like, it gets put on the scales, there's some haggling (but only a bit because you're only negotiating about the amount of work that's gone into your piece, not the price of the gold). Don't go before sundown. That's when the shops light up in all their exotic brilliance, and the customers, lots of Indians and covered Arab women with bags and baggages, really get in the mood to shop. *Daily 9.30am-1pm and 4-10pm | Sikkat Al Khail Street | Metro Green Line: Al Ras | Deira | ⌘ V4*

19 SOUK AL BAHAR ★

Very close to the Burj Khalifa and just a few steps from Dubai Mall, on the tiny Old Town Island in the middle of Dubai Lake: even Souk Al Bahar's location can't be beaten. The architecture, decorations and design of the entire souk, with its lanes of shops, is based on that of an Arab souk from the 12th to 17th centuries. As soon as you enter, you'll slip from the 21st century into a fantasy oriental world of the imagination. Arcades, dim lighting, the quiet splashing of water, the whiff of incense and lavish copper lanterns combine to create the desired Arabian Nights atmosphere.

> **INSIDER TIP — Food lovers' hotspot**
> The 17 hand-picked restaurants and bars of the *Time Out Market* (timeoutmarket.com) on the first floor

are also exciting and refreshing in terms of styling – a mixture of food halls and New York loft. *Sat-Thu 10am-10pm, Fri 2-10pm | 1 Sheikh Mohammed bin Rashid Blvd, opposite Dubai Mall | soukalbahar.ae | Metro Red Line: Dubai Mall | Downtown Dubai | ⌘ S5*

20 SOUK KHAN MURJAN

An attraction in Wafi Mall. The Arabian souk is in the basement and ranged over two floors. It offers Islamic-

SHOPPING

inspired arts and crafts, plus Arab jewellery, carpets and furniture. *Sun–Wed 10am–10pm, Thu–Sat 10am–midnight | Oud Metha Road/off Sheikh Zayed Road | Wafi | Metro Green Line: Healthcare City |* Umm Hurair *| ☐ U6*

TRADITIONAL SOUKS

Genuine rather than elegant: they're cramped and hectic, and the merchants are (mostly) charming and masters at making promises. In the *Bur Dubai Souk (between the abra stops on the Creek |* Bur Dubai *| ☐ V4)*, also called *Grand* or *Old Souk*, the goods are mainly textiles. In the *Spice Souk (Al Ras Street |* Deira *| ☐ V4)* exotic spices from Asia and Arab countries are sold in packages or from huge jute sacks at prices lower than in the supermarkets. Ask for Egyptian kohl kajal in the Spice Souk – an inexpensive, original gift or an indispensable cosmetic utensil for henna evenings at home. The *Perfume Souk (Sikkat Al Khail |* Deira *| ☐ V4)* has oriental scented oils and perfumes that customers can also mix themselves.

INSIDER TIP: Eyes like Cleopatra

A great variety of Eastern scents and smells: the Spice Souk

NIGHTLIFE

The hip alongside the traditional – Dubai's hallmark combination also applies to evening entertainment. You can find everything from shisha cafés to trendy clubs on the top floors of high-rise hotels and river dinner cruises on ships bathed in lights.

Aside from the big international DJs, who fly in for only a few days to heat things up at mega parties in the city's best clubs, many locally known DJs – such as David Craig, Da Sendri, Smokingroove, Charl Chaka and Mark Pickup – are popular performers in Dubai. The

> You'll find all the venues in this chapter on the pull-out map 📖

There's plenty of nightlife around the Dubai Marina

interiors of the city's numerous clubs and bars are usually stunning. You can always turn night into day here, but the busiest days are Thursdays to Saturdays. Meanwhile, teetotal nationals and (Muslim) expats meet in the evenings for mocktails and tea at the many shisha lounges with outdoor seating. Alcoholic drinks are only available at licensed pubs and hotels. In the month of Ramadan, so-called *Ramadan tents* open after dark offering an opulent buffet (for *iftar*, the meal that breaks the fast), folklore performances and shishas

WHERE TO GO OUT IN DUBAI

MARCO POLO HIGHLIGHTS

★ **BUDDHA BAR**
New Age music and a touch of Zen
➤ p. 84

★ **MERCURY LOUNGE**
Rooftop bar with magical views ➤ p. 86

★ **DINNER CRUISE**
Dine as you glide gently past the city skyline ➤ p. 87

★ **DINNER IN THE DESERT**
Action and romance outside the city
➤ p. 88

★ **DUBAI OPERA HOUSE**
The new star of Downtown Dubai ➤ p. 91

DUBAI MARINA

Easy-going waterside lifestyle. Here, beneath the palm trees, Dubai is particularly relaxed

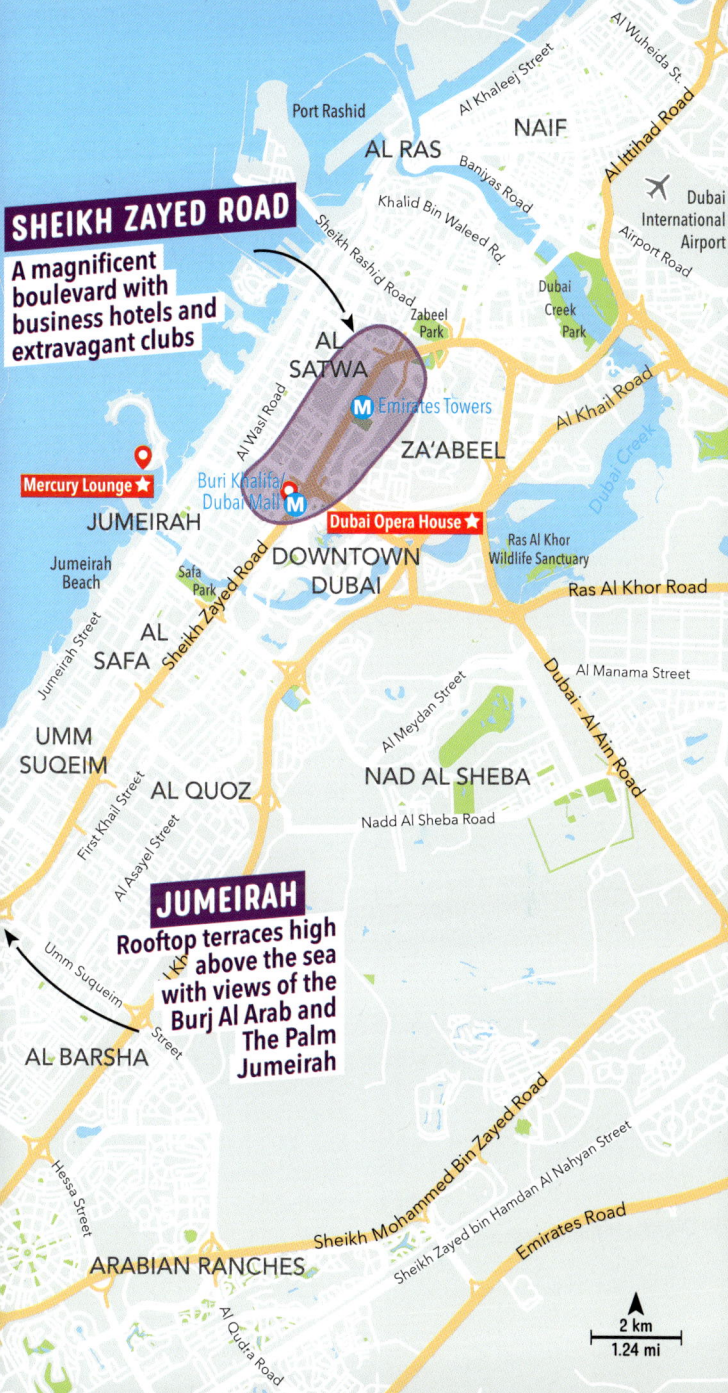

BARS

Because of the taxes, drinks are really expensive in Dubai. It's cheaper if you go out during one of the (frequent) happy hours.

However, Dubai is also good for a night out with the girls because of *Ladies' Night (ladiesnight.dubai.com)*, usually midweek, when there is less going on around town and women's drinks arev free. From 6pm onwards, bars and dance clubs admit only persons over 21 years of age. Some bars do a check on every guest. It's important to note that anyone who appears to be drunk in public runs the risk of arrest. Going out in baggy jeans and a T-shirt is taboo if you want to go clubbing. So put on your high heels and wear a glittery top and tight jeans.

WHERE TO START?

New hotspots with great bars and clubs are constantly popping up in the city. With night-time temperatures often around 30°C, partying outdoors is particularly enjoyable. The rooftop bars of **Downtown Dubai** and **Dubai Marina** are great for this purpose, as are those along **Sheikh Zayed Road** and the beach clubs of **Jumeirah** and **The Palm Jumeirah**. In Dubai, people go out early. The **Nasimi Beach** in the Atlantis Hotel is a good place to start, but no matter where you begin, many Western residents like to head to the **Barasti Bar** for one last drink on the beach before going home.

For information on what's on, pick up a copy of *Time Out Dubai (timeoutdubai.com)*.

BARS

1 ALTA BADIA
Two lifts take you straight to the 51st floor and the minimalist-style bar of the elegant Jumeirah Emirates Towers hotel. As the sun goes down, you can enjoy a marvellous view while you try to decide which of 200 (!) classic cocktails and newcomers to choose. Perhaps the Fraisini – rosé champagne with strawberry purée? By the way, you can smoke here, too. *Daily 5.30pm–1.30am | Emirates Towers Hotel, 51st floor | Sheikh Zayed Road | jumeirah.com | Metro Red Line: Emirates Towers | Downtown Dubai | T5*

2 BAR 44
Romantic and just the place for couples: the Dubai view looks even better by candlelight and with live piano music, especially from as high up as this. *Sun–Thu 6pm–1am, Fri/Sat until 2am | Grosvenor House, 44th floor | West Marina Beach | Al Sufouh Road | bar44-dubai.com | Metro Red Line: Damac | Dubai Marina | J4*

3 BUDDHA BAR ★
"Love and compassion" in Dubai. This theme, imported from Paris, goes down well in the desert, too. Specially made New Age compilations with Asian influences are played in the lounge and bar, and a Zen restaurant is part of it all, along with the view of

NIGHTLIFE

You'll need a hefty wallet for an evening here: Skyview Bar at the Burj Al Arab

the marina and an enormous statue of Buddha. *Sun-Thu 7pm-1am, Fri until 2am, Sat 1.30-4.30pm and 8pm-2am | Hotel Grosvenor House | Al Sufouh Road | tel. 04 3 99 88 88 | buddhabar.com | Metro Red Line: Damac | Dubai Marina | ☐ J4*

4 CHILLOUT ICE LOUNGE

Dubai's coolest bar. Everything is made of ice, several feet thick: the seats, tables, walls and bar itself are all frozen. The atmosphere is reminiscent of a Star Wars film, which is partly down to the fluorescent lighting. In the acclimatisation room, guests slip into padded jackets and gloves before entering the bar, where the temperature is -6°C. Hot chocolate has never tasted as good as when it's served with cardamom and cream topping in this cool bar. Yum! We'll count the calories later. *Daily 10am-10pm, Thu/Fri 10am-midnight | admission 80 Dh | Times Square Center | Sheikh Zayed Road, between Interchanges 3 and 4 | chilloutindubai.com | Metro Red Line: FGB | Al Manara | ☐ O5*

INSIDER TIP — Hot chocolate on ice

5 THE ROOFTOP

Candles, seating on oriental cushions and high-class lounge furnishings on the roof terrace of a luxury hotel, the Royal Mirage. Beneath the stars and high above Jumeirah Beach you can sip cocktails while listening to cool rhythms. *Daily 5.30pm-1am | Arabian Court of the Royal Mirage Hotel | Al Sufouh Road | short.travel/dub10 | Metro Red Line: Nakheel | Jumeirah Beach | ☐ K3*

6 SKYVIEW BAR

A view to die for: see the Palm Jumeirah and the coast from a height of 200m. This place sets its sights on wealthy customers. A drink called "27,321" costs 27,321 Dh, which

CLUBS

translates as around £5,970 – it's Scotch served in a glass made of 18-carat gold. New cocktails can be created individually for each guest in the mobile trolley bar by the mixologist. *Daily 6–11pm, booking required | Burj Al Arab hotel | Jumeirah Road | tel. 04 3 01 76 00 | jumeirah.com | Metro Red Line: FGB | Jumeirah Beach | N3*

CLUBS

7 BARASTI BEACH BAR
The classic of all Dubai beach clubs, one of the favourite venues for partying with friends, listening to music and enjoying a relaxed beach atmosphere. Barasti makes a pleasantly unstyled impression in highly polished Dubai and the in-house rock band usually plays old songs on weekdays. Top DJs also play at special events, and the weekends are party time. *Sun–Thu 9am–2am, Fri/Sat until 3am | Le Meridien Mina Seyahi Beach Resort & Marina | Al Sufouh Road | barastibeach.com | Metro Red Line: DMCC | Jumeirah Beach | K3*

8 CLUB BOUDOIR
In Dubai, it's "ladies drink free all night" one day a week in most clubs. This place, with its romantic, extravagant styling in French Renaissance style, is the place to enjoy Dubai's "hottest ladies' night". DJs spin and the dancefloor is buzzing. *Daily 9pm–3am | Jumeirah Road (near the Jumeirah Mosque) | Dubai Marine Beach Resort | clubboudoirdubai.com | Metro Red Line: World Trade Centre | Jumeirah Beach | T3-4*

9 MERCURY LOUNGE ★
Enjoy a cocktail, feel the gentle sea breeze and enjoy the DJs' music. The top location, attentive service and fabulous views of the Arabian Gulf or the city's skyscrapers more than justify the higher prices. *Sat–Tue 6pm–2am, Wed–Fri until 3am | Four Seasons Hotel | Jumeirah Road | mercurydubai.com | Metro Red Line: Business Bay | Jumeirah 2 | R4*

10 WHITE BEACH
Not cheap, but great: even when the sun is still over the horizon. After lunch at the weekend, the in-house DJs play dance and house music and by sunset at the latest, you'll be completely addicted to the location on the white sandy beach. *Mon–Wed 10am–8pm, Fri–Sun 10am–midnight, Fri/Sat DJ from 2pm | Hotel Atlantis | atlantisthepalm.com | Metro Red Line: Nakheel | The Palm Jumeirah | K1*

11 NIKKI BEACH
Lounge music, a swim, good drinks and then enjoy the sunset: just like in Ibiza, St Tropez and other lifestyle destinations, people meet up in this all-white club for a pool party and enjoy top compilations with one of the trendy cocktails. *Daily 11am–8pm | Nikki Beach Resort | Pearl Jumeirah | dubai.nikkibeach.com | Metro Red Line: Al Jafiliya | Pearl Jumeirah | T3*

12 WHITE DUBAI
A little distance away, but well worth the effort to get here. This is an absolutely fabulous rooftop club with views of the skyline in a top location high

NIGHTLIFE

above the Meydan Race Course. Laser shows, dance performances and energising sounds for a stylish international audience. Best to share a taxi with several people to get here. *Daily 8pm–3am, hours vary during events | Meydan Racecourse Grandstand Rooftop | Nad Al Sheba 1 | whitedubai.com | Metro Red Line: Business Bay | Al Marqadh | R7*

13 ZERO GRAVITY

Come for a beach brunch, after work drinks or a full night of clubbing. The modern club on the beach regularly attracts internationally renowned DJs and pop stars. Fatboy Slim, Clean Bandit, James Arthur and John Newman have already done the honours. The live broadcasts of international football tournaments are both loud and fun. *Sat–Tue, Thu 10am–9pm, Fri until 2am | King Salman Bin Abdulaziz Al Saud Street/ Dubai Marina | 0-gravity.ae | Metro Red Line: Damac | Dubai Marina | J3*

DINNER SPECIALS

14 DINNER CRUISE ★ ▶

Gaily illuminated dhows sail from the mouth to the end of the Creek. First you enjoy a sundowner on the upper deck, then have dinner on the air-conditioned deck below, where an extensive buffet with Arab and international dishes is laid on. The sight of night-time Dubai gliding past is a good reason to go back to the upper deck to puff on a shisha.

The boats can be found on the Deira side between the Sheraton Hotel and the Radisson Blu *(Al Mansour | tel. 04 222 71 71 | Metro Green Line, Red Line: Union Square)*, in Bur Dubai on Al Seef Road *(Danat | tel. 04 3 51 11 17*

A spectacle of light and water: a dinner cruise on the Creek

DINNER SPECIALS

| *Metro Red Line: Burjuman)* and in the *Al Boom Tourist Village (tel. 04 3 43 30 00 | Metro Green Line: Healthcare City). Prices: 150–200 Dh*

A more expensive version, modern with all-round glazing, is *Bateaux Dubai (Banias Road | 350 Dh | tel. 04 8 14 55 53 | bateauxdubai.com | Metro Red Line, Green Line: Union Square).*

15 DINNER IN THE DESERT ★ ⚑

Watch the sun go down from the top of a sand dune and then dine under the stars – an experience that no visitor to Dubai should miss. The procedure doesn't vary much: a 4WD accommodating up to six passengers picks you up in the afternoon at your hotel and takes you into the desert, up and down across the crests of dunes that can be over 100m high. Ideally, you should only wear light sandals that you can quickly take off to trudge through the sand. Make a great souvenir by filling the empty jar you brought with you (from the breakfast honey at the hotel, say) with desert sand. Then the sun sets: a truly magical moment.

After that, it's on to the Bedouin camp. Surrounded by high dunes, there are camels, tents are pitched and a camp is set up, lit by torches. You make yourself comfortable on cushions, help yourself to the buffet (salads, Arabic starters, steaks and the typical meat dishes of the region), listen to the music and watch the belly dancers. Never ridden a camel before? Now is your chance! Get a free henna tattoo from the Bedouin women in the desert camp. You can also have your photo taken with a falcon on your arm. At around 10pm you will return to civilisation in a motorcade.

Packages including pick-up from the hotel are on offer from all the city's travel agents and hotels *(from 350 Dh per person)*, for example *Oasis Palm Tourism (Riqqa Road | Deira | tel. 04 2 62 88 89 | oasispalmdubai.com)* or *Arabian Adventures (Emirates Holidays Building 1st floor | Sheikh Zayed Road | tel. 04 3 03 48 88 | arabianadventures.com | Metro Red Line: DMCC).*

INSIDER TIP
Henna highlight

NIGHTLIFE

Delicacies on the sand: everything is laid out ready for dinner in the desert

GOLF BY FLOODLIGHT

16 EMIRATES GOLF CLUB

Tee off with a dream view of Dubai's skyline. The 18-hole course is one of the best in the region and the only one to offer night-time golf. *Green fees 450 Dh (18 holes) | tel. 04 4 17 98 00 | dubaigolf.com | Metro Red Line: Nakheel | Emirates Hills | K4*

JAZZ

17 BLUE BAR

Despite the name, they play more jazz than blues here. Guests can keep an eye on everything from a high stool or loll around on a comfy sofa. *Daily 2pm–2am | Novotel Hotel | Sheikh Zayed Road (behind the World Trade Centre) | Metro Red Line: Trade Centre | Trade Centre | T5*

18 COOZ

Repeatedly voted one of the best bars in Dubai. Intimate cocktail lounge with a jazz pianist and singer. *Daily 6pm–2am | Grand Hyatt Hotel | Al Qutaeyat Road | dubai.grand.hyatt.com | Metro Green Line: Healthcare City | Umm Hurair | U6*

19 UP ON THE TENTH

A favourite with jazz lovers: intimate and romantic, and up on the tenth floor with an uninterrupted view of the Creek. A changing roll call of jazz musicians perform, sometimes for an evening of solo piano music. *Daily 6.30pm–2am | Radisson Blu Hotel,*

CINEMAS

Dubai Opera House: glamour and gravitas for Dubai's cultural scene

10th floor | Beniyas Road Deira | dubai.radissonblu.com | Metro Green Line, Red Line: Union Square | Deira | ⌑ V4

CINEMAS

Dubai has several multiplex cinemas, with up to two dozen screens each. Most films are shown in English, and tickets cost 20–30 Dh. To give a varied population what it wants, all sorts of international films are screened. Whether Hollywood blockbuster or the latest Bollywood romcom, there's hardly a cheaper way to spend an evening. Two of the 14 cinemas at *Vox Cinemas (Mall of the Emirates)* are "Vox Gold Class", which means fabulously comfortable lounge-style seats with recliners, and the in-house restaurant's food is brought to your seat!

INSIDER TIP — Movie relaxation

20 CINEMA ON THE SAND

Chilled out! You're sitting on cushions on the beach, with the glowing skyscrapers of Dubai Marina in front of you and the giant screen is showing *Titanic* or *Top Gun*. At *Zero Gravity* (see p. 87), one of Dubai's most popular beach clubs, films are shown every Sunday evening from 8pm during the season. *Oct–May | 75 Dh | King Salman Bin Abdulaziz Al Saud Street | Skydive Dubai, Dubai Marina | 0-gravity.ae | Metro Red Line: DAMAC Properties | Dubai Marina | ⌑ J3*

NIGHTLIFE

PUB

21 IRISH VILLAGE
A green lawn, Van Morrison songs and good Irish beer on draught: the Irish community in Dubai comes here for all sorts of events. English and Irish visiting musicians and bands often perform here too. *Daily 11am–1.30am | 31 A Street | north of the Garhoud Bridge next to the Tennis Stadium | theirishvillage.com | Metro Red Line: GGICO | Al Garhoud | V6*

THEATRE

22 DUBAI COMMUNITY THEATRE & ARTS CENTRE
A non-profit organisation puts on art exhibitions and performances, ranging from Disney's *High School Musical* to performances by touring British chamber orchestras and karaoke competitions for schoolkids. *Mall of the Emirates, Level 2 | tel. 04 3 41 47 77 | ductac.org | Metro Red Line: Mall of the Emirates | Al Barsha | M4*

23 DUBAI OPERA HOUSE ★
Sparkling and hyper-modern – the Opera House is a new eye-catcher for the city. An amazing building, light and airy, and not unlike … a dhow, of course, as locals will tell you right away. There is capacity for 2,000 to enjoy moving world premières in a concert hall with unbeatable acoustics. In addition to ballet and opera, there are also musicals and concerts by British symphony orchestras. Tickets are bought online. *Mohammed bin Rashid Blvd | dubaiopera.com | Metro Red Line: Burj Khalifa/Dubai Mall | The Opera District, Downtown Dubai | R5*

24 THE JUNCTION
A top address for the growing number of international artists in Dubai, whether soul singers, Bollywood actors or performers from London's Globe Theatre, as well as a venue for local amateur performances. The theatre has 160 seats, and is in the ultra-popular arty area of Al Quoz. *Alserkal Av., 8 Street | tel. 04 3 38 85 25 | thejunction.com | Metro Red Line: Noor Bank | Al Quoz | O5*

WINE BARS

25 CIN CIN
This horseshoe-shaped wine bar has an avant-garde-style decor and a legendary wine list, with 350 fine and famous vintages. Savour them to the alternating sounds of European dance music and soul. *Daily 7pm–2am | Fairmont Hotel | Sheikh Zayed Road | fairmont.com/dubai | Metro Red Line: Trade Centre | Trade Center | T5*

26 VINTAGE
The place to be if you fancy a cosy and intimate lounge atmosphere: sink deep into a sofa, enjoy a good red wine from New Zealand or South Africa, and finger food such as Japanese tempura or Italian cheese. Incidentally, this is one of the few places where smoking is permitted. *Daily 1pm–1am | The Pyramids, Wafi | Metro Green Line: Healthcare City | Umm Hurair | U6*

ACTIVE & RELAXED

Much more than just hot air: a different kind of desert trip

SPORT & WELLNESS

BEACHES & BEACH SPORTS

A white sandy beach, parasols and sun loungers for hire, showers and changing rooms, and a great setting against the backdrop of the skyscrapers of the Jumeirah Beach Residence: Dubai's most famous public beach is the lively *The Beach (thebeach.ae)*. *La Mer (lamerdubai.ae)* at the start of Jumeirah Beach Road is relaxed and decidedly hip. The 1.6km-long *Palm West Beach (westbeach.ae)* on the trunk of The Palm Jumeirah is also great for strolling and eating out. The spacious 👯 *Kite Beach (Jumeirah | kitebeach.ae)*, with a superb view of the Burj Al Arab is a relaxed place with a wide range of sports on offer (kayaking, trampoline, volleyball).

KITESURFING & STAND-UP PADDLE BOARDING

Alongside yoga, beach volleyball, jogging and skating, kitesurfing and stand-up paddle boarding are among Dubai's trendy sports, which is why part of the super-groomed 👯 *Umm Suqeim Beach* is now only known as *"Kite Beach"*. If you don't want to come out as a greenhorn, *Dukite (dukite.com)* offers quick tuition for beginners.

SKIING & SANDBOARDING

This is fun: bare legs, tanned skin and shorts – and travelling on skis. On a mono-ski (sandboard), you ski down the sand dunes in the nearby desert, which are up to 100m high. An off-road vehicle then takes you back up to the dune crest. Even beginners can go down an easy slope for a few seconds after a short briefing. Extreme cooling off awaits you on the *Ski Dubai* alpine downhill run (see p. 48) in the Mall of the Emirates. In addition to tow lifts, there is a proper gondola lift operation. Children and teenagers love

Dubai has beautiful routes for joggers

sliding downhill on plastic tyres in the snow park or watching the penguins. Snowboarders enjoy the 90m-long halfpipe.

WALKING, JOGGING, SKATING, CYCLING

The *Jumeirah Corniche Walk* stretches for 14km along the sea, parallel to Jumeirah Beach Road, from Dubai Marina Beach Resort to Burj Al Arab. Walkers along this promenade have a 5m-wide pavement next to a 4m-wide track for joggers and in-line skaters. Kiosks and shady benches make the walk a popular meeting place. It is directly next to a sandy beach where you can go for a quick dip or take advantage of the water sports on offer. *Wolfi's Bike Shop (Sheikh Zayed Road/ exit 46 | next to the Audi showroom | tel. 0 43 39 44 53 | wbs.ae)* will guide cyclists to suitable routes.

WELLNESS

Hotels spoil you with spas where the quality of the treatments is excellent and the surroundings are magical. The Turkish steam baths at some luxury hotels can become addictive. Visit, for example, the *Sensasia Urban Spa (The Village Mall | sensasiaspas.com | ⊞ T4)*, which is designed in Asian minimalist style, or the lavishly decorated *Talise Ottoman Spa (Hotel Jumeirah Zabeel Saray | jumeirah.com | ⊞ J2)*. It's worth making a reservation here and indulging yourself. At the *One & Only Spa (Residence & Spa, Hotel Royal Mirage | oneandonlyresorts.com | ⊞ K3–4)* the hammam ritual is one of the most beautiful treatments on the spa menu. *Cleopatra's Spa (Wafi Centre | cleopatraspa.com | ⊞ U6)* is Dubai's largest and most renowned day spa.

INSIDER TIP: Relax in the hammam

FESTIVALS & EVENTS

Festivals and public holidays mainly follow the Islamic calendar. Friday is the weekly day of rest, and the weekend also includes Saturday.

CHANGEABLE DATES

Ramadan, the holy month for Muslims, is a time of fasting and prayer. After sunset, people break their fast at *iftar*. In Dubai people often meet in restaurants for particularly sumptuous buffets. *28 Feb–30 March 2025, 18 Feb–19 March 2026.*

Eid Al-Fitr is the three-day festival at the end of Ramadan, which is celebrated with fireworks, fairs and folk dances. *30 March–1 April 2025, 20–23 March 2026*

JANUARY/FEBRUARY

Professional golfers arrive for the **Dubai Desert Classic golf tournament**, part of the European PGA Tour. *End Jan/early Feb | dubaidesertclassic.com*

★ ⚑ **Dubai Shopping Festival:** this 30-day festival is the ultimate spree. The shops (some 30,000 of them) offer discounts of between 20 and 70 per cent. Fairy lights, fireworks and countless (free) events attract more than three million visitors from all around the world. *mydsf.ae*

Dubai Marathon: an absolute dream event for Dubai fans and runners. The starting signal is given within sight of the Burj Al Arab. With around 30,000 runners from 150 nations, you will be a part of a well-organised race. In addition to the full marathon, shorter distances are also offered. The finish line is at the Dubai Marina. *dubaimarathon.org*

FEBRUARY

The **Dubai Tennis Championships** pull in tennis fans from all over the world. *2nd half Feb | dubaidutyfree tennischampionships.com*

Magnificent fireworks over the Dubai skyline

Even Sting has been known to stop by the **Dubai Jazz Festival**. *3 days at the end of the month of Eid Al-Fitr | dubaijazzfest.com*

MARCH
You won't believe your eyes when you see the yachts on show at the **Dubai International Boat Show**. *5 days early March | boatshowdubai.com*

The **Dubai World Cup** boasts the world's biggest prize money for a horse race. *End March | dubaiworldcup.com).*

At **Art Dubai**, around 90 galleries in Madinat Jumeirah delight audiences with exciting and amusing art exhibitions from the region, and also from Africa and southern Asia. *4 days second half May | artdubai.ae).*

OCTOBER TO APRIL
In the winter season, **horse and camel races** take place at weekends. Camel races are held Thu–Sat from 2.30pm; spectators are also welcome to watch the training beginning from 7.30am. On Thu/Fri evening everyone meets at the horse races (see p. 50).

Between November and March, acrobats from Mongolia and geishas from Kyoto, ghost trains and old-fashioned chairoplanes await visitors at the **Global Village** *(Sheikh Zayed Road/Dubailand | globalvillage.ae)*. Over 70 "countries" sell their typical goods in imaginatively styled pavilions. There are also cultural shows, live music and lots of food stands.

2 DECEMBER
National Day: at numerous festivals and events, the locals wear their national colours, good luck wishes are painted in the sky by plane, and there are discounts and bargains in the malls and at the Dubai Duty Free.

SLEEP WELL

ISLAND DREAMS
Take a hotel boat to the *Anantara World Islands Resort (70 suites and villas | 4km off the coast, transfer from the associated Anantara The Palm Dubai Resort | tel. 04 5 67 87 77 | anantara. com | £££ | P-Q2)*. The beach villas with private pools have a Maldives vibe – and a view of the Dubai skyline. The secluded location on the artificial archipelago cannot be beaten.

SITAR SOUNDS IN OLD DUBAI
Little India and a Sikh doorman await you at the *Arabian Courtyard Hotel (173 rooms | Al Fahidi Street | Meena Bazar | tel. 04 3 51 91 11 | arabiancourtyard.com | Metro Green Line: Al Fahidi | ££ | Bur Dubai | V4)*. And the location is fantastic: this large hotel complex is sited in the middle of the labyrinth of lanes of the lively Meena Bazar, opposite the Dubai Museum and in the heart of historic Dubai.

GARDEN BY THE SEA
Peacocks strut through the tropical park, there is a riding club, tours are offered from the marina and there is a wonderful walk through the palm-strewn gardens to the hotel's own golf course: the *JA Beach Hotel (235 rooms | exit no.13 Sheikh Zayed Road | tel. 04 8 14 55 55 | jaresortshotels. com | Metro Red Line: UAE Exchange | £££ | Jebel Ali | F3)* is the best address for a relaxing beach holiday.

AMONG SEAHORSES
With seemingly endless gold leaf adorning the walls, the famous *Atlantis (1539 rooms | Crescent Road | tel. 04 4 26 20 00 | atlantisthepalm. com | £££ | The Palm Jumeirah | K-L1)* is a pink fairy-tale palace on an artificial palm island. Even the door handles here are shaped like sea creatures, and the chandeliers ... well, you will find out for yourself!

Welcome to the underwater world of the Atlantis Hotel!

THE NAME SAYS IT ALL

At the *Orient Guest House (10 rooms | Sikka 15c | Al Fahidi Street at the R/A | tel. 04 3 51 91 11 | heritage dubaihotels.com | Metro Green Line: Al Fahidi | ££ | Bur Dubai | V4)* you leave modern Dubai behind. Arab-style accommodation in a historic two-storey building in the Bastakiya district. Tastefully furnished rooms are grouped around a courtyard.

BOTH TRADITIONAL & AVANT-GARDE

The art-loving *XVA Gallery (7 rooms | Al Fahidi Street | at the R/A (behind the Arabian Teahouse) | tel. 04 3 53 53 83 | xvahotel.com | Metro Green Line: Al Fahidi | ££ | Bastakiya | V4)* combines tradition with lots of art. The rooms around the patio of this wind-tower house are furnished with witty objects and old toys, each one different and always original.

A VISIT TO THE BUDDHA

Ganesh statues, many Nepalese regulars and a great location in the middle of Old Dubai characterise the pleasantly run, small *Lumbini Guest House (18 rooms | Al Suq Street | Meena Bazar | tel. 04 2 43 73 88 | £ | Bur Dubai | V4)*. The rooms are simple and clean, the atmosphere is completely atypical of Dubai, almost like the birthplace of the Buddha, in Lumbini.

SHEHERAZADE ON A BEACH HOLIDAY

A fairy-tale palace in its own park by the sea. The *One & Only Royal Mirage (246 rooms | Al Sufouh Road | tel. 04 3 99 99 99 | oneandonlyresorts.com | Metro Red Line: Nakheel | £££ | Al Sufouh | K3–4)* makes your oriental fantasies come true. In the evening, the resort is lit up by thousands of tiny lights, and even the many palm trees are incorporated into the scenery.

DISCOVERY TOURS

Want to get under the skin of this city? Then our discovery tours are the ideal guide – they provide advice on which sights to visit, tips on where to stop for that perfect holiday snap, a choice of the best places to eat and drink, and suggestions for fun activities.

Sharks in the desert at the Dubai Mall

DISCOVERY TOURS OVERVIEW

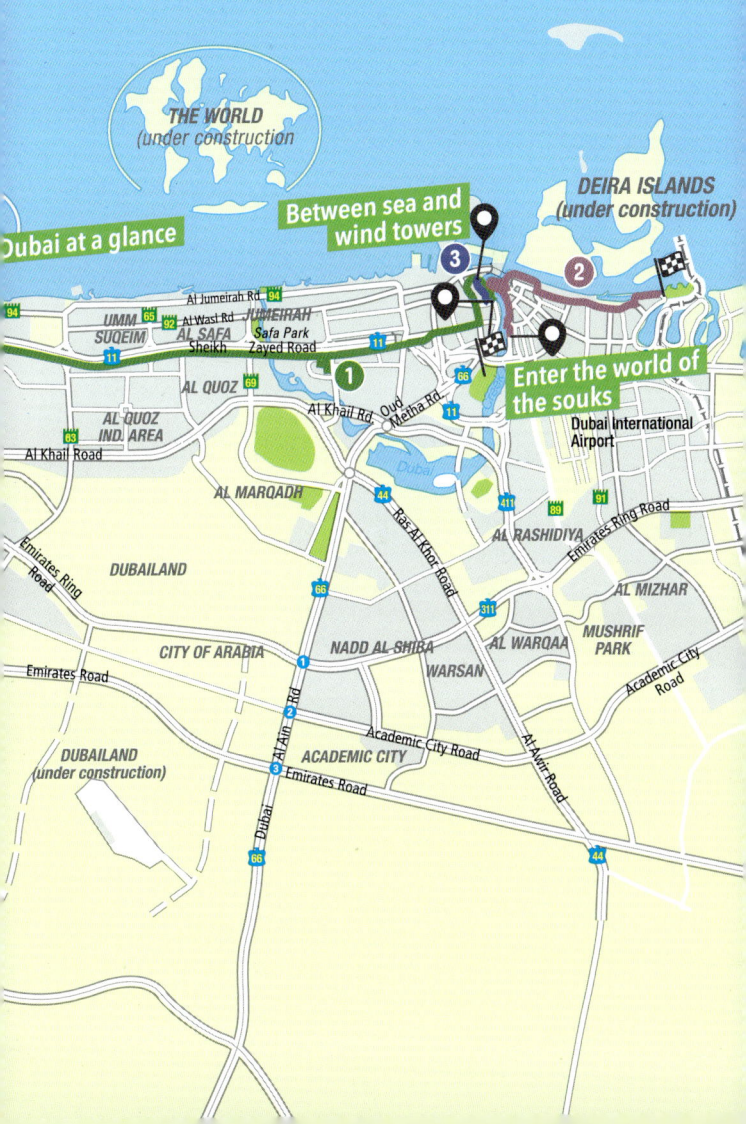

❶ DUBAI AT A GLANCE

- ➤ Take the lift to the 124th floor of the Burj Khalifa
- ➤ Whizz along an artificial palm-shaped island on a monorail
- ➤ Marvel at the skyscraper skyline of the Dubai Marina

📍 Arabian Tea House

🏁 Buddha Bar

➡ 60km

🚶 1 day (total walking time 4 hours)

ℹ Costs: 750 Dh per person for admission fees, Metro, taxi and monorail, snacks and dinner.
Important tips: You save time and money if you book your tickets for the Burj Khalifa online.
The Palm Monorail runs about every 15 minutes between 10am and 10pm.
Plan to return to the hotel from the Dubai Marina by Metro, which runs Sat–Wed until 11pm, Thu/Fri until midnight.

❶ Arabian Tea House

❷ Bastakiya

❸ Dubai Museum

START YOUR DAY THE ARAB WAY

Begin the day in Middle Eastern style by treating yourself to a mint tea beneath a sandalwood tree in the courtyard of the fittingly decorated ❶ **Arabian Tea House ➤ p. 58**. Afterwards, stroll through ❷ **Bastakiya ➤ p. 30**, where the city's historic roots are on display. Old, painstakingly restored merchants' palaces and houses with wind towers in soft desert colours are now home to galleries, boutiques and restaurants, as well as two hotels. The impressive historic **Al Fahidi Fort** is *just a short walk along Al Fahidi Street from Bastakiya*. Here you will find the fabulous ❸ **Dubai Museum ➤ p. 30**, part of which is housed in a newly created underground passageway. Make sure to check out the exhibits depicting life in the desert, as well as the replicas of an old craftsmen's street and a Quranic school.

DISCOVERY TOURS

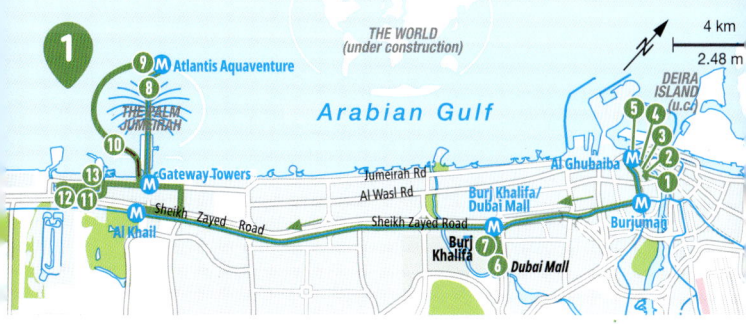

ON THE WAY TO MODERN DUBAI

Walk through the souk streets to the Dubai Creek, which smells of diesel fuel and the sea. Migrant workers from India and Pakistan sit along the shoreline, but you should snag a table on the terrace of the old trading house ❹ Bayt Al Wakeel ➤ p. 61 and order a tasty drink, such as a fizzy lime juice, to enjoy as you watch all the activity on the waterfront. Duly refreshed, *stroll towards the shore to get to the next Metro station* ❺ Al Ghubaiba, and take note of the fact that it differs noticeably from the other stations because of its old Arabic design. *Hop aboard the Metro, change from the Green Line to the Red Line at Burjuman station*, and sit back and enjoy the ride on the ultra-modern Metro *along Sheikh Zayed Road to the Dubai Mall and Burj Khalifa*.

❹ Bayt Al Wakeel

❺ Al Ghubaiba

ADMIRE DUBAI'S SUPERLATIVES

Head first to the ground floor of the ❻ Dubai Mall ➤ p. 39, p. 76 and enjoy a coffee on the outdoor terrace of one of the cafés with a view of Burj Khalifa square, for example Tim Horton's *(daily | LG Waterfront | £)*. Afterwards, stroll through the elegant wings of the mall and take a look at the Dubai Aquarium ➤ p. 40, which stretches over two floors. Don't miss out on so-called "Fashion Avenue" before heading on to the real highlight of the day: the Burj Khalifa ➤ p. 38. Take the lift to the 124th floor. The glass viewing platform ❼ At the Top offers a view that you won't forget in a hurry. When your eyes have had their fill, head back down again.

❻ Dubai Mall

❼ At the Top

OFF TO PALM ISLAND

Take the Metro to Nakheel station and then hail a taxi for the short trip to the Gateway monorail station for The Palm Jumeirah ➤ p. 45. The ⑧ **Palm Monorail** will take you across the water to the man-made island shaped like a palm tree. From its elevated tracks, you can enjoy a superb view of the sea, the yachts and the villas as you travel to the most spectacular hotel, the ⑨ **Atlantis** ➤ p. 45. Make sure to check out the "Lost Chambers", underwater worlds housed in aquariums that you view from a series of rooms. It is surrounded by luxury boutiques as well as fast-food restaurants, but you should only stop for a quick drink because it's time to *get a taxi to the next stop on the tour, the* ⑩ **101 Dining Lounge & Bar** *(daily | oneandonlyresorts.com/the-palm | £££)*. It is part of the impressive **One & Only The Palm** and over-looks the sea on a teak deck in a private marina. Take a seat under the awning and enjoy tapas with a cocktail.

FEEL THE JET SET ATMOSPHERE

Since you were a guest at the restaurant, you can *take the hotel's shuttle boat to its affiliate hotel, the Royal*

Gigantic residential project à la Dubai. The Palm Jumeirah

DISCOVERY TOURS

Mirage, opposite. From there, take a taxi to the nearby ⑪ **Dubai Marina ➤ p. 44**. Enjoy the view of the glittering buildings and skyscrapers, as well as the palm trees lining pathways that are illuminated by countless tiny lights.

⑪ **Dubai Marina**

DINE ABOVE THE WATER AND DANCE WITH THE BUDDHA

For a fitting end to the day, have dinner at the ⑫ **Dubai Marina Yacht Club** *(dubaimarinayachtclub.com | ££)* located at the Dubai Marina Promenade. You can almost imagine you are aboard a yacht as you dine on the terrace above the water. After your meal, stroll a bit further to the ⑬ **Buddha Bar ➤ p. 84** at the Grosvenor Hotel. It's high time to enjoy Dubai's brilliant nightlife.

⑫ **Dubai Marina Yacht Club**

⑬ **Buddha Bar**

❷ ENTER THE WORLD OF THE SOUKS

- ➤ Made entirely of wood: marvel at heavily laden dhows on the Creek
- ➤ Try perfume oils and incense in the souks
- ➤ Delicious and super-cheap: enjoy street food

📍 Sheraton Dubai Creek

 Al Mamzar Beach Park

➡ 14km

🚶 8 hours (total walking time 4 hours)

ℹ Costs: 250 Dh per person for admission fees, lunch, tea and coffee breaks, evening picnic and taxi.

YESTERDAY'S BARGES, TODAY'S RESTAURANTS

Start from the ❶ **Sheraton Dubai Creek** *(Baniyas Street | short.travel/dub13 | £££)*. Built in 1975, it is the grande dame of the local luxury hotel scene, and still a top favourite among locals and expats. To get a sense of the enormous proportions of the open foyer, stop for a drink in the lobby café. *Afterwards, stroll along the Creek, past the numerous dhows anchored here*

❶ **Sheraton Dubai Creek**

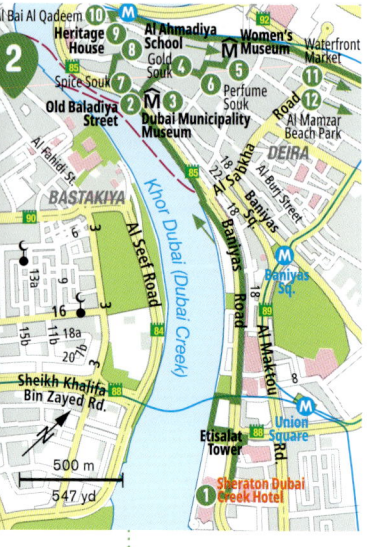

– traditional wooden boats, many now converted into floating restaurants. Why not take advantage of the opportunity to board one later on for an evening dinner cruise ➤ p. 87?

ON THE WAY TO THE SOUKS AND INTO DUBAI'S HISTORY

For now, continue your stroll along the Creek for 2.5km – if it's too hot, you can take a taxi – along the Corniche until you come to ❷ Old Baladiya Street. There are small shops here selling street food and mango and papaya juice in a square. You can also stock up on small water bottles for just 2 Dh. Spices are sold from open jute sacks, but it is the exotically sweet perfume oils that pervade the air with frankincense and other notes. It is now time for a taste of local culture with a tour of the small ❸ Municipality Museum *(Sat-Thu 9am–5pm | Baniyas Road | admission free | Metro Green Line: Al Ras)*, in the building that used to house the city administration offices. Displays show the rise of Dubai through historic photos.

DISCOVER THE HIDDEN WORLD OF THE EMIRATE'S WOMEN

Continue walking along Old Baladiya Street until Sikkat Al Khail Street appears to the right, with the entrance to the covered ❹ Gold Souk ➤ p. 36, p.78. Even during the day, the shops nestled together are quite busy, but the streets are most crowded in the evening. If you are spending a larger amount of money in a shop, the dealer will send one of the Indian errand boys to buy you tea and cola. *At the end of Sikkat Al Khail Street, a street branches off to the left leading to the* ❺ Women's Museum ➤ p. 37, the only museum on the Arabian Peninsula dedicated to women. It is full of portraits of the fascinating, yet often still unknown, women who stood alongside the powerful men of Arab countries while remaining in the shadows.

DISCOVERY TOURS

EASTERN ESSENCES

Return to Sikkat Al Khail Street and head to the ❻ **Perfume Souk** ➤ p. 79; sniff your way through the hundreds of different scented oils, frankincense and incense sticks – it's a good place to pick up a touch of Arabia to take home. For just a few dirhams, you can also buy kohl kajal (traditional eye make-up) in old-fashioned packaging, as well as henna paste and plastic stencils to make patterns on the skin. *As you walk back to the Creek,* you will pass the ❼ **Spice Souk** ➤ **p. 36, p. 79**, where once again the tempting smells of spices waft through the air. Indian and Pakistani merchants sell cardamom, cinnamon, nuts, saffron and henna powder, as well as baskets and pottery.

❻ Perfume Souk
❼ Spice Souk
❽ Al Ahmadiya School
❾ Heritage House
❿ Al Bait Al Qadeem
⓫ Waterfront Market

A look into the past: Al Ahmadiya School

SOME HISTORY TO ROUND IT ALL OFF

Al Ras Road lies beyond Old Baladiya Street; the parallel street to the north, *Al Ahmadiya Street,* is home to the oldest school in the city, ❽ **Al Ahmadiya School** ➤ **p. 34**, with the worthwhile ❾ **Heritage House** ➤ **p. 35** next door. Both buildings are a must-see because they are historic remnants of the old Dubai that have been authentically restored. Afterwards, head for a late lunch at ❿ **Al Bait Al Qadeem** ➤ **p. 60**, housed in a skilfully restored townhouse. Take a seat in one of the high-ceilinged rooms or shady courtyards and enjoy the delicious (and cheap) Arabic food.

LOOK, SHOP AND MARVEL AT THE HUGE SELECTION

Take a taxi to the ⓫ **Waterfront Market** ➤ **p. 37** *on the Deira Corniche, 11km away.* Locals shop here, as do the city's hotels and restaurants. Nowhere else in the emirates is there a greater selection of fresh spices, fruit,

⑫ Al Mamzar Beach Park

vegetables and fish. If you are tired of all the sightseeing and photographing, you can refresh yourself in one of the cafés overlooking the Creek.

SUNSET ON A DREAMLIKE BEACH

Afterwards, take a taxi to ⑫ **Al Mamzar Beach Park** *(daily 8am–10pm | Mon and Wed women and children only | dm.gov.ae).* On its beautiful, unspoilt beaches and palm-lined promenades on the border with Sharjah, a chilled-out end to an eventful day awaits you. You can buy snacks at the small kiosks and enjoy them in the picnic areas. Look out over the sea and let yourself be captivated by the romantic atmosphere between dusk and sunset.

An early skyscraper: the Al Shindagha watch tower is a reminder of Dubai's past

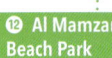

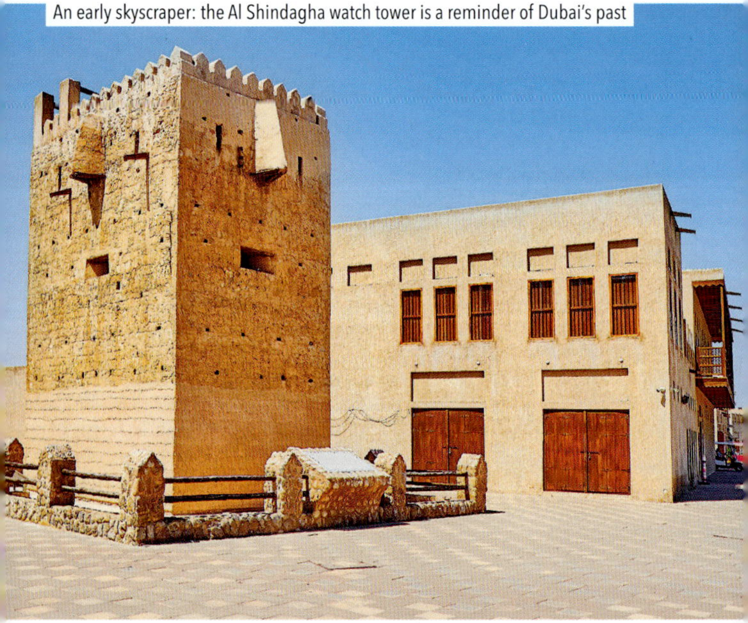

DISCOVERY TOURS

❸ BETWEEN SEA AND WIND TOWERS

➤ Into the bustling centre of Bur Dubai
➤ Culture you can touch: the museum in Al Fahidi Fort
➤ Sipping a cappuccino amid avant-garde art

📍 Al Ghubaiba 🏁 XVA Gallery

➡ 2km 🚶 4 hours (total walking time 30 minutes)

ℹ Costs: 100 Dh per person for admission fees, tea/coffee break, lunch.
Important tips: the best way to get to the starting point is with the Metro Green Line. Al Fahidi Fort and the Dubai Museum were closed for renovation at the time of going to print.

SIT BY THE CREEK WITH ARABIC DELICACIES

The starting point is the Metro station of ❶ **Al Ghubaiba**, which is built in traditional Arabic style, with added wind towers. *From here walk about 300m towards the Creek to the* ❷ **Al Shindagha Watchtower**, a real eye-catcher and a reminder of Dubai's bygone days. Although you can't go inside, it's an excellent backdrop for a selfie. From there you can see the ❸ **Al Ghubaiba Marine Station**. It gets really busy here in the afternoon, with ships docking until midnight. You might even see the modern Dubai Ferry come in, a futuristically styled high-speed catamaran. *Head right and stroll along the shore to the* ❹ **Blue Barjeel Café & Restaurant** (daily 10am–1am | Al Gubaiba Road, Creek Waterfront | tel. 04 3 54 25 08). The Arabic delicacies that are served here look irresistible and taste even better.

ABRA TO THE SOUKS AND A MUSEUM

Continue walking along the waterside. The scene becomes livelier: there is usually a crush of people of all nations at the ❺ **Bur Dubai Abra Station**, where

- ❶ Al Ghubaiba
- ❷ Al Shindagha Watchtower
- ❸ Al Ghubaiba Marine Station
- ❹ Blue Barjeel Café & Restaurant
- ❺ Bur Dubai Abra Station

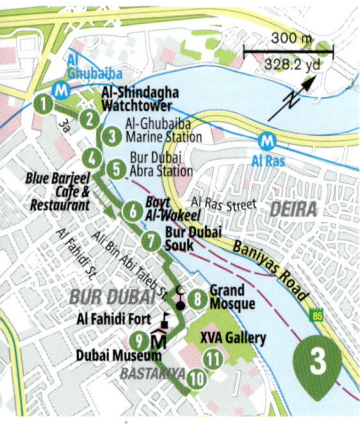

lots of boats wait, ready to cross to the other side. As you walk along the Creek, you will pass the historic trading house ❻ Bayt Al Wakeel ➤ p. 29, p. 61. Its wooden terrace is a good place to enjoy a touch of the old Dubai with a glass of chai.

EXPLORE GALLERIES AND SHOPS IN OLD BASTAKIYA

The route then continues through the covered ❼ Bur Dubai Souk ➤ p. 29, p. 79. In many of the tailors' shops, clothes are made according to individual specification and everything is custom-fitted. You can also buy T-shirts emblazoned with "I love Dubai" for 10 Dh and cheap pashmina scarves. *Go past the next station, Bur Dubai Old Souk Abra, to the* ❽ Grand Mosque *(Ali Bin Abi Taleb Street | near the Ruler's Court)*, whose domes can be seen from afar. You can look around the outside, but if you're not Muslim you will not be permitted inside.

❻ Bayt Al Wakeel
❼ Bur Dubai Souk
❽ Grand Mosque

Bur Dubai Souk. What would a Dubai holiday be without a shopping spree?

DISCOVERY TOURS

INTO THE SEMI-DARKNESS OF A SOUK ALLEYWAY AT THE DUBAI MUSEUM

From the side of the Grand Mosque that faces away from the Creek continue on to the magnificent **Al Fahidi Fort**, the oldest building in the city. It now houses the ❾ **Dubai Museum** ➤ p. 30, the largest and most significant museum in the United Arab Emirates. Head downstairs and take a trip into the past as dim lamps light your way through a replica of an old souk alleyway. When you're finished at the museum, walk further along Al Fahidi Street to ❿ **Bastakiya** ➤ p. 30. This historic quarter between the Al Fahidi roundabout and the Creek is full of carefully restored houses made of coral stone and clay that have been converted into galleries, cafés, restaurants and hotels. The last stop on the walking tour is the patio of the ⓫ **XVA Gallery** ➤ p. 74. Sit in a typically Arab atmosphere, surrounded by inspiring art, and enjoy a first-class vegetarian meal.

- ❾ Dubai Museum
- ❿ Bastakiya
- ⓫ XVA Gallery

❹ BEACH LIFE À LA DUBAI

- ➤ Morning refreshment on Jumeirah beach
- ➤ A round of shopping on the Palm promenade
- ➤ Incredible scenery at the Dubai Marina

📍 Double Tree Hotel
🏁 Hilton Hotel
→ 7km
🚶 3 hours (total walking time 1¾ hours)

Costs: 3 Dh for the waterbus and 20 Dh/hr per person to rent a go-kart or bike.

ℹ️ Go-kart and bike rental: *q8byky.com*
You can reach the Dubai Marina area via the Metro Red Line, stop Damac or DMCC *(thewalkdubai.com)*

YACHTS, SKYSCRAPERS AND A MIAMI FEELING

- **1** Double Tree Hotel
- **2** Marina Beach
- **3** Cheesecake Factory
- **4** Al Fattan Marine Towers

From the **1** Double Tree Hotel *to the west of The Walk, walk past the Sheraton and turn left before the Amwaj Rotana hotel to the public part of* **2** Marina Beach. This is an opportunity to dip your feet in the water or even go for a refreshing swim in the sea. You can enjoy the sweeping view of The Palm Jumeirah and the Bluewater Island peninsula with the Ain Dubai Ferris wheel, which is accessible via a bridge. For a caffè latte, take a seat on the fantastic terrace of the **3** Cheesecake Factory *(daily 10am–1am, The Beach JBR, ££).*

After the break, *take a walk along the seaside promenade that runs parallel to The Walk to the Hilton Hotel.* The public beach ends here as it turns into a private hotel beach. *Head to the right to get back to The Walk* and then continue past the Meydan Beach Club towards the Ritz Carlton. The shop windows of the expensive boutiques in the **4** Al Fattan Marine Towers will

Maritime flair and huge skyscrapers: Dubai Marina

DISCOVERY TOURS

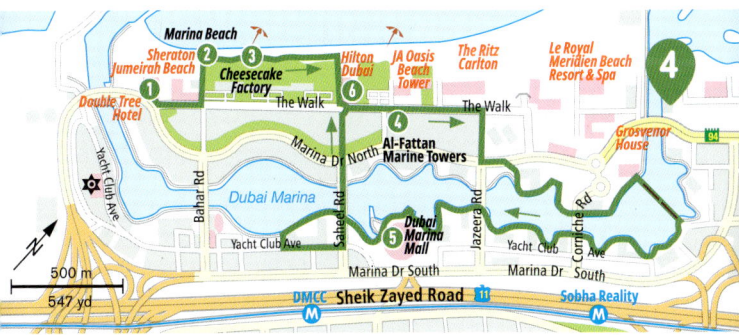

surely catch your eye. The building is also home to the famous Gallery One *(Store GMO2 | Mon–Fri 9am–10pm, Sat/Sun 9am–noon | The Walk | g-1.com),* the address for contemporary art in the region. *In front of the Ritz Carlton Hotel, turn to the right in the direction of a road bridge over the Dubai Marina. Before the bridge, go down to* the Dubai Marina Promenade, which runs along both sides of the long man-made lagoon harbour, with its mega-yachts, high-rise buildings, palm trees, pleasant cafés and shops.

EXPLORE THE DUBAI MARINA IN A WATERBUS

Take the waterbus, which runs around the marina, from the Marina Terrace station across to the Marina Walk station on the other side and continue your walk from there. After you pass the designer hotel The Address, you will come to the ❺ Marina Mall, a small but chic shopping mall. Expats love to meet up here in Le Pain Quotidien *(daily | lepainquotidien.ae | ££)* to sit on the terrace above the marina and enjoy coffee and chocolate muffins. In front of the Dubai Marina Mall, you can rent bicycles and pedal go-karts for use on the car-free promenade. Take note of the spectacular design of the Dubai Marina Yacht Club, p. 107 *as you walk past on your way to Al Gharbi Street, which crosses the Dubai Marina, and back to the JBR Walk,* where this tour ends by the ❻ Hilton Hotel.

❺ Marina Mall

❻ Hilton Hotel

GOOD TO KNOW
HOLIDAY BASICS

ARRIVAL

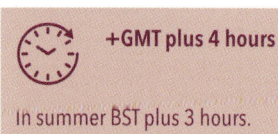

+GMT plus 4 hours

In summer BST plus 3 hours.

GETTING THERE
Emirates (emirates.com) has many daily flights (7 hours) from London Heathrow to Dubai, and flies three times daily from London Gatwick. British Airways (britishairways.com) flies three times daily from Heathrow. Emirates has a non-stop service to Dubai from New York. Other direct flights from Britain to Dubai are operated by Virgin Atlantic, with daily flights during the winter holiday season (virgin-atlantic.com). Qatar Airways (qatarairways.com) flies direct from London Heathrow, and from Manchester with one stop. You can also fly with Kuwait Airways (kuwait-airways.com), Gulf Air (gulfair.com), Qatar Airways, Oman Air (omanair.com) or Etihad (etihadairways.com) and combine a trip to Dubai with a stay in Kuwait, Bahrain, Qatar, Muscat or Abu Dhabi. The budget airline Fly Dubai (flydubai.com) has low-price connections between Dubai and Bahrain, Qatar, Kuwait and Muscat (Oman).

IMMIGRATION
On arrival in Dubai British and US passport holders will be given an entry visa (free) that's valid for 30 days. Your passport's expiry date must be at least six months after arrival in the UAE. There are no border controls between emirates.

CLIMATE & WHEN TO GO
In summer it's very hot and humid on the coast (around 40°C or more) and

A breathtaking sight: a bird's-eye view of Dubai

hot and dry in the interior. The best time for travelling is therefore winter: between October and April. In that period the weather is mild, with lots of sunshine and daytime average daytime temperatures around 28°C, with night time temperatures around 20°C.

CLOTHING

Even in winter, the weather is very warm, and summer clothes are adequate. However, in the chilly air-conditioning of hotels, restaurants and shopping malls, you will need a pullover or a jacket. Local etiquette frowns on short trousers, naked shoulders, and for women anything that is short, tight-fitting or see-through.

CUSTOMS

Visitors can import 400 cigarettes and 2 litres of alcohol into Dubai. For personal allowances of alcohol and cigarettes that can be imported when returning to the UK, see *gov.uk*. You can also bring in other goods worth up to £390. You can normally take US$800-worth of goods into the USA, including 2 litres of alcoholic drinks; see *cbp.gov* for details.

 Adapter type G

220–240 V, 50 Hertz; most sockets are three pins (English style).

GETTING AROUND

CARS & CAR HIRE

Traffic congestion is bad in Dubai and parking is often a problem. As taxis are cheap, there is not a lot of point in using a hire car in the city. To hire (from US$35 per day) you need a national driving licence, and, for a trip outside the UAE to Oman, an international licence. It is usually cheaper to book a hire car before you leave home. Petrol is cheap and the highways are wide and well signposted. Maximum speed 120kmh, and 50 or 60kmh in built-up areas. Those on a roundabout have right of way. In case of an accident, you must wait for the police to arrive. The alcohol limit for drivers is zero.

CITY BUSES

Dubai has many bus routes *(rta.ae)*, which are mainly used by Asian workers. A journey costs 2–5 Dh. Bus 401 goes from the airport to the hotels in Deira, bus 402 to Bur Dubai *(both routes 3 Dh)*. From the Deira bus station there are connections to the Jubail bus station in the centre of Sharjah *(10 Dh)*.

RESPONSIBLE TRAVEL

It doesn't take a lot to be environmentally friendly whilst travelling. Don't just think about your carbon footprint while flying to and from your holiday destination *(myclimate.org, routerank.com)* but also about how you can protect nature and culture abroad. As a tourist it is especially important to respect nature, look out for local products, cycle instead of driving, save water and much more. If you would like to find out more, please visit: *ecotourism.org*.

OVERLAND BUSES

Emirates Express connects Dubai (stops in Deira and Bur Dubai) with Abu Dhabi and Hatta (Dubai) hourly. Connections with Muscat (Oman) and Fujairah City (Fujairah) run four times daily, with buses to Al Ain (Abu Dhabi) six times daily (25–50 Dh).

METRO & TRAM

The trains of the *Dubai Metro* run on an elevated track 4m high and in a tunnel in the city centre. The ticket price consists of a once-only payment for a magnetic card (Nol card) of 2 Dh and then up to 6 Dh per single journey, depending on the zones. Passengers can store credit on the card and use it for journeys *(rta.ae)*. A *day pass* (unlimited journeys) costs 20 Dh. The *Weekly Silver Class Nol* costs 25 Dh, and can be used on buses, the monorail, the water bus and trams. The Metro operates until midnight Saturday to Wednesday, and until 2am on Thursday and Friday. Some compartments are reserved for women and children when there is less crowding at rush hour, and there are first-class compartments ("gold class").

The *Palm Jumeirah Monorail* elevated train travels from Gateway station on the Al Sufouh Road 4.5km over to the Palm Jumeirah and the Atlantis. A single journey costs 15 Dh, a return 25 Dh. It runs about every 15 minutes from 10am to 10pm.

The ultra-modern *Dubai Tram* runs along an 11km-long track between the Jumeirah Beach Residence and around the Dubai Marina. It continues along Sufouh Road to the monorail that speeds on to The Palm Jumeirah.

GOOD TO KNOW

WATERBUS

Air-conditioned boats (35 passengers) run on five routes on the western Creek between Deira (Sabkha, Beniyas) and Bur Dubai (Shindagha, Al Seef Street) as well as in the Dubai Marina. *Daily 6–11pm | 4 Dh per trip.*

A tourist waterbus runs the entire route between Shindagha and Creekside Park (25 Dh).  You can see the whole harbour if you take the Waterbus on its "tourist route" from Shindagha to Al Seef Street. *Daily, hourly 8am–midnight | 45 mins return | 25 Dh | Metro Green Line: Al Ghubaiba.*

CITY TOURS

A semi-open-top *double-decker bus (The Big Bus: May–Sept daily 3–8pm, Oct–April daily 9am–5pm, every 30 mins | 240 Dh, under-15s 100 Dh, family (2+2) 580 Dh | bigbustours.com)* leaves the Wafi Centre and Deira City Centre every hour to tour the main sights of Bur Dubai and Deira. There are three routes and numerous stops where passengers can hop on and off. The price includes a dhow trip on the Creek, a guided walk in Bur Dubai and free admission to the Dubai Museum. The programme also includes a two-hour night tour.

TAXI

Taxis have yellow number plates. The basic charge is 12 Dh (20 Dh from the harbour; 25 Dh from the airport) plus 1.80 Dh per km. 20 Dh is added when you go to Sharjah. The minimum fare is 12 Dh. If the meter is not switched on, the journey must not be charged; a notice to this effect is displayed in every taxi. In Dubai there are also taxis for women (and children), recognisable by the pink roof and pink interior (and the driver is a woman). At malls, shoppers often have to queue for a taxi.

EMERGENCIES

EMBASSIES & CONSULATES
UAE EMBASSY IN UK (ALSO SERVING IRISH CITIZENS)
1–2 Grosvenor Crescent, London SW1X 7EE | tel. 020 7581 1281 | mofa.gov.ae

UAE EMBASSY IN USA
3522 International Court NW, Suite 400, Washington, DC 20008 | tel. 202 243 2400 | uae-embassy.org

UAE EMBASSY IN CANADA
125 Boteler Street, Ottawa K1N 0A4 | tel. 613 565 7272 | mofa.gov.ae

BRITISH EMBASSY IN DUBAI
Al Seef Road, Bur Dubai, PO Box 65 | tel. 04 309 4444 | gov.uk/world/organisations/british-embassy-dubai.

IRISH EMBASSY IN SAUDI ARABIA
PO Box 94349, Plot No. 3114, Al Idrisi, Assafarat District, Riyadh 12513 | tel. +966 11 407 1530 | ireland.ie/en/saudiarabia

US EMBASSY IN DUBAI
8 Al Seef Street, near corner Sheikh Khalifa bin Zayed Street | Umm Hurair 1 | tel. 971 4 309 4000 | ae.usembassy.gov

CONSULATE GENERAL OF CANADA
Jumeirah Emirates Towers (Business Tower), 19th floor, Sheikh Zayed Road | tel. 971 4 404 844 | international.gc.ca/country-pays/uae-ea

HEALTH
No vaccinations are required, but protection against tetanus, polio and hepatitis A is advisable. The risk of malaria applies only to remote wadis with stagnant water. Hygiene is excellent, even in basic restaurants, but as you may be unaccustomed to some of the food, consider taking something with you for stomach problems. The standard of medical care in Dubai is also excellent. Most doctors speak English. The *American Hospital* is highly rated *(19th Street or emergency department 15th Street, Oud Metha | tel. 971 43 77 55 00 | ahdubai.com)*. Emergency treatment is free of charge in state hospitals.

EMERGENCY SERVICES
Police: tel. 999; 8 00 44 38 (in English)
Ambulance and emergency doctor: tel. 998 and 999
Fire brigade: tel. 997

ESSENTIALS

BANKS & MONEY
Cash points (ATMs) can be found everywhere, credit cards are widely accepted.

HOTELS
Dubai has more than 500 hotels, including many in the upper price bracket. However, due to the constant increase in capacity, prices have been falling since the beginning of 2019. Some bargains can therefore be found on the usual booking portals.

Prices are made up of the room rate and 10–15 per cent service, plus 10 per cent tax and a 7–20 Dh (depending on the hotel category) "tourism dirham fee" per person and room. From May to September, hotel prices fall, in July/August even by as much as half. If you'd prefer to stay in a beach hotel, you'll find luxury hotels located along Jumeirah Beach or Palm Jumeirah are your best bet.

INFORMATION
DEPARTMENT OF TOURISM AND COMMERCE MARKETING
For UK and Ireland: *4 Nuffield House | 41–46 Piccadilly, London W1J 0DS | tel. 0207321 6110 | visitdubai.com*

In Dubai: *P.O. Box 594 | Al Fattan Plaza (Airport Road), Al Garhoud | tel. 04 2 82 11 11*

Welcome kiosks at the airport (24 hrs) and in the shopping malls Deira City, Burjuman, Hamanrain, Wafi and Mercato (all 10am–10pm).

TimeOut Dubai, weekly, 12 Dh, timeoutdubai.com

Concierge Dubai, monthly, free, myconcierge.com

Discover Dubai, monthly, free, with coupons for restaurants, travel agents and other services, discover-dubai.ae

Event Guide, monthly, free, visit dubai.com

What's On Dubai, monthly, 10 Dh, whatson.ae/dubai

GOOD TO KNOW

INTERNET ACCESS & WIFI
Almost all hotels offer their guests free Wi-Fi, and increasingly this is also the case with restaurants. Hotspots can be found at: *hotspot-locations.com*. The malls, as well as Kite Beach, JBR Walk, and Metro and bus stations also offer Wi-Fi.

NATIONAL HOLIDAYS

27 Jan 2025, 16 Jan 2026	*Leilat al-Miraj* (ascension of the Prophet Mohammed)
30 March 2025, 20 March 2026	*Eid Al-Fitr* (festival at the end of Ramadan)
6 Aug	*Accession Day* (when President Sheikh Zayed took office)
25–26 June 2025, 16–17 June 2026	*Hijri New Year*
5 Sept 2025, 26 Aug 2026	*Mawlid al-Nabi* (birthday of the Prophet Mohammed)
2 Dec	*National Day* (foundation of the UAE in 1971)
25 Dec	*Christmas*

OPENING HOURS
Banks: *Sun–Thu 8am–1pm*; authorities: *Sun–Thu 7.30am–2.30pm*; shopping malls: *Sat–Thu 10am–10pm, Fri 2–10pm*; shops: *Sat–Thu 9am–1pm and 4–8pm*

PHONES & MOBILE PHONES
The country code for Dubai from Europe is 00971 4, from Dubai to the UK 0044, to Ireland 00353, to the USA and Canada 001. Local landline calls are free. If you call other emirates (or call Dubai from there) you have to dial the 0 of the respective country code.

The mobile network in Dubai is GSM, and the national phone company is *Etisalat (tel. 04 101 | etisalat.com)*. European mobile phones work in Dubai. In Etisalat shops and supermarkets you can buy a local prepaid SIM card for 75 Dh with a 25 Dh call credit; a passport is required when purchasing.

PRICES & CURRENCY
The UAE's currency is the *dirham (Dh or AED)*, divided into 100 *fils*. Dubai is not a cheap holiday destination, and hotels are particularly expensive. On the other hand, there are enormous price differences. If you travel off-season and stay in Bastakiya or in Deira, and visit restaurants favoured by Asian expatriates, you can travel cheaply. Unfortunately, prices for clothing and electronics are consistently higher than in European countries, even in the malls, and you can only buy items cheaply during the annual sales.

HOW MUCH IS IT?

Coffee	£2.75–£4.50 for a cup
Beer	£7–£9 in a hotel
Snack	£1.75–£3.50 for a shawarma
Metro	£4.50 for a day pass
Souvenir	from £1.75 for a T-shirt
Gold	approx. £47.50 for 1 gram, 22 carat

SPELLING
Transliteration from Arabic script means that the way words are

rendered in English can vary: Jazeera or Jazirah, for example. MARCO POLO uses the version most often used locally and corresponding generally to an English style of spelling. We've tried to follow what you'll see in Dubai on public signs, which use both Latin and Arabic script.

TIPPING

In restaurants it is usual to give 10 per cent if you are satisfied and no service charge was included on the bill. In taxis, tips are not expected, but it's a good idea to round up the amount. Porters get 5 Dh per item of luggage at the hotel and 20 Dh at the airport. Room cleaners – always male in Dubai – are happy to receive 5 Dh per night, which is handed to them during their stay or left on the bedside table on departure.

IMPORTANT INFORMATION

ALCOHOL

In Dubai you can be served a variety of alcoholic drinks in many restaurants and in the hotels. Enjoy it, but take care: anyone who is obviously drunk in public can expect to be arrested and imprisoned.

BEACHWEAR

It is strictly forbidden to go topless on a beach or at a hotel pool, and taking photos on public beaches is also a punishable offence. When visiting beach restaurants, wear something smart, as swimming trunks and bikinis are taboo away from the beach and pool.

DESERT

If you have a hire car that's not a 4 x 4, resist the temptation to leave the road and drive into the desert, because you might put your life at risk. The sand may be flat and look as if it's hard, but the unpractised eye fails to see the soft patches, and all of a sudden, you're stuck.

Tours through the desert and into the wadis by 4WD vehicles destroy the plants that manage to grow on this barren soil under the blazing sun. A favourite bit of fun on these expeditions is to drive through watercourses and watering holes. This is very bad for the environment – and unfortunately the Emiratis don't set a good example.

MEN

Particular restraint is required towards local women, who should not be approached or photographed. If local women are travelling as hotel guests, men are advised not to try and talk to them or look at them for too long, as this could be interpreted as staring.

PERSONAL SAFETY

Dubai is an extremely safe place, where fraud and harassment are unusual. *Dubai Tourism and Commerce Marketing* has a dedicated telephone number, free of charge, for tourists wishing to make a complaint: *tel. 8 00 70 90*.

GOOD TO KNOW

PHOTOGRAPHY

Do not take photos of people without their permission. Local women and girls are likely to be particularly unhappy if you try to do so. Military installations, police stations, harbours and airstrips are also off limits. At the royal family's palaces it's best to ask the guards first before you reach for your camera.

UNMARRIED & SAME-SEX COUPLES

It is actually illegal for unmarried couples to stay together in a hotel room, but this is not enforced with tourists. Homosexuality is illegal in Dubai and can be punished with several years in prison. Hugging and holding hands must therefore be avoided in public, and you are not allowed to come out as gay or lesbian. Booking a shared hotel room is not a problem, but it is advised that you ask for separate beds.

WOMEN

Being a woman alone is not a problem in Dubai – providing you observe some basic rules. It's best to avoid flirting or giving any signal you might welcome attention, including looking into men's eyes – sunglasses help here! Women should not dress too revealingly outside of beach hotels and clubs. Sadly, in the event of sexual harassment or assault, it is not advisable to contact the police as this usually leads to further difficulties.

WEATHER IN DUBAI

High season / Low season

	JAN	FEB	MARCH	APRIL	MAY	JUNE	JULY	AUG	SEPT	OCT	NOV	DEC
Daytime temperature	20°	21°	24°	28°	33°	35°	37°	38°	36°	32°	27°	22°
Night-time temperature	14°	15°	17°	21°	26°	28°	29°	30°	27°	24°	21°	16°
Sunshine hours/day	8	8	8	10	12	12	10	10	10	10	9	8
Rainy days/month	1	2	1	2	0	0	0	0	0	0	1	1
Water temperature in °C	19	18	23	27	27	27	29	32	27	27	25	24

ARABIC WORDS & PHRASES

SMALLTALK

yes/no	na'am/la oder: kalia	نعم/لا، كلا
please/thank you	minfadlak/schukran	من فضلك/شكرا
Excuse me!	'afwan	عفوا
Good morning/	sabba l-chair/	صباح الخير/مساء الخير
good afternoon	masa l-chair	
Goodbye!	ma'a s-salama	مع السلامة
My name is ...	ismi ...	اسمي
I come from	ana min ...	انا من
I don't understand you	ana la afhamuka [ki]	انا لا افهمك
How much is it?	kam jukallif dhalika	كم يكلّف ذلك
Where can I find ...?	'afwan alna ...	عفوا اين

1 wahid (واحد)١	5 chamsa (خمسة)٥	9 tis'a (تسعة)٩
2 itnan (اثنان)٢	6 sitta (ستّة)٦	10 'aschra (عشرة)١٠
3 talata (ثلاثة)٣	7 sab'a (سبعة)٧	20 'ischrun (عشرون)٢٠
4 arba'a (اربعة)٤	8 tamanija (ثمانية)٨	100 mia (مئة)١٠٠

SYMBOLS

The beauty of Arabic script celebrated at one of Dubai's many museums

HOLIDAY VIBES
FOR RELAXATION & CHILLING

FOR BOOKWORMS & FILM BUFFS

📖 ARABIAN SANDS
British adventurer Wilfred Thesiger, who travelled with Bedouins through the deserts of the emirates in the mid-20th century, whets the appetite for discoveries beyond the city (1959).

🎥 MISSION: IMPOSSIBLE – GHOST PROTOCOL
In this US action film, directed by Brad Bird, Tom Cruise climbs around the spectacular tip of the Burj Khalifa. Other sites that appear in the movie include the Palm Jumeirah, with the Zabeel Saray hotel, and the desert (2011).

🎥 GOING TO HEAVEN
In his moving, multiple award-winning film, director Saeed Salmeen Al-Murry tells the story of an Emirati boy looking for familiar warmth after losing his mother, in a society that is struggling with a loss of traditional communication and human interaction in favour of consumption and new technology (2015).

📖 DUBAI TALES
These short stories by Muhammad Al Murr provide an insight into life in the emirate, with a focus on the often-conflicting claims of modernism and tradition (2008).

PLAYLIST ON SHUFFLE

0:58

▌ **HUSSAIN AL JASSMI – BASSBOR AL FOURGAKOM**
All of Dubai loves this catchy tune by the Emirati singer.

▶ **EIDA AL MENHALI – MOTASOA**
This Emirati singer's favourite hit.

▶ **CHRISTOPHER YETU – BABA YETU**
World music played at the Dubai Fountains.

▶ **DJ MARETIMO – NIGHTFLIGHT DUBAI**
Lounge music by the German DJ.

▶ **MEHAD HAMAD – SAMA DUBAI**
The emirate's most successful singer is an icon for all those who love tradition and romance.

▶ **JASIM FEAT. ADEL EBRAHIM – EMARATI – DUBAI EXPO 2020 SONG**
Almost everyone in Dubai knows this catchy tune.

Your holiday soundtrack can be found on **Spotify** under **MARCO POLO UAE**

Or scan this code with the Spotify app

ONLINE

MONDLY
With this (free) language app from Apple you will soon be mastering everyday phrases. *In-shallah?* No, not "God willing" – it's up to you!

DUBAI MALL
1,200 shops and 200 cafés and restaurants – with this app you can plan your visit, and then navigate yourself to the shops you want.

FOCUS.HIDUBAI.COM
This mainly business-based website also has useful information on restaurants, resorts and shopping.

DUBAI.COM
Local news, plus information on tours, festivals and events, and a look at the emirate's restaurants, nightlife and shopping scenes.

DUBAI CALENDAR
The variety of events, festivals, exhibitions and concerts on this app is great – you always know what's going on and can order tickets straight away.

DOINDUBAI.COM
A blog on living, travelling and eating in Dubai, by a long-time resident.

TRAVEL PURSUIT
THE MARCO POLO HOLIDAY QUIZ

Do you know your facts about Dubai? Here you can test your knowledge of the little secrets and idiosyncrasies of this city and its people. You will find the correct answers below, with further details on pages 18 to 23 of this guide.

❶ Who has the most prestige among Dubai locals?
a) A sheikh, as the head of a large clan
b) An emir, as this indicates political importance
c) A sultan, as the holder of an Islamic ruler's title

❷ Which weather conditions usually lead to chaos on the roads in Dubai?
a) Light snowfall between January and March
b) Sandstorms during the Christmas period
c) Unforeseen sudden rain

❸ What was the original aim of Arabic calligraphy?
a) To create harmony between the spoken word and the written word of the Quran
b) To write in a way that is easy to read
c) To create artistic wall decorations

❹ What do men in Dubai like to do in their spare time?
a) Camel racing with remote-controlled robots as jockeys
b) Camel racing with female jockeys
c) Horse racing with remote-controlled robots as jockeys

Answers: 1a, 2c, 3a, 4a, 5b, 6b, 7b, 8c, 9c, 10c

An ivory beauty: the Jumeirah Mosque

❺ Which of these is a traditional beauty treatment for women?
a) A good pedicure
b) Henna tattoos on hands and feet
c) A henna tattoo on the back and stomach

❻ What do Dubai men do with their falcons in the desert?
a) Release them into the wild
b) Use them to hunt rabbits and other prey
c) Take them for exercise as there are few opportunities to fly in Dubai's city centre

❼ Which large desert does Dubai border?
a) The Sahara
b) The Rub Al Khali
c) The Bub Al Sahli

❽ How do the state and government organisations help people in need?
a) With soup kitchens
b) With relaxed asylum regulations
c) With internationally active charitable organisations

❾ What is a *majlis*?
a) A doctor's waiting room
b) A place where local women meet their friends
c) A reception room where Sheikh Mohammed meets his subjects

❿ Which of these is a popular trend among Western expatriates in Dubai?
a) Bungee jumping from a skyscraper
b) Strolling with French bulldogs
c) Learning yoga and meditation

INDEX

Ain Dubai 43
Al Ahmadiya School 34, 109
Al Fahidi Fort 8, 104, 111, 113
Al Fattan Marine Towers 114
Al Khor Corniche 37
Al Mamzar Beach Park 110
Al Seef 32
Al Shindagha Museum 28
Al Shindagha Watchtower 111
Aquaventure 10, 46
Atlantis 45
Bastakiya 11, 15, 28, 30, 53, 104, 113
Bayt Al Wakeel 29, 61, 105, 112
Big Red 10, 51
Bur Dubai 28, 56, 111, 118, 119
Bur Dubai Souk 29, 72, 79, 112
Burj Al Arab 47
Burj Khalifa 11, 15, 24, 38, 104, 105
Coffee Museum 31
Creekside Park 32, 119
Crossing the Creek 10, 34
Deira 22, 34, 56, 118, 119
Deira City Centre Mall 9
Downtown Dubai 15, 24, 28, 38, 84
Dubai Aquarium & Underwater Zoo 8, 9, 40, 105
Dubai Creek 10, 107, 119
Dubai Creek Golf & Yacht Club 37
Dubai Creek Tower 16
Dubai Fountain 9, 38
Dubai Frame 33
Dubai Mall 8, 9, 15, 24, 39, 72, 76
Dubai Marina 44, 84, 104, 107, 113
Dubai Marina Promenade 115
Dubai Museum 8, 30, 104, 113, 119
Dubai Opera 25
Dubai Water Canal 16, 41
Etihad Museum 41
Gate Village 40
Gold Souk 8, 36, 78, 108

Grand Mosque 112
Heritage House 35, 109
Hindi Lane 29
Jumeirah 25, 42, 84
Jumeirah Beach 11, 42, 113
Jumeirah Corniche Walk 95
Jumeirah Mosque 41
Karachi Darbar 9, 67
Kite Beach 10, 56, 94
La Mer 16, 48, 94
Legoland Dubai 10, 50
Madinat Jumeirah 46
Mall of Emirates 9, 77
Marina Beach 114
Marina Mall 115
Meydan Racecourse 9, 50
Municipality Museum 108
Palm Jumeirah 11, 21, 42, 45, 84, 118, 126
Palm West Beach 94
Perfume Souk 79, 109
Ras al Khor Wildlife & Waterbird Sanctuary 49
Safa Park 48
Sharjah Old Town 50
Sheikh Mohammed Centre for Cultural Understanding 62
Sheikh Saeed Al Maktoum House 28
Shindagha 119
Ski Dubai 8, 48, 94
Souk Al Bahar 8, 72, 78
Souk Khan Murjan 8
Spice Souk 8, 36, 79, 109
The Beach 94
The Walk at JBR 43
Waterfront Market, Deira 37, 109
Women's Museum 37, 108

INDEX & CREDITS

WE WANT TO HEAR FROM YOU!

Did you have a great holiday? Is there something on your mind? Whatever it is, let us know! Whether you want to praise the guide, alert us to errors or give us a personal tip – MARCO POLO would be pleased to hear from you. Please contact us by email:

sales@heartwoodpublishing.co.uk

We do everything we can to provide the very latest information for your trip. Nevertheless, despite all of our authors' thorough research, errors can creep in. MARCO POLO does not accept any liability for this.

PICTURE CREDITS
Cover photo: Burj Khalifa (Look/age fotostock)
Photos: R. Freyer (36, 112); Getty Images/Maremagnum (80/81); R. M. Gill (30, 87); huber-images: M. Borchi (79), M. Rellini (114), Schmid (11); Laif: M. Amme (47), Brunner (20), L. Jäckel (18, 52/53, 57, 66), T. Linkel (31), T. & B. Morandi (76), M. Sasse (63); Laif/Loop Images: P. Tyson (44); Laif/robertharding: K. Kozlowski (12/13, 34), N. Tondini (58); Look/travelstock44 (40); mauritius images: J. Kellermann (14/15), Mirau (24/25), R. Mirau (128/129); mauritius images/age (100/101); mauritius images/age fotostock: G. Piccinetti (92/93); mauritius images/Alamy (46, 48/49, 68/69, 98/99), P. Chonya (90), A. Dallett (110), J. Gojda (106, 116/117), M. House (126/127), B. Lewis (109), N. Marcutti (51), L. Masterton (42, 64), H. Slavinska (96/97), K. Sriskandan (85), G. Vaughn (2/3); mauritius images/Alamy/AllOver ventures (8); mauritius images/Alamy/Dubai (89); mauritius images/Alamy/Gallo Images (22); mauritius images/Alamy/Oneinchpunch (10); mauritius images/Alamy/PictoKraft (94/95); mauritius images/Alamy/Smoxx (6/7); mauritius images/Alamy/Urbanmyth (33); mauritius images/imagebroker: Tack (9); mauritius images/Imagebroker: J. Tack (73); mauritius images/robertharding: F. Hall (Klappe vorne außen, Klap); alfaori/Shutterstock (23); Kateryna Galkina/Shutterstock (125)

3rd Edition – fully revised and updated 2024
Worldwide Distribution: Heartwood Publishing Ltd, Bath, United Kingdom
www.heartwoodpublishing.co.uk

Authors: Birgit Müller-Wöbcke, Manfred Wöbcke
Editor: Jens Bey
Picture editor: Gabriele Forst
Cartography: © MAIRDUMONT, Ostfildern (pp. 102–103, outside jacket, inside jacket; DuMont Reisekartografie, Fürstenfeldbruck © MAIRDUMONT, Ostfildern (pp. 105, 108, 112, 115, pull-out map); © MAIRDUMONT, Ostfildern, using data from OpenStreetMap, licence CC-BY-SA 2.0 (pp. 26–27, 29, 35, 39, 43, 54–55, 70–71, 82–83)
Cover design and pull-out map cover design: bilekjaeger_Kreativagentur with Zukunftswerkstatt, Stuttgart
Page design: Langenstein Communication GmbH, Ludwigsburg

Heartwood Publishing credits:
Translated from the German by Thomas Moser, John Sykes, Jennifer Walcoff Neuheiser and Mo Croasdale
Editors: Rosamund Sales, Kate Michell and Felicity Laughton
Prepress: Summerlane Books, Bath
Printed in India

All rights reserved. No part of this book may be reproduced, stored in a retrieval system or transmitted in any form or by any means (electronic, mechanical, photocopying, recording or otherwise) without prior written permission from the publisher.or by any means (electronic, mechanical, photocopying, recording or otherwise) without prior written permission from the publisher.

MARCO POLO AUTHOR
BIRGIT MÜLLER-WÖBCKE

Birgit Müller-Wöbcke has known and loved Dubai ever since she landed here on her way to India almost 30 years ago. The travel journalist has written several guides about her favourite destination. She continues to look for new jogging routes in this great city every winter and to explore exciting new hotels and clubs: and all of this on six hours of sleep a night!

DOS & DONT'S

HOW TO AVOID SLIP-UPS & BLUNDERS

DON'T GET SADDLED WITH A LIMO SERVICE
It happens in shopping malls, outside hotels and at the airport: you ask for a taxi, and are offered a limousine. Even if you check, you'll be told, "Yes, it's a taxi." But of course, the ride in a luxury vehicle costs much more than the same journey in a normal taxi.

DON'T BOOK A SUMMER BARGAIN
Sure, you can book a five-star hotel at a bargain price in summer, but the fun is limited if you burn your feet on the way from the deckchair to the pool. 50°C is simply too hot!

DON'T VISIT DOWNMARKET BARS
Prostitution is big business in Dubai, and is discreetly tolerated. Sex workers, particularly from Eastern Europe and Asia, work in the city's bars, restaurants and hotels, especially the cheaper venues. This is one of the reasons why – despite the price of the drinks – it's better to stick to the bars and lounges of the five-star hotels.

DON'T VISIT DURING RAMADAN
During the annual fasting month of Ramadan, public life in Dubai is very restricted. Shops and restaurants don't open until after dark, the hotel lobby is empty, and it's hard to find a taxi. Food and drink are only available after dusk – or from room service.

DO WAIT TO BE SEATED AT A RESTAURANT
Even in a small and simple Asian restaurant, you shouldn't seat yourself without asking. Do as everyone else does and wait for the staff to guide you to your table.